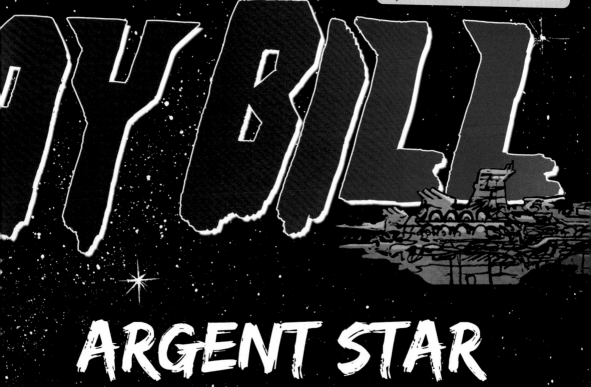

ARGENT STAR

DANIEL WARREN JOHNSON
WRITER/ARTIST

MIKE SPICER
COLOR ARTIST

VC's JOE SABINO
WITH DANIEL WARREN JOHNSON
LETTERERS

DANIEL WARREN JOHNSON &
MIKE SPICER
COVER ART

STACIE ZUCKER
LOGO DESIGN

KAT GREGOROWICZ
ASSISTANT EDITOR

WIL MOSS
EDITOR

JENNIFER GRÜNWALD COLLECTION EDITOR • DANIEL KIRCHHOFFER ASSISTANT EDITOR
MAIA LOY ASSISTANT MANAGING EDITOR • LISA MONTALBANO ASSISTANT MANAGING EDITOR
JEFF YOUNGQUIST VP PRODUCTION & SPECIAL PROJECTS • JAY BOWEN BOOK DESIGNER
DAVID GABRIEL SVP PRINT, SALES & MARKETING • C.B. CEBULSKI EDITOR IN CHIEF

INTRODUCTION

It has been nearly a decade since I last wrote something for Daniel Warren Johnson.

Daniel and I started our careers in comics at the exact same time in a little book that I wrote and he drew called *The Ghost Fleet*. It was an absolutely insane book about truckers and demons and hell and rage and friendship and love and…well, come to think of it, I don't think either of us has really stopped writing about those things since.

But now…Daniel and I have found ourselves in new, strange, wonderful lands, far from the fields we know. If we weren't before, Daniel and I are warbound now. Back-to-back, brothers of Asgard, facing down the fires of Muspelheim, Hel damned and hammers raised.

(Damn, that's cool.)

When editor Wil Moss and I started breaking down the big beats that would begin to shape my run on THOR, I knew that Beta Ray Bill would play a large role. I absolutely **adore** that character. Which of course means that I would have to be cruel to him.

Sorry. Those are the rules.

I knew he would lose his hammer. I knew that he would be brought low before eventually taking his place as Asgard's Master of War. The breaking of Stormbreaker was initially there to show how desperate Thor had become in his trials as Asgard's king — his crown would weigh so heavy that it would turn him away from even his closest of allies.

That, in short…he would find himself on a path to becoming Odin. To being alone. And bitter.

But perhaps more importantly than that….it allowed us an excuse to try something new. Without Stormbreaker…well, Bill would need something new and ferocious to wield, right? Something fearsome. Something enormous and utterly insane. What the Hel could we put in Beta Ray Bill's hands that would rival the *famed Stormbreaker?!*

Well. I had no clue. BUT….

Enter **Daniel Warren Johnson**. If you know Daniel's work (and if not, you're about to), you know he has this incredible LOUD QUIET LOUD to his work that very few people in this industry can thread like he can. It's a delicate balance of over-the-top action set pieces and, almost seamlessly nestled within and around them, the quietest, most gentle of character moments. Doom Metal sludging through an opera house. A valentine wrapped in napalm.

Beautiful. Brutal. Brilliant.

THAT is a Daniel Warren Johnson book. And no one does it better. And this one here is no different.

You guys, seriously. This book opens with a symbiote-covered dragon punching a talking spaceship out of the air and THEN things get crazy.

It's my favorite Beta Ray Bill story that has ever been told. Promise.

But listen…enough of me. There's a reason I haven't written anything for Daniel in ten years. I just get in the way.

And, as honored as I am to be asked to write this, I cannot FATHOM why you are wasting time reading this introduction.

Because honestly?

Daniel doesn't need one.

Just turn the page already.

—Donny Cates

BETA RAY BILL
ARGENT STAR

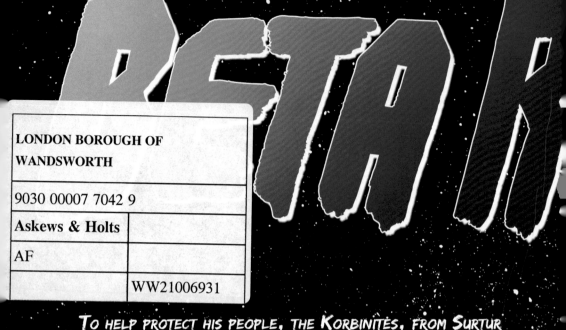

To help protect his people, the Korbinites, from Surtur the fire god, Beta Ray Bill was transformed into a powerful, horse-like cyborg. When he first encountered Thor, Bill surprised everyone by being able to lift Mjolnir, earning him the respect of All-Father Odin, who made Bill his own hammer, Stormbreaker. Odin's enchantment let Bill revert to his humanoid form whenever he struck the hammer on the ground.

Thor has since become the All-Father of Asgard, and recently, during a disagreement with Bill, Thor shattered Stormbreaker. The two friends made amends, and Thor asked Bill to become Asgard's "Master of War." Living on Asgard again, Bill has begun to rekindle his old romance with Lady Sif.

Currently, Thor is on Earth fighting the King in Black and his symbiote-possessed army. But the King in Black has not forgotten about Asgard...

BETA RAY BILL: ARGENT STAR. Contains material originally published in magazine form as BETA RAY BILL (2021) #1-5. First printing 2021. ISBN 978-1-302-92812-4. Published by MARVEL WORLDWIDE, INC., a subsidiary of MARVEL ENTERTAINMENT, LLC. OFFICE OF PUBLICATION: 1290 Avenue of the Americas, New York, NY 10104. © 2021 MARVEL No similarity between any of the names, characters, persons, and/or institutions in this magazine with those of any living or dead person or institution is intended, and any such similarity which may exist is purely coincidental. **Printed in Canada.** KEVIN FEIGE, Chief Creative Officer; DAN BUCKLEY, President, Marvel Entertainment; JOE QUESADA, EVP & Creative Director; DAVID BOGART, Associate Publisher & SVP of Talent Affairs; TOM BREVOORT, VP, Executive Editor; NICK LOWE, Executive Editor, VP of Content, Digital Publishing; DAVID GABRIEL, VP of Print & Digital Publishing; JEFF YOUNGQUIST, VP of Production & Special Projects; ALEX MORALES, Director of Publishing Operations; DAN EDINGTON, Managing Editor; RICKEY PURDIN, Director of Talent Relations; JENNIFER GRÜNWALD, Senior Editor, Special Projects; SUSAN CRESPI, Production Manager; STAN LEE, Chairman Emeritus. For information regarding advertising in Marvel Comics or on Marvel.com, please contact Vit DeBellis, Custom Solutions & Integrated Advertising Manager, at vdebellis@marvel.com. For Marvel subscription inquiries, please call 888-511-5480. Manufactured between 8/20/2021 and 9/21/2021 by SOLISCO PRINTERS, SCOTT, QC, CANADA.

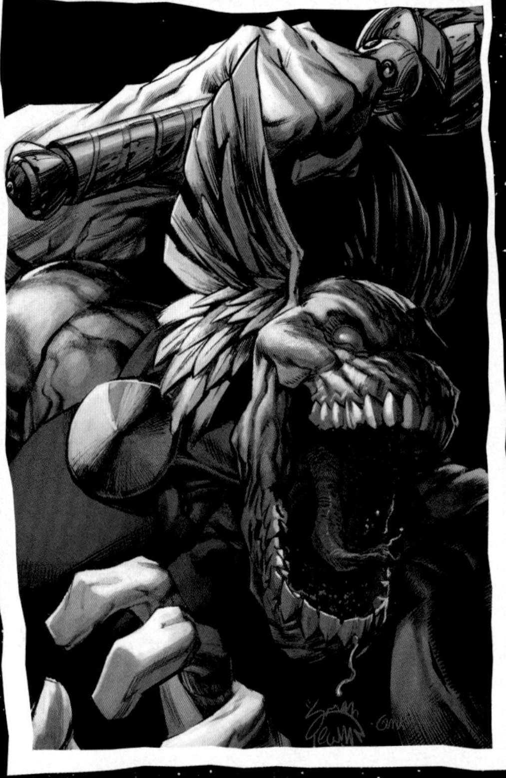

#1 VARIANT BY RYAN STEGMAN & FRANK MARTIN

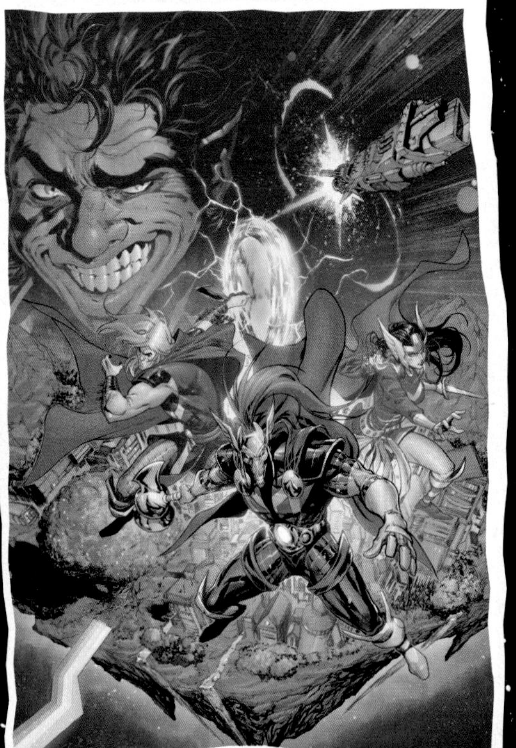

#1 STORMBREAKER VARIANT BY IBAN COELLO & JESUS ABURTOV

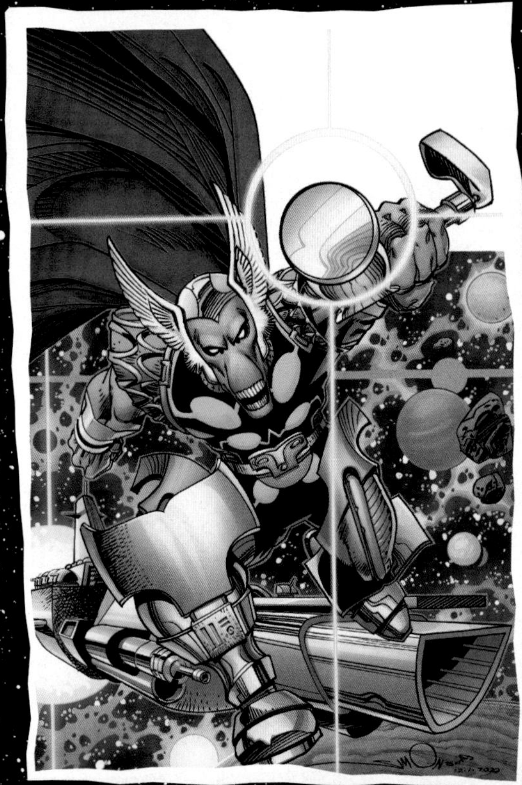

#1 VARIANT BY WALTER SIMONSON & LAURA MARTIN

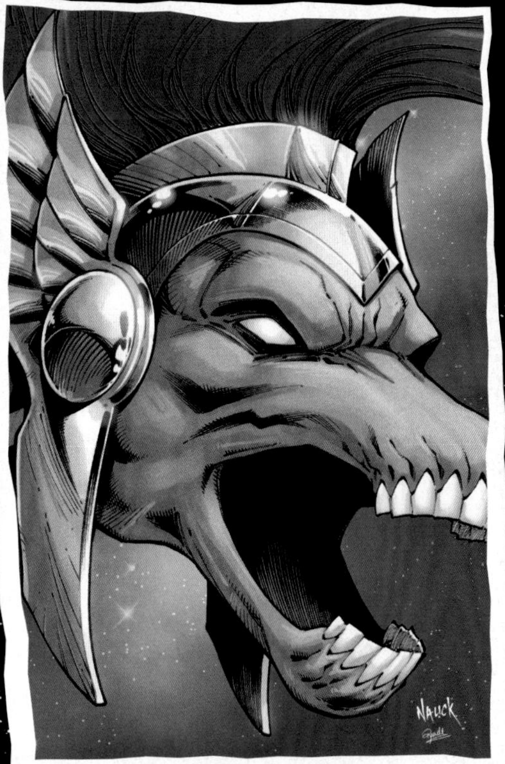
NAUCK

#1 HEADSHOT VARIANT BY TODD NAUCK & RACHELLE ROSENBERG

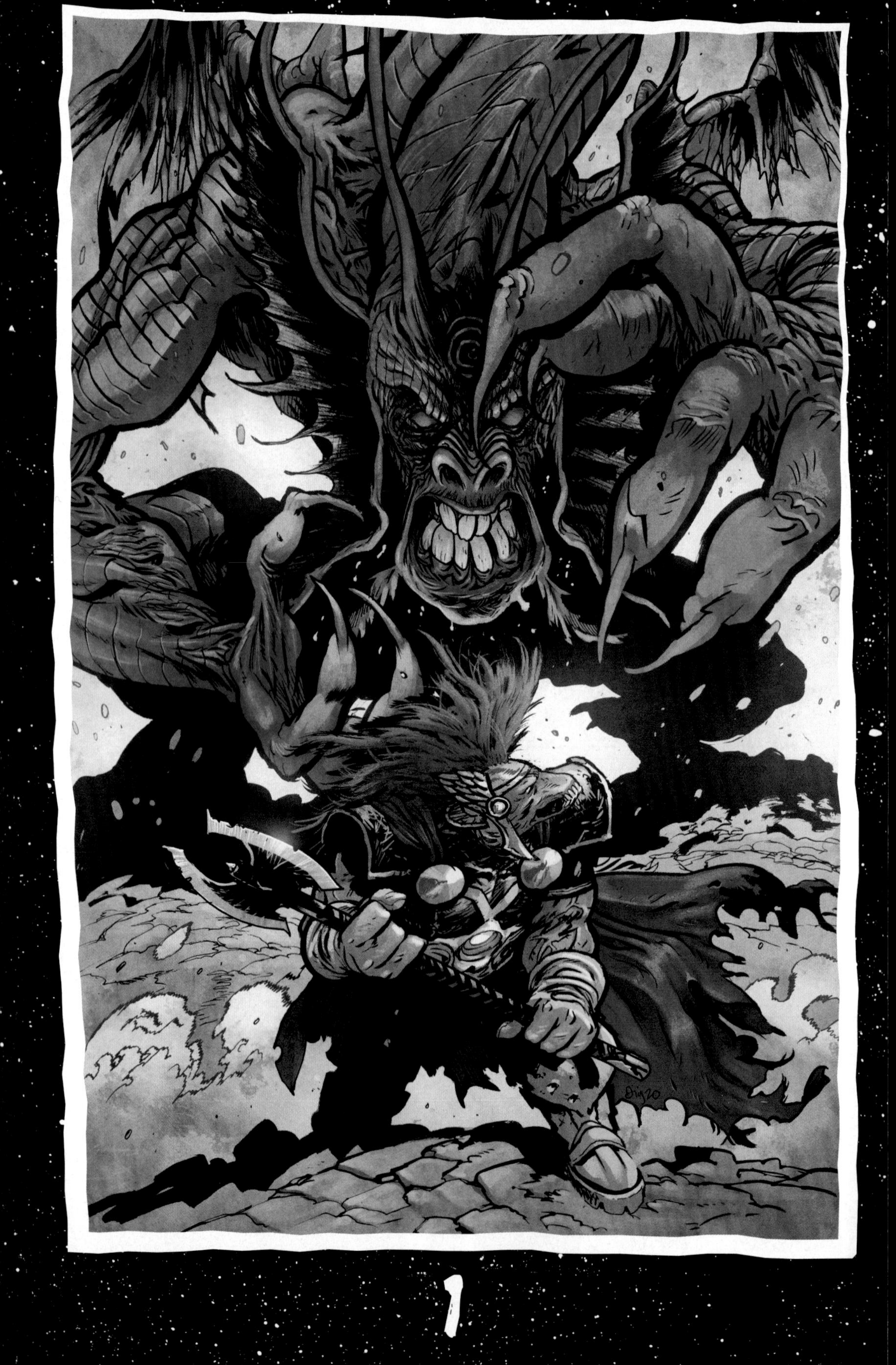

1

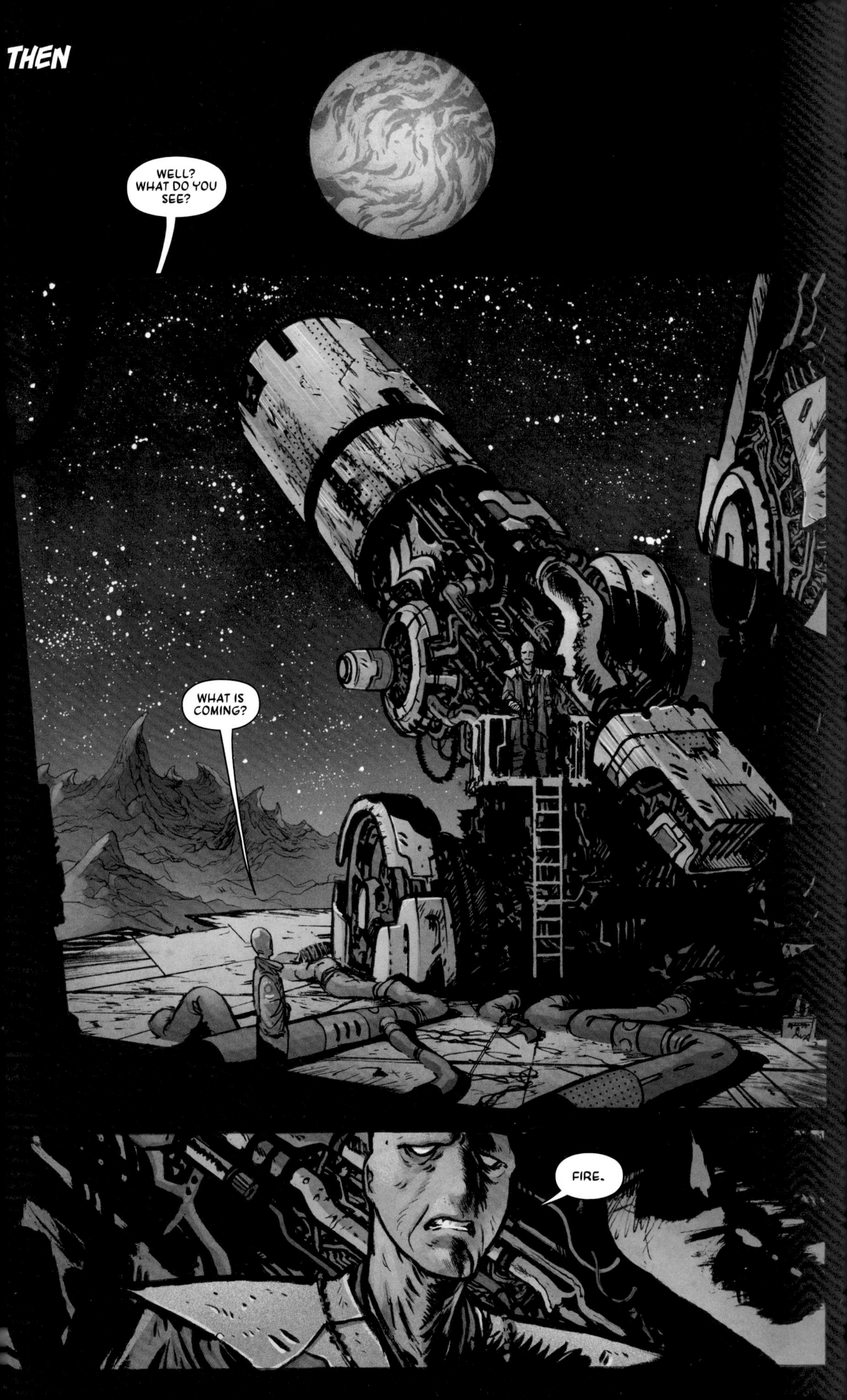
THEN
WELL? WHAT DO YOU SEE?
WHAT IS COMING?
FIRE.

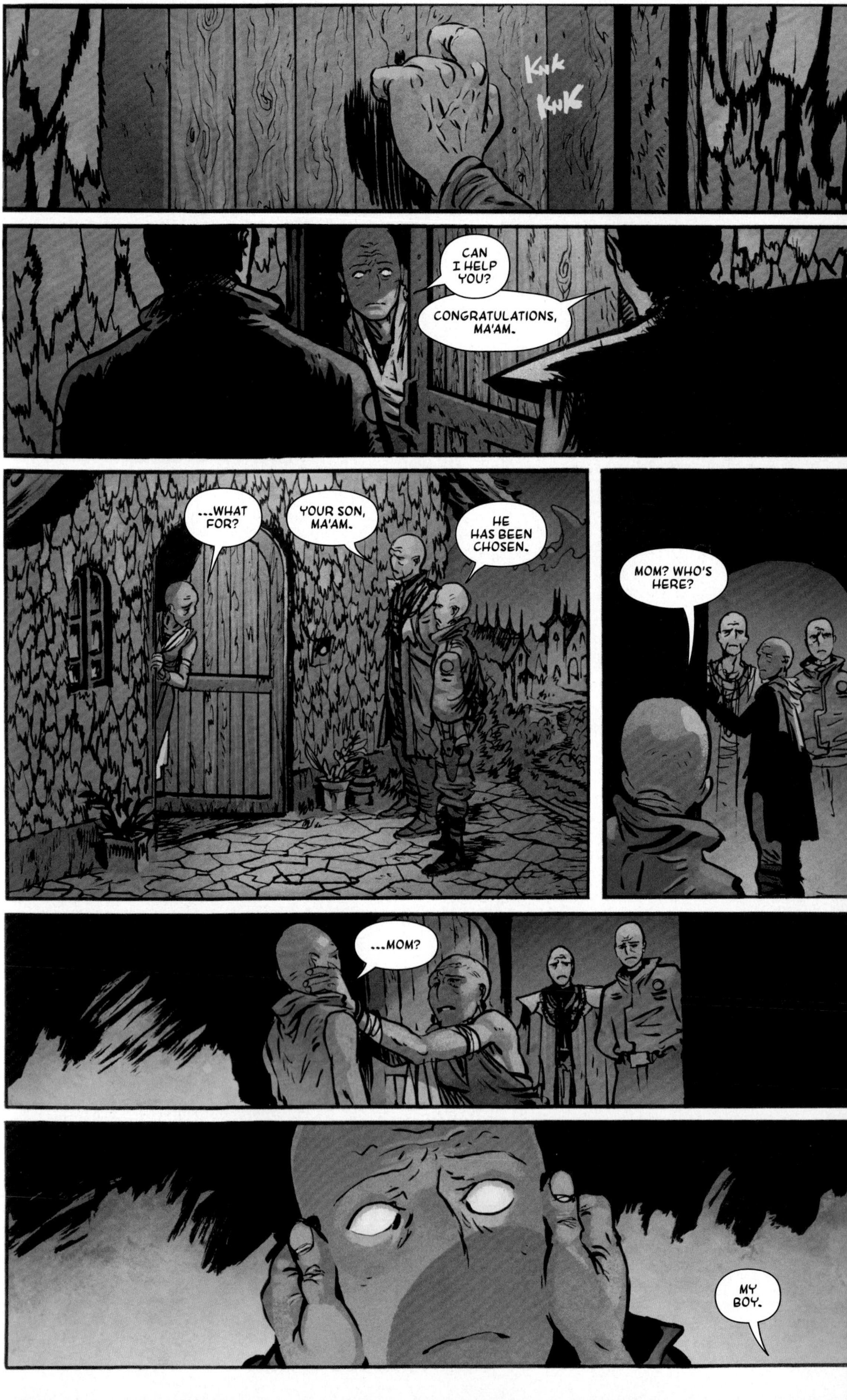
KNK
KNK
CAN I HELP YOU?
CONGRATULATIONS, MA'AM.
...WHAT FOR?
YOUR SON, MA'AM.
HE HAS BEEN CHOSEN.
MOM? WHO'S HERE?
...MOM?
MY BOY.

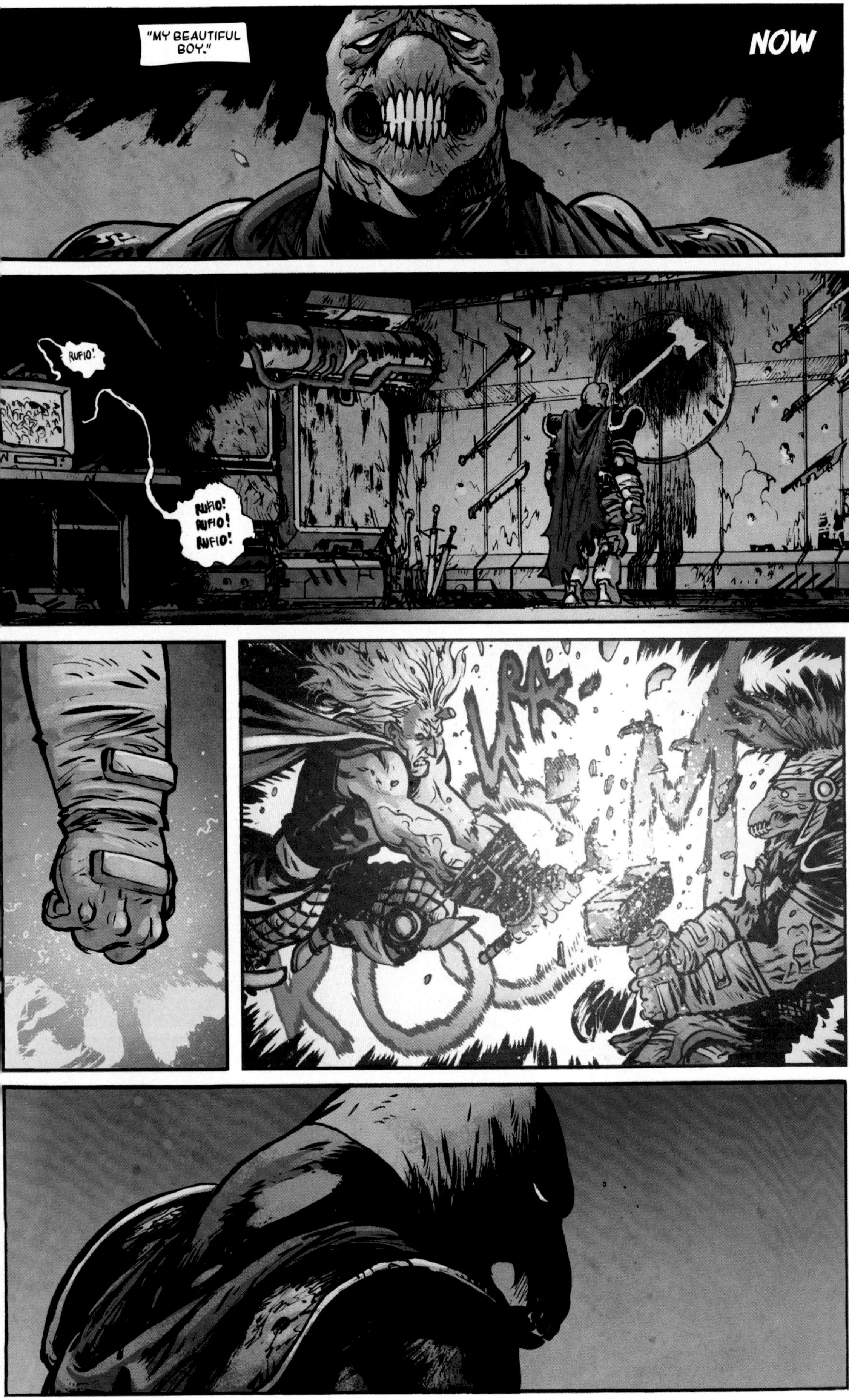
"MY BEAUTIFUL BOY."
NOW
RUFIO!
RUFIO! RUFIO! RUFIO!

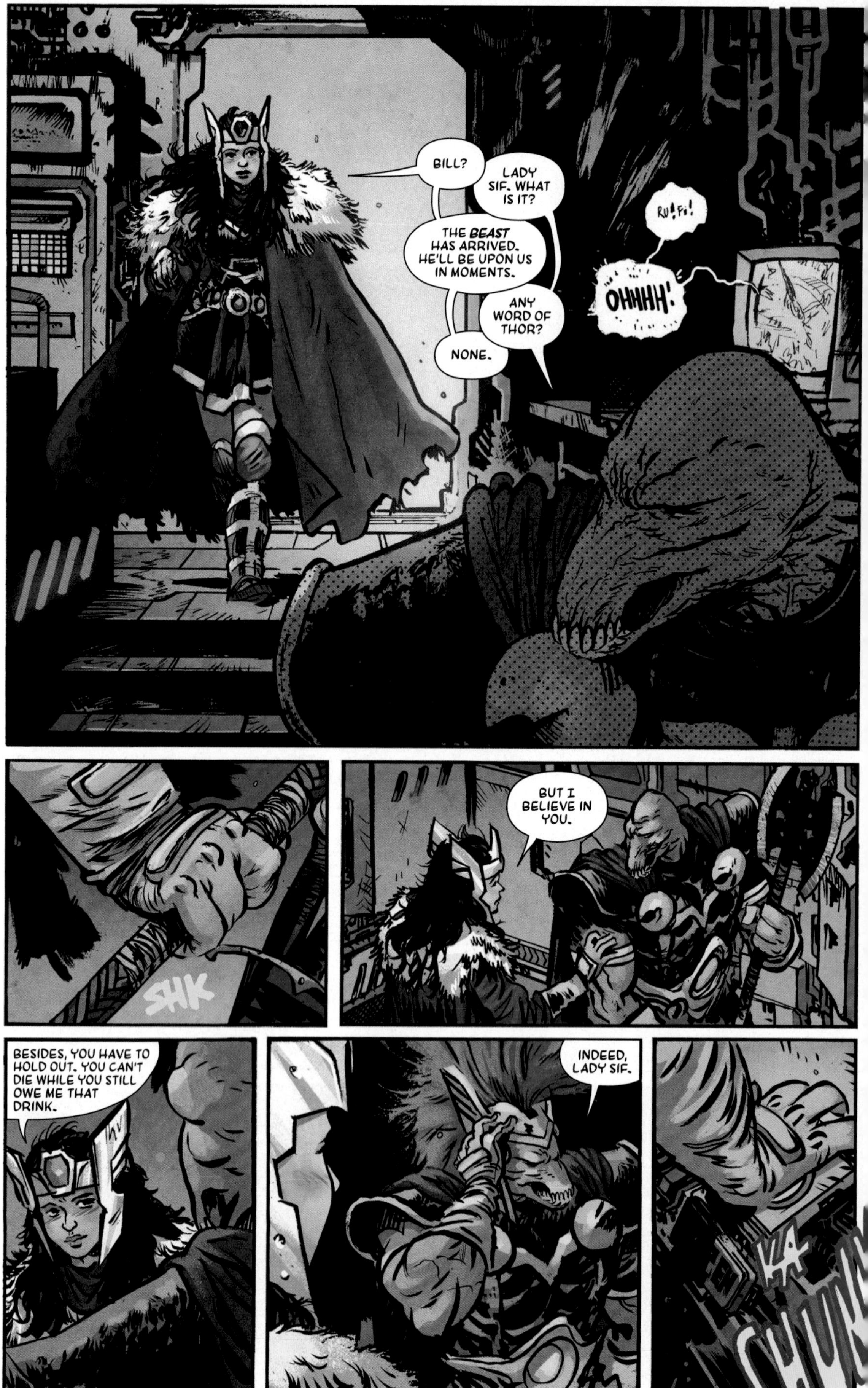
BILL?
LADY SIF. WHAT IS IT?
THE BEAST HAS ARRIVED. HE'LL BE UPON US IN MOMENTS.
ANY WORD OF THOR?
NONE.
RU!Fi!
OHHHH!
SHK
BUT I BELIEVE IN YOU.
BESIDES, YOU HAVE TO HOLD OUT. YOU CAN'T DIE WHILE YOU STILL OWE ME THAT DRINK.
INDEED, LADY SIF.
KA
CHUN

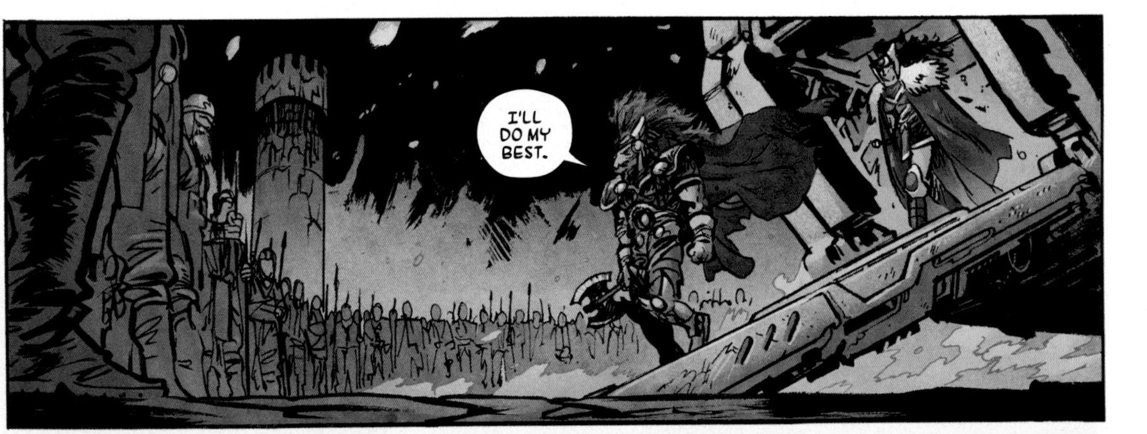
I'LL DO MY BEST.

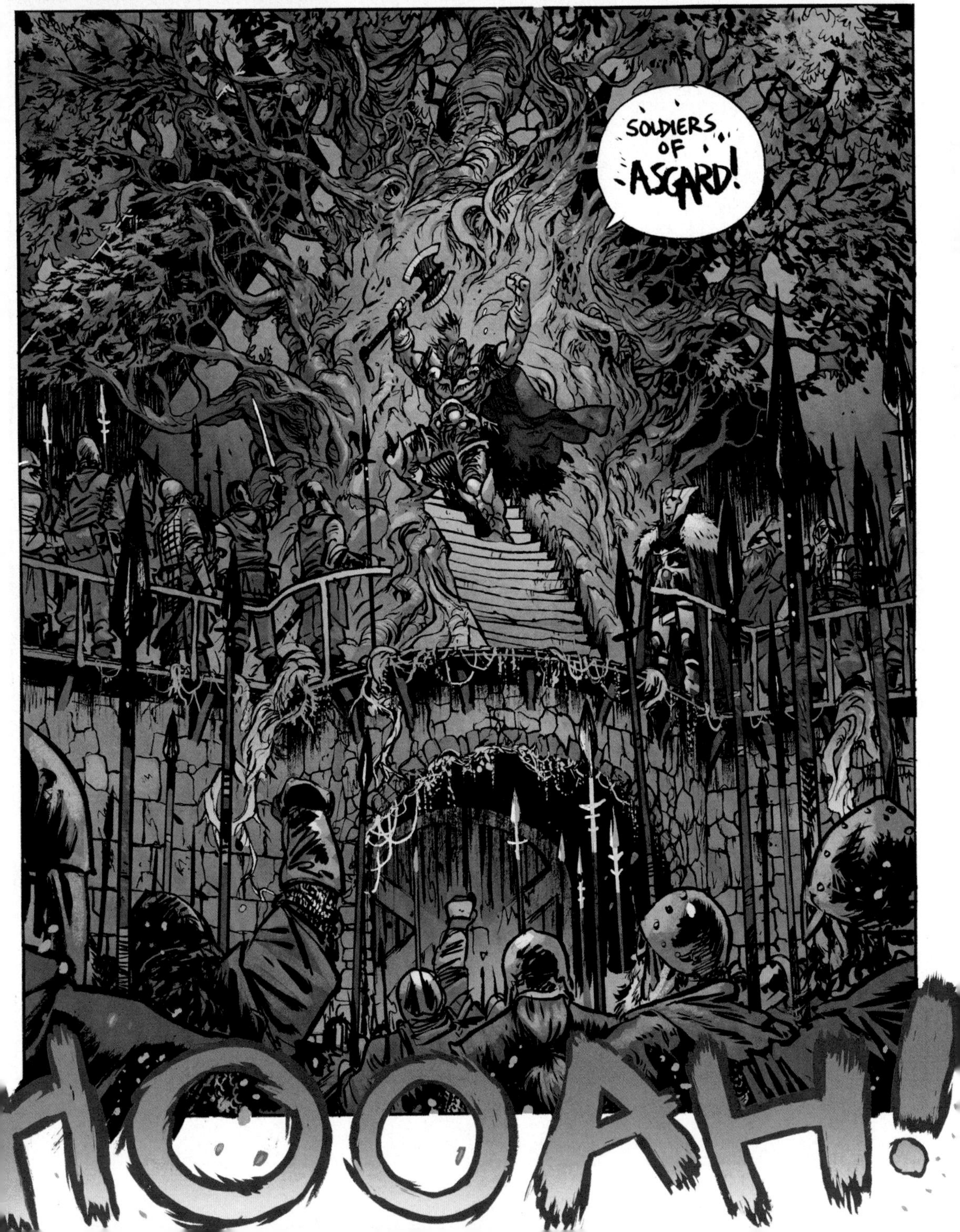
SOLDIERS OF ASGARD!
HOOOAH!

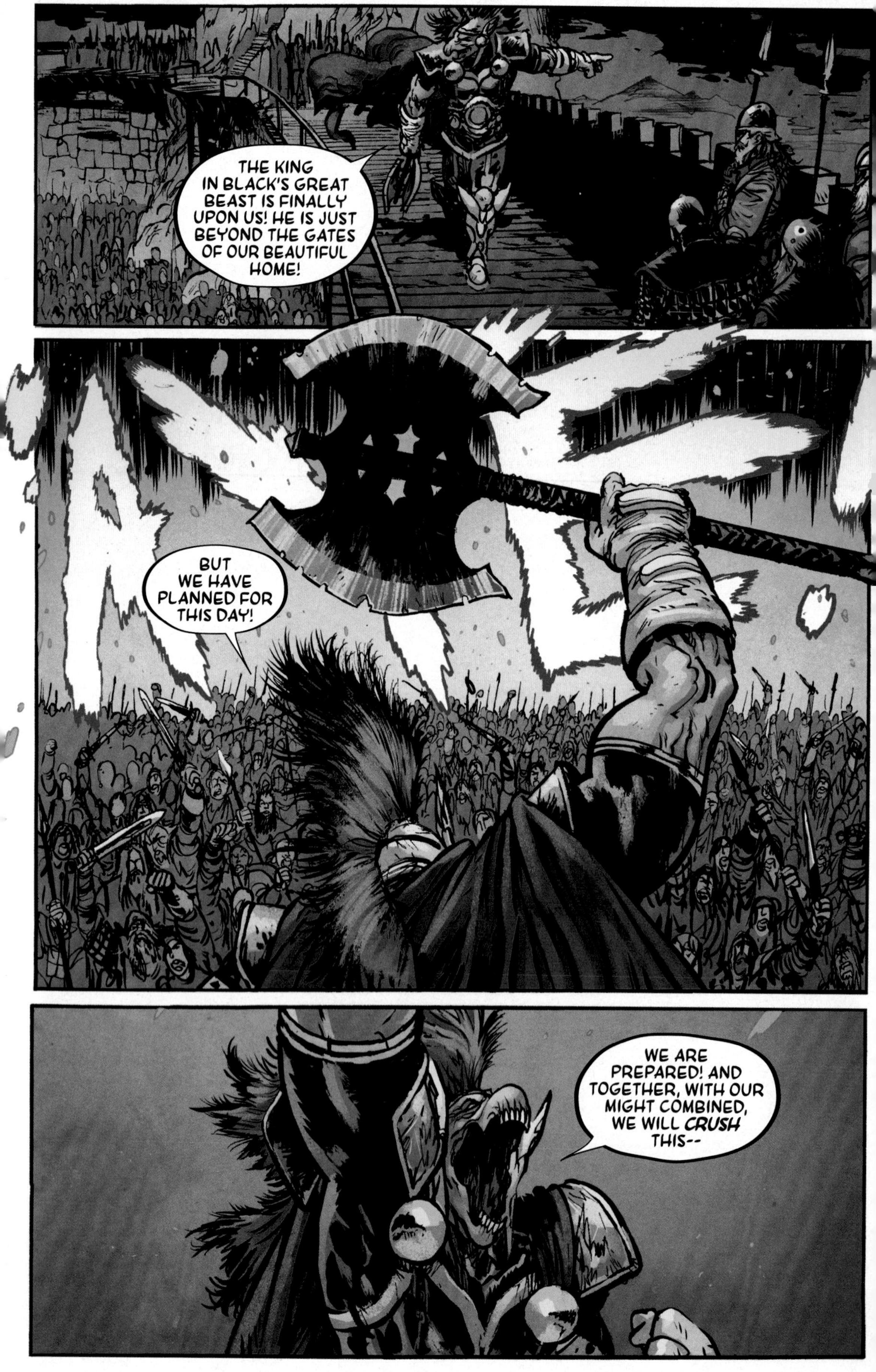

THE KING IN BLACK'S GREAT BEAST IS FINALLY UPON US! HE IS JUST BEYOND THE GATES OF OUR BEAUTIFUL HOME!
BUT WE HAVE PLANNED FOR THIS DAY!
WE ARE PREPARED! AND TOGETHER, WITH OUR MIGHT COMBINED, WE WILL *CRUSH* THIS--

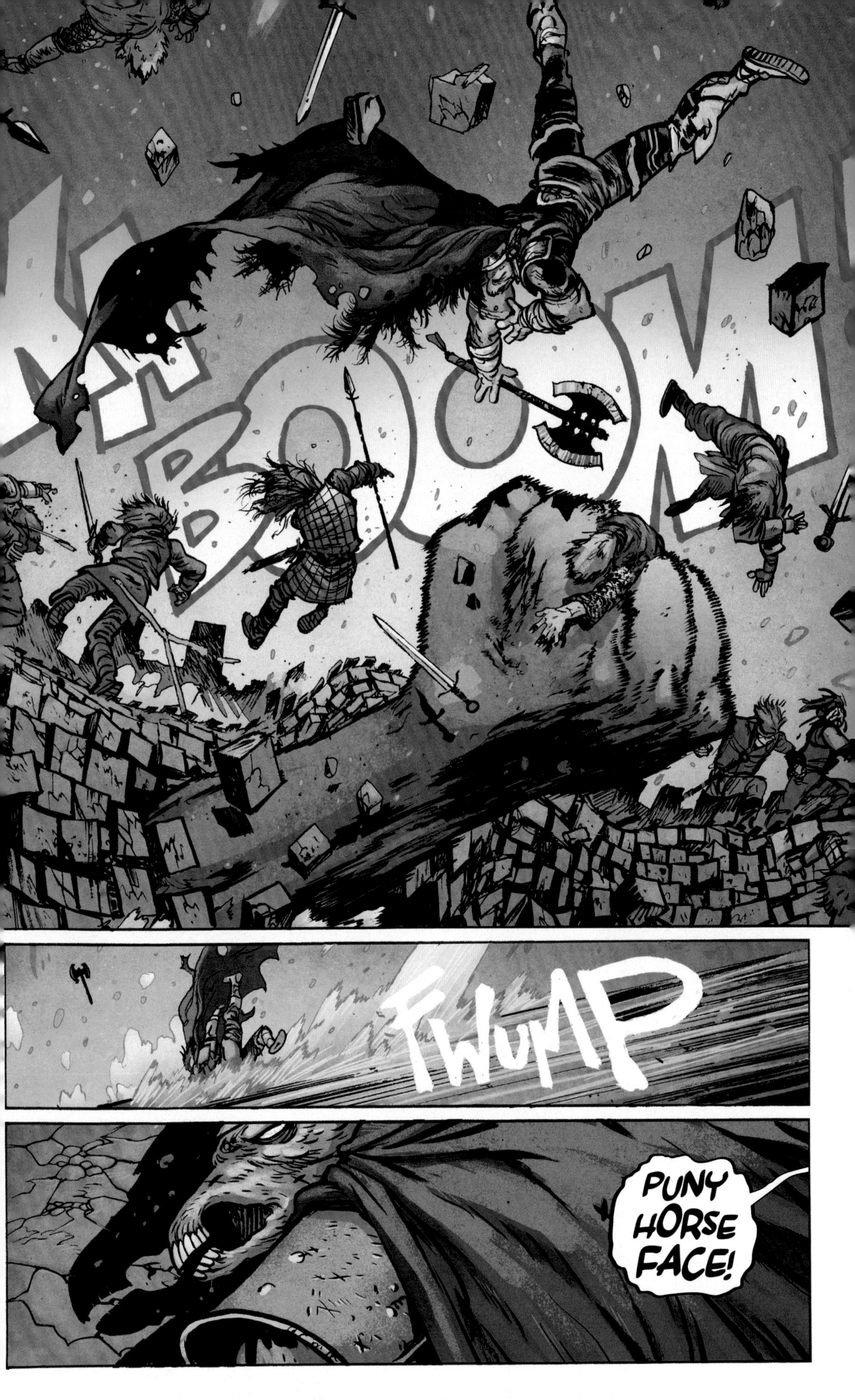
BOOM
FWUMP
PUNY HORSE FACE!

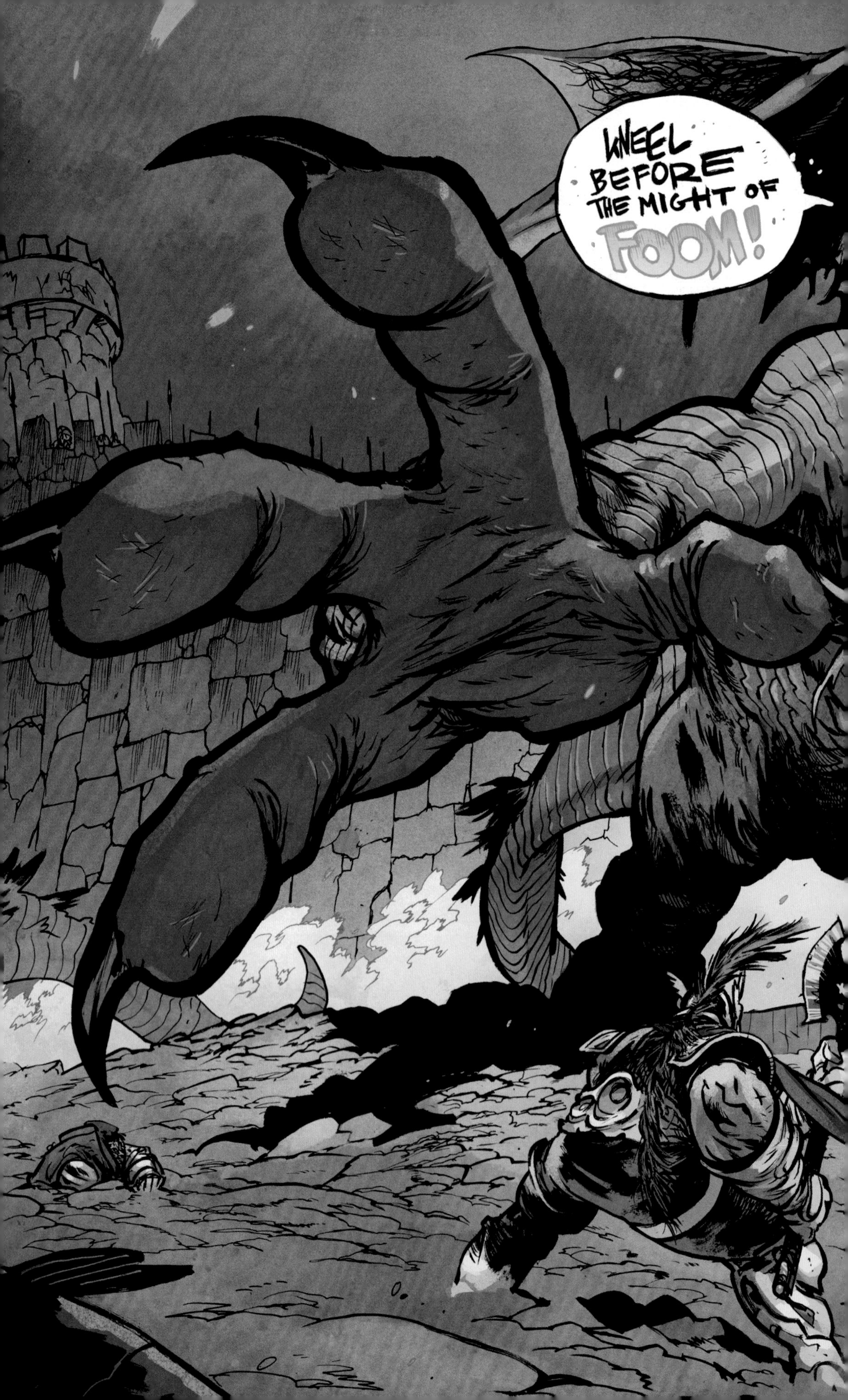
KNEEL BEFORE THE MIGHT OF FOOM!

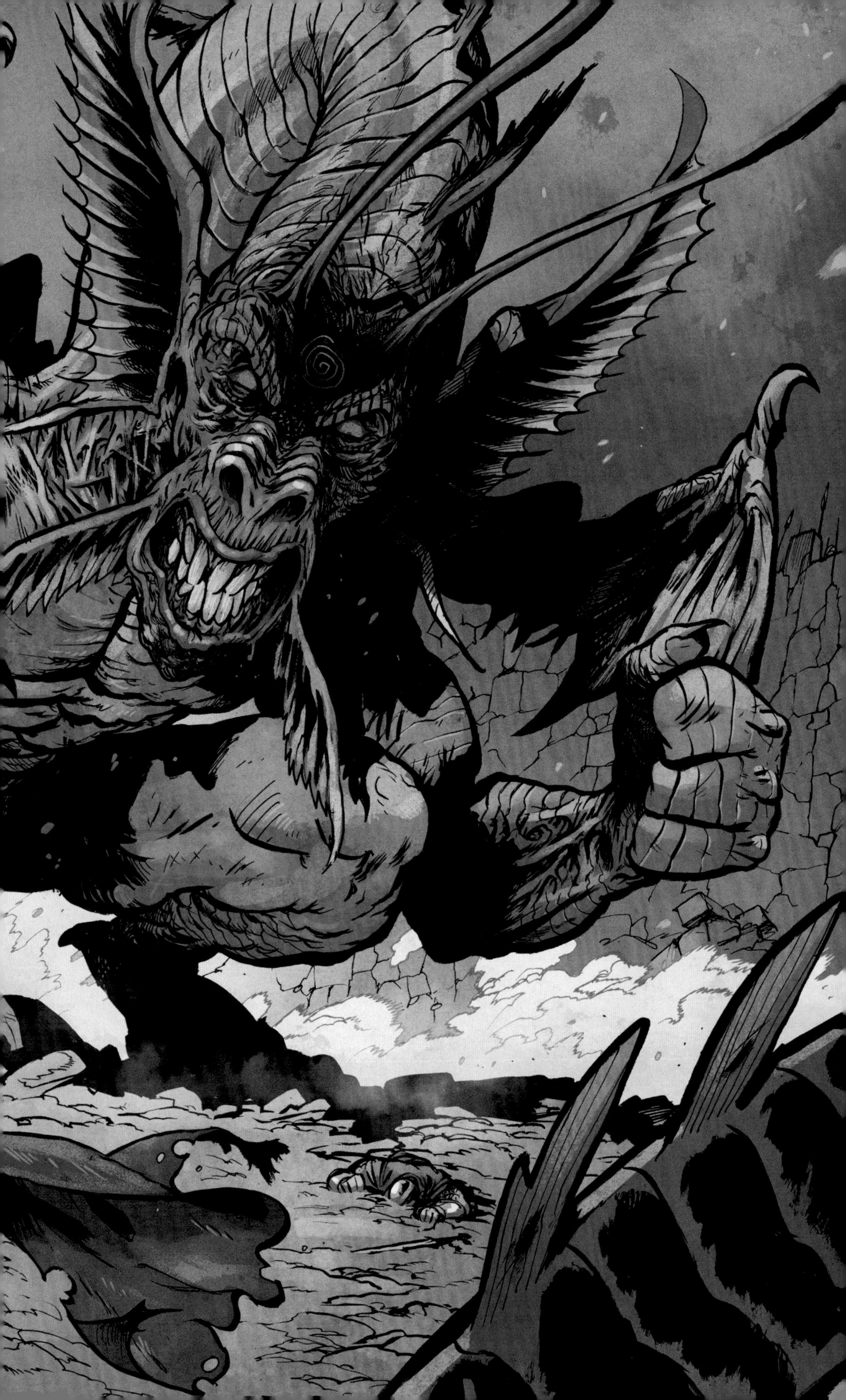

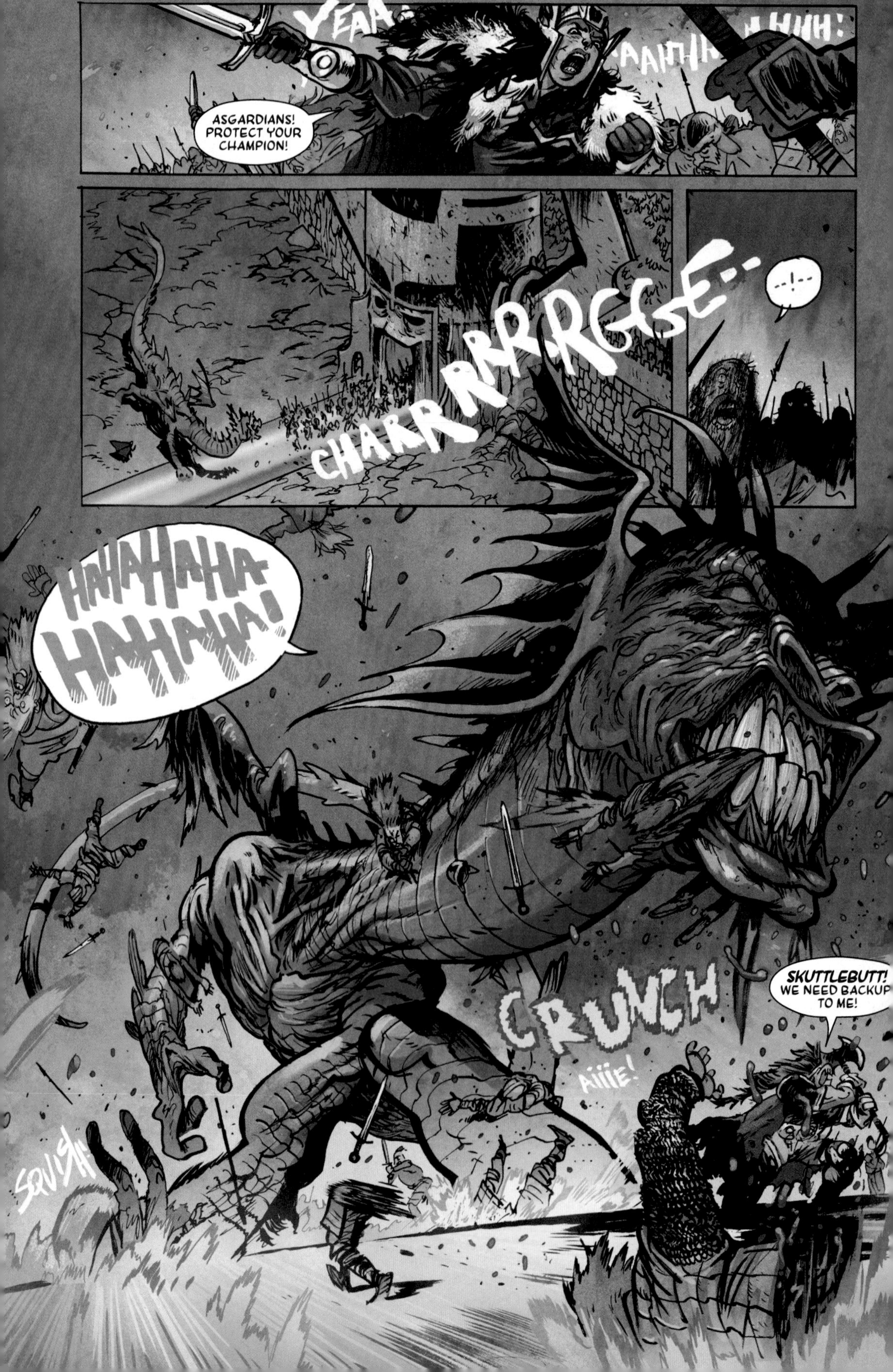
YEAA
AAHHH
HHHH!
ASGARDIANS! PROTECT YOUR CHAMPION!
CHARRRRRRGGSE...
--!--
HAHAHAHA HAHAHA!
CRUNCH
SKUTTLEBUTT! WE NEED BACKUP TO ME!
AIIIE!
SQUISH

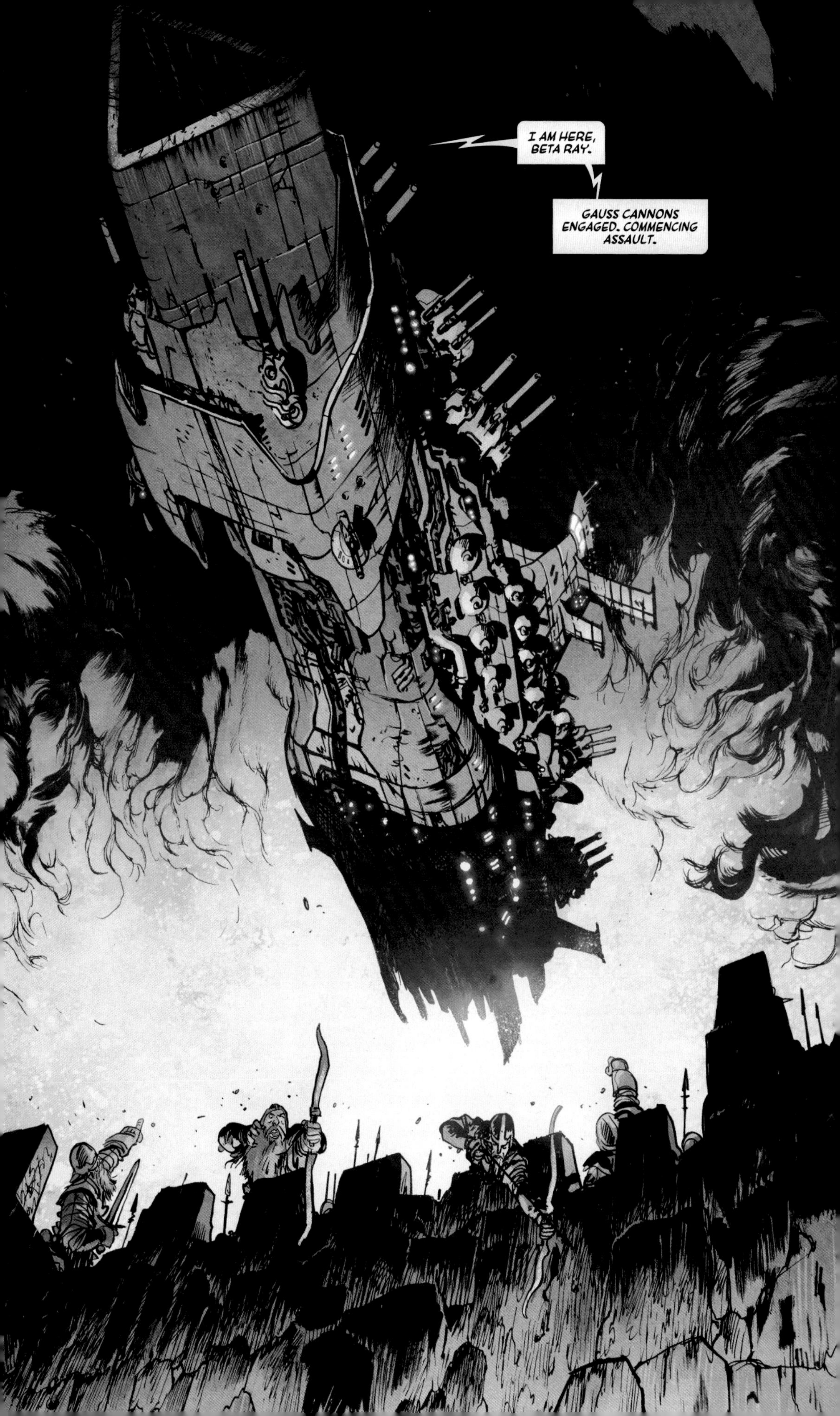
I AM HERE, BETA RAY.
GAUSS CANNONS ENGAGED. COMMENCING ASSAULT.

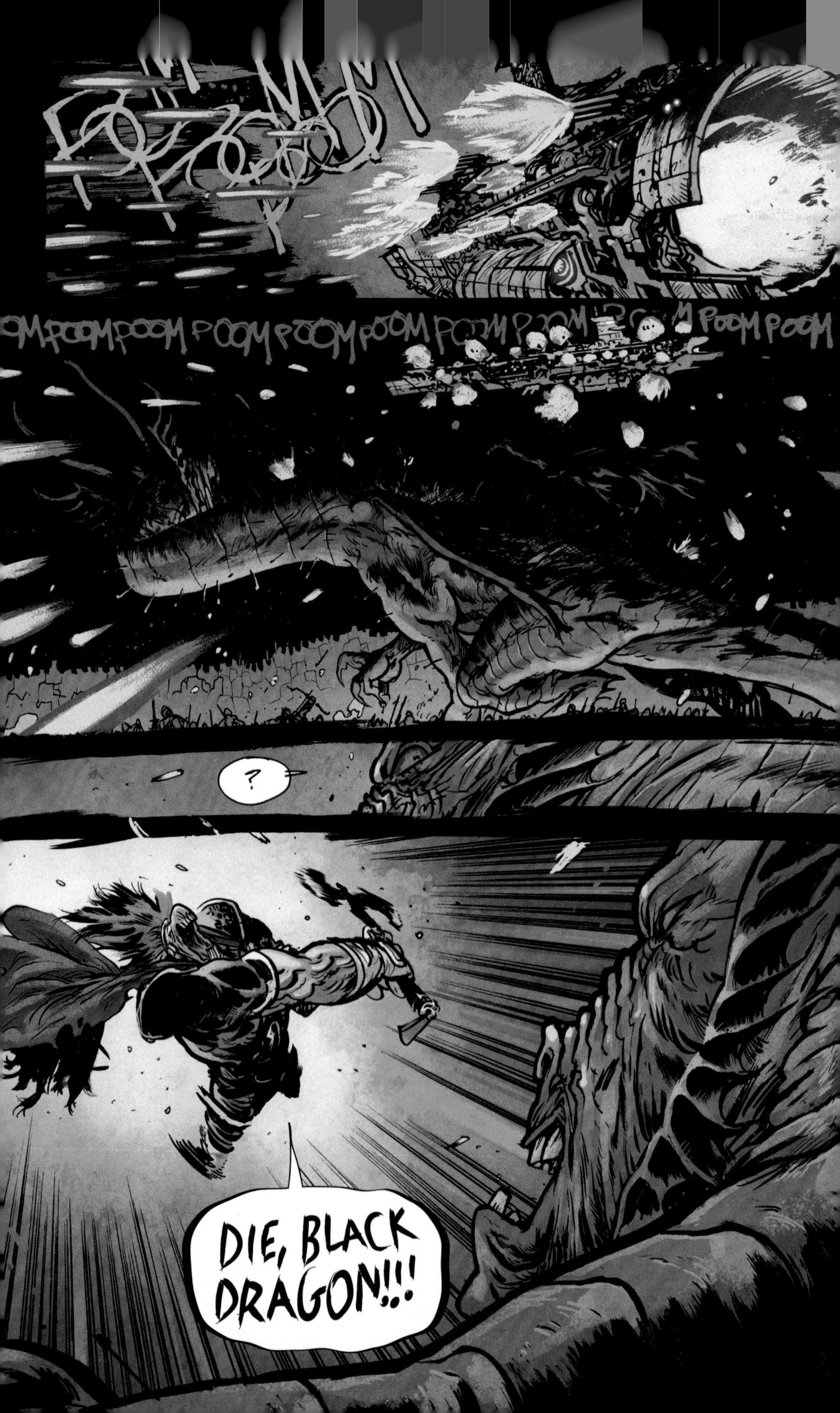
POOM POOM POOM POOM POOM POOM POOM POOM
?
DIE, BLACK DRAGON!!!

GRAHHH!

BOOM!

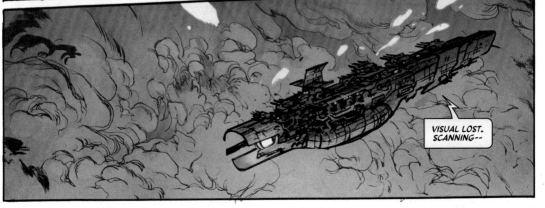

VISUAL LOST. SCANNING--

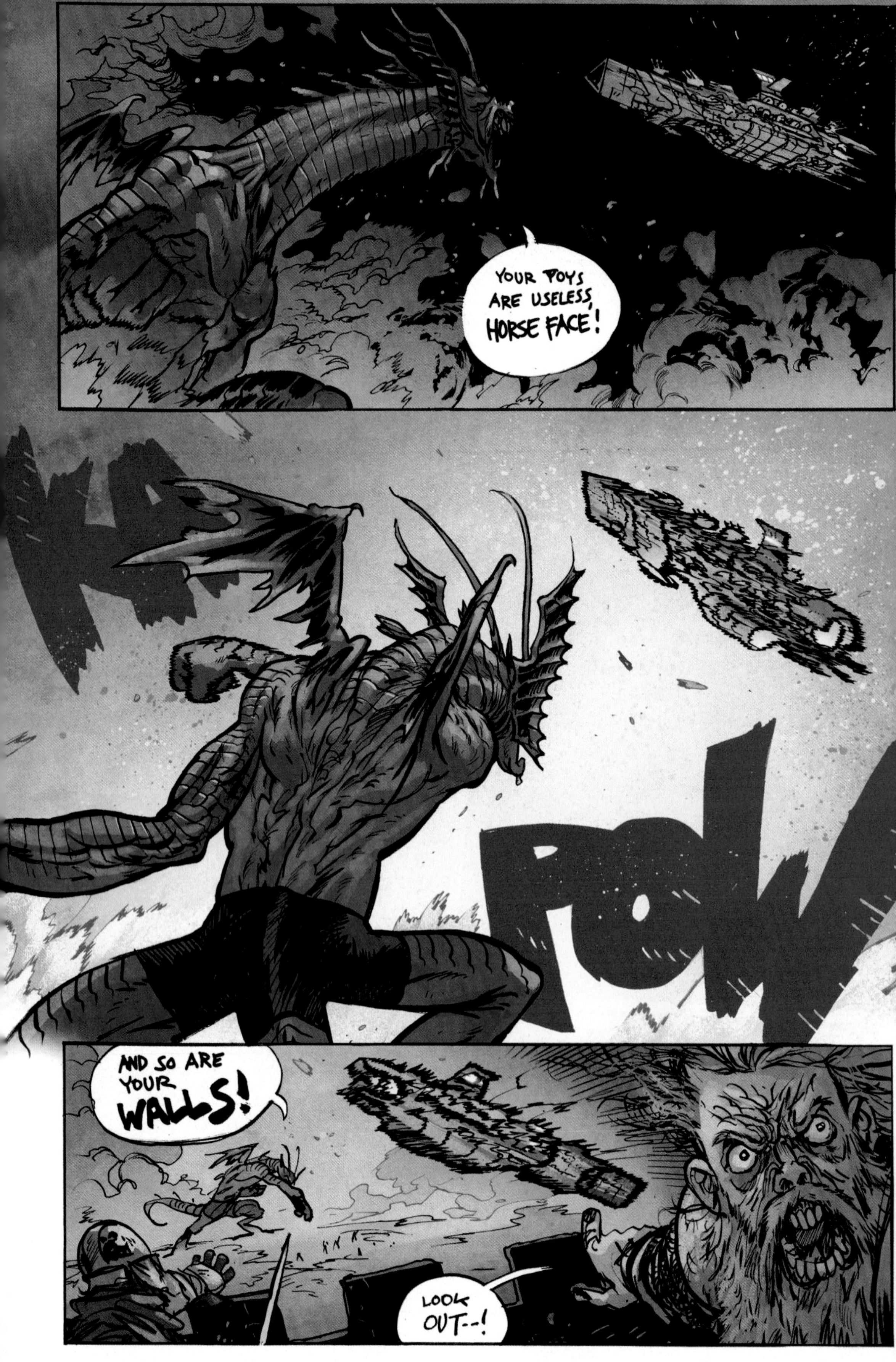
YOUR TOYS ARE USELESS, HORSE FACE!
KA
PO
AND SO ARE YOUR WALLS!
LOOK OUT--!

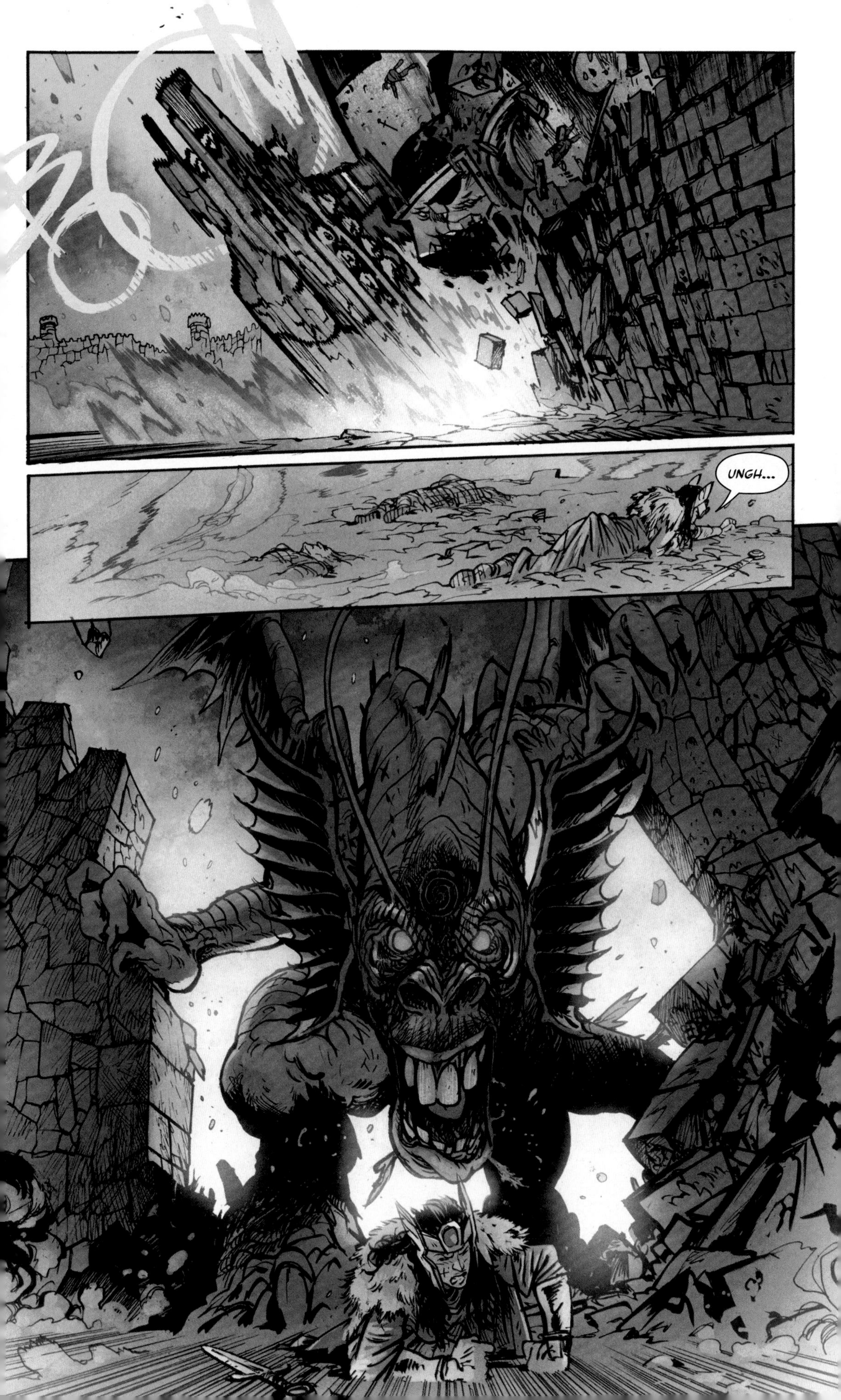
BOOM
UNGH...

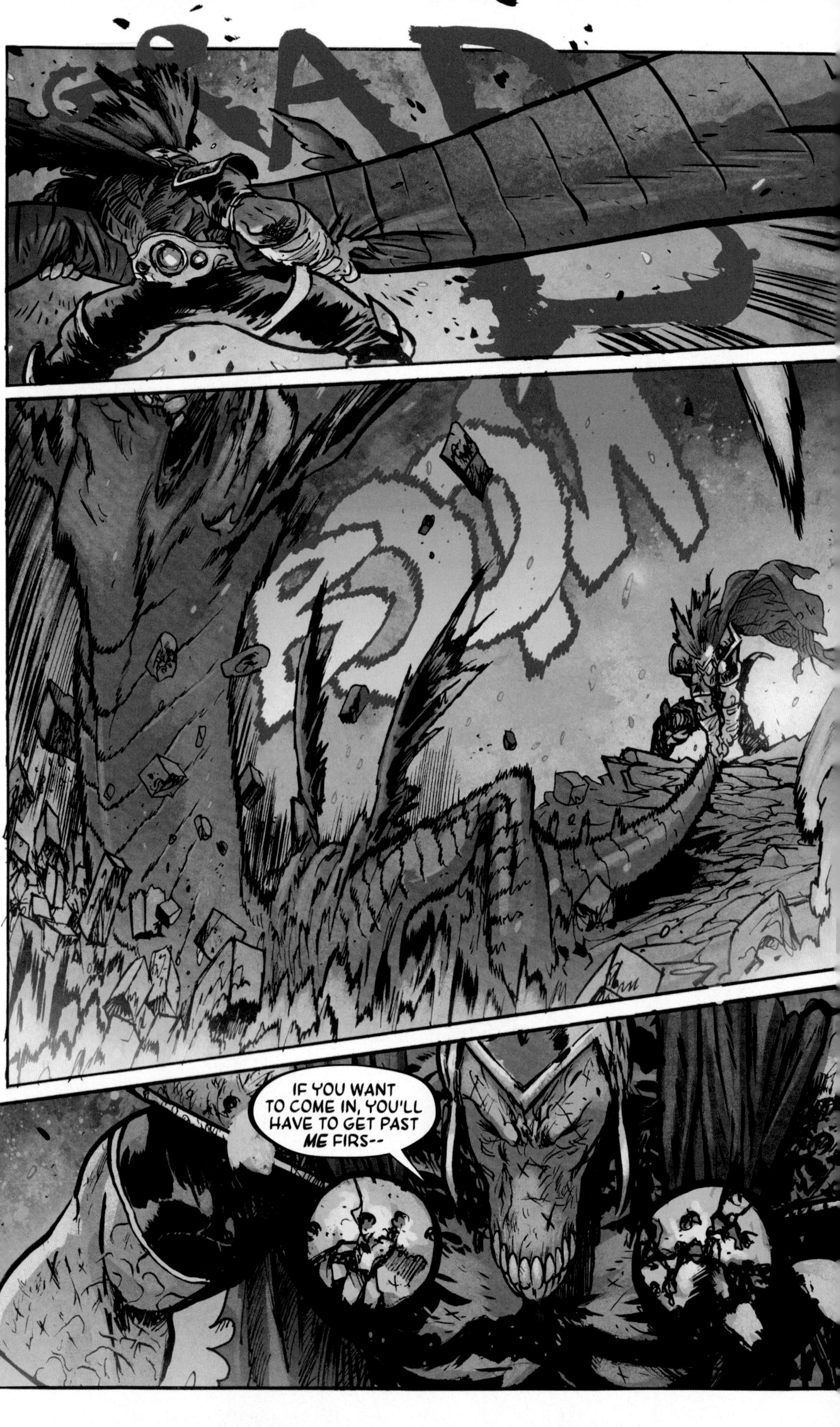
IF YOU WANT TO COME IN, YOU'LL HAVE TO GET PAST *ME* FIRS--

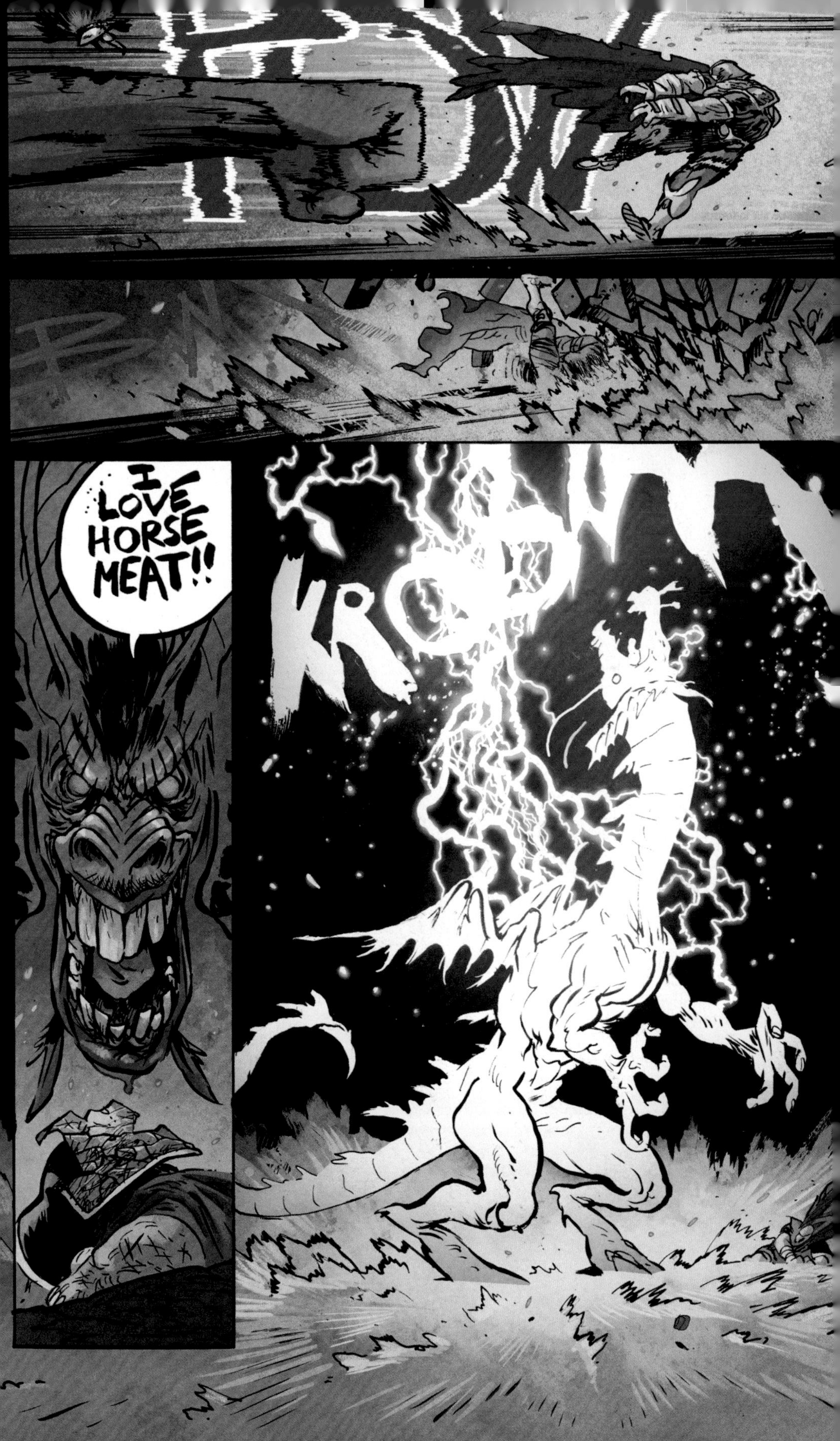
I LOVE HORSE MEAT!!
KROOM

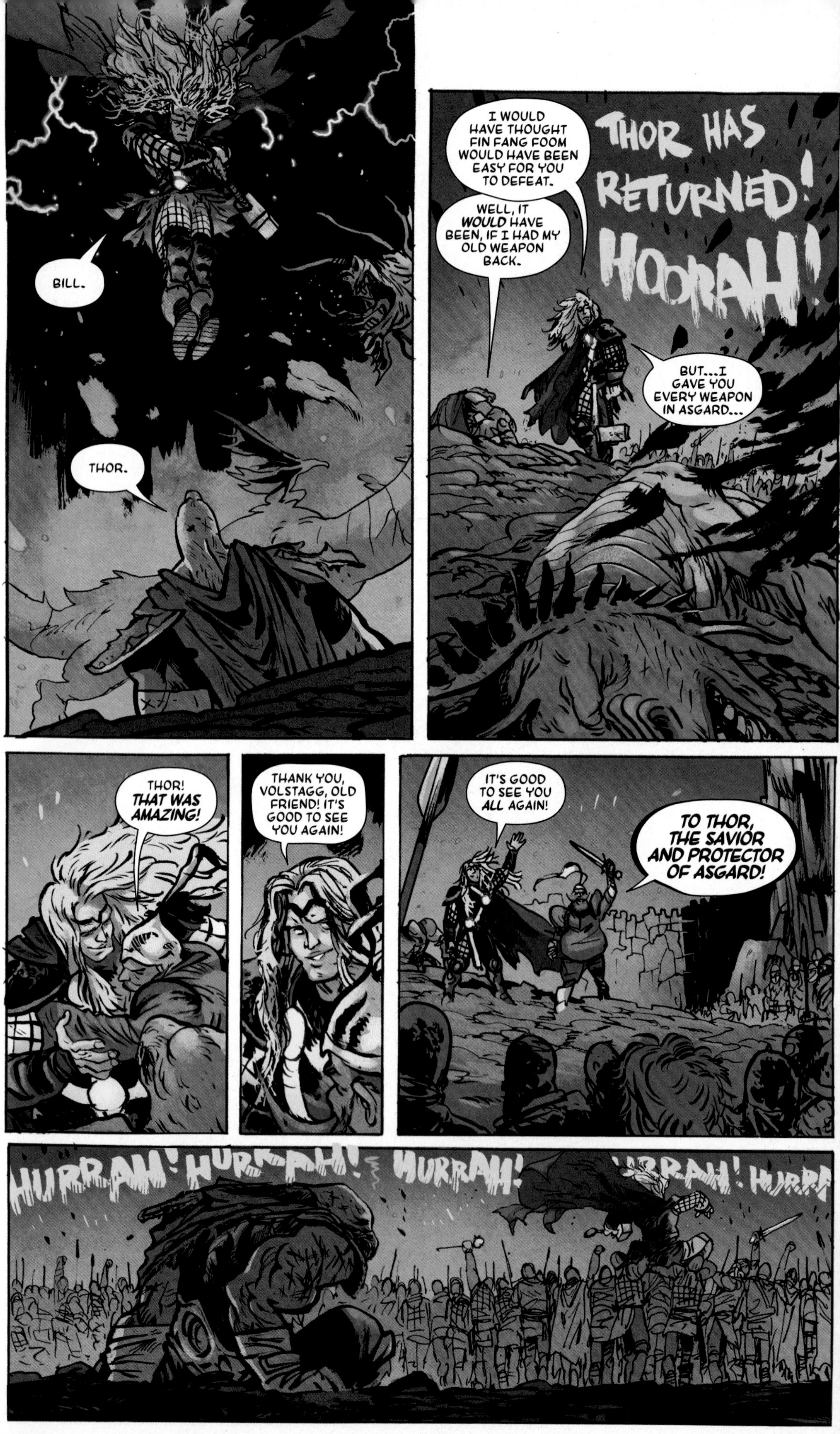
BILL.
THOR.
I WOULD HAVE THOUGHT FIN FANG FOOM WOULD HAVE BEEN EASY FOR YOU TO DEFEAT.
WELL, IT WOULD HAVE BEEN, IF I HAD MY OLD WEAPON BACK.
THOR HAS RETURNED! HOORAH!
BUT...I GAVE YOU EVERY WEAPON IN ASGARD...
THOR! THAT WAS AMAZING!
THANK YOU, VOLSTAGG, OLD FRIEND! IT'S GOOD TO SEE YOU AGAIN!
IT'S GOOD TO SEE YOU ALL AGAIN!
TO THOR, THE SAVIOR AND PROTECTOR OF ASGARD!
HURRAH! HURRAH! HURRAH! HURRAH! HURR

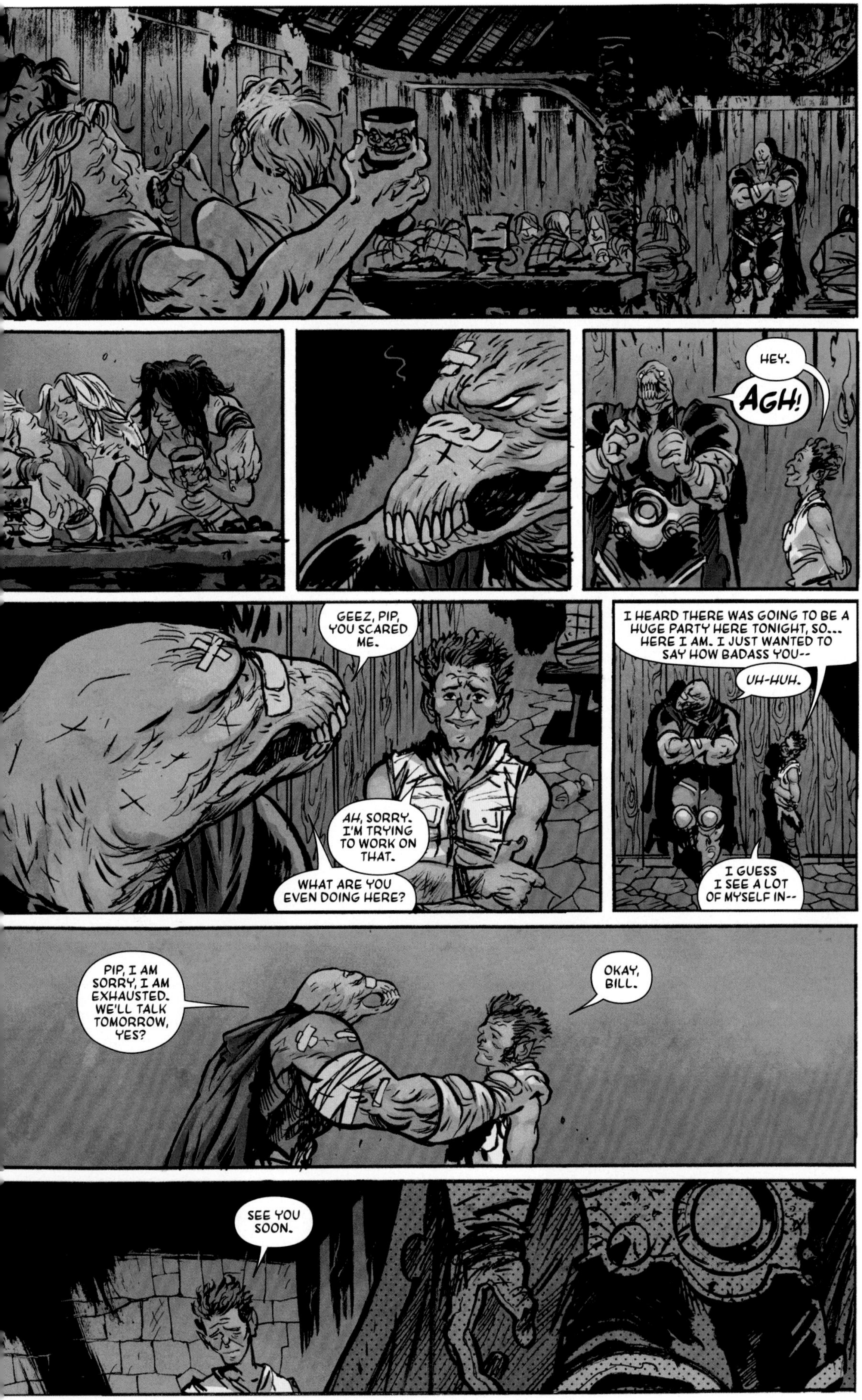

HEY.
AGH!
GEEZ, PIP, YOU SCARED ME.
AH, SORRY. I'M TRYING TO WORK ON THAT.
WHAT ARE YOU EVEN DOING HERE?
I HEARD THERE WAS GOING TO BE A HUGE PARTY HERE TONIGHT, SO... HERE I AM. I JUST WANTED TO SAY HOW BADASS YOU--
UH-HUH.
I GUESS I SEE A LOT OF MYSELF IN--
PIP, I AM SORRY, I AM EXHAUSTED. WE'LL TALK TOMORROW, YES?
OKAY, BILL.
SEE YOU SOON.

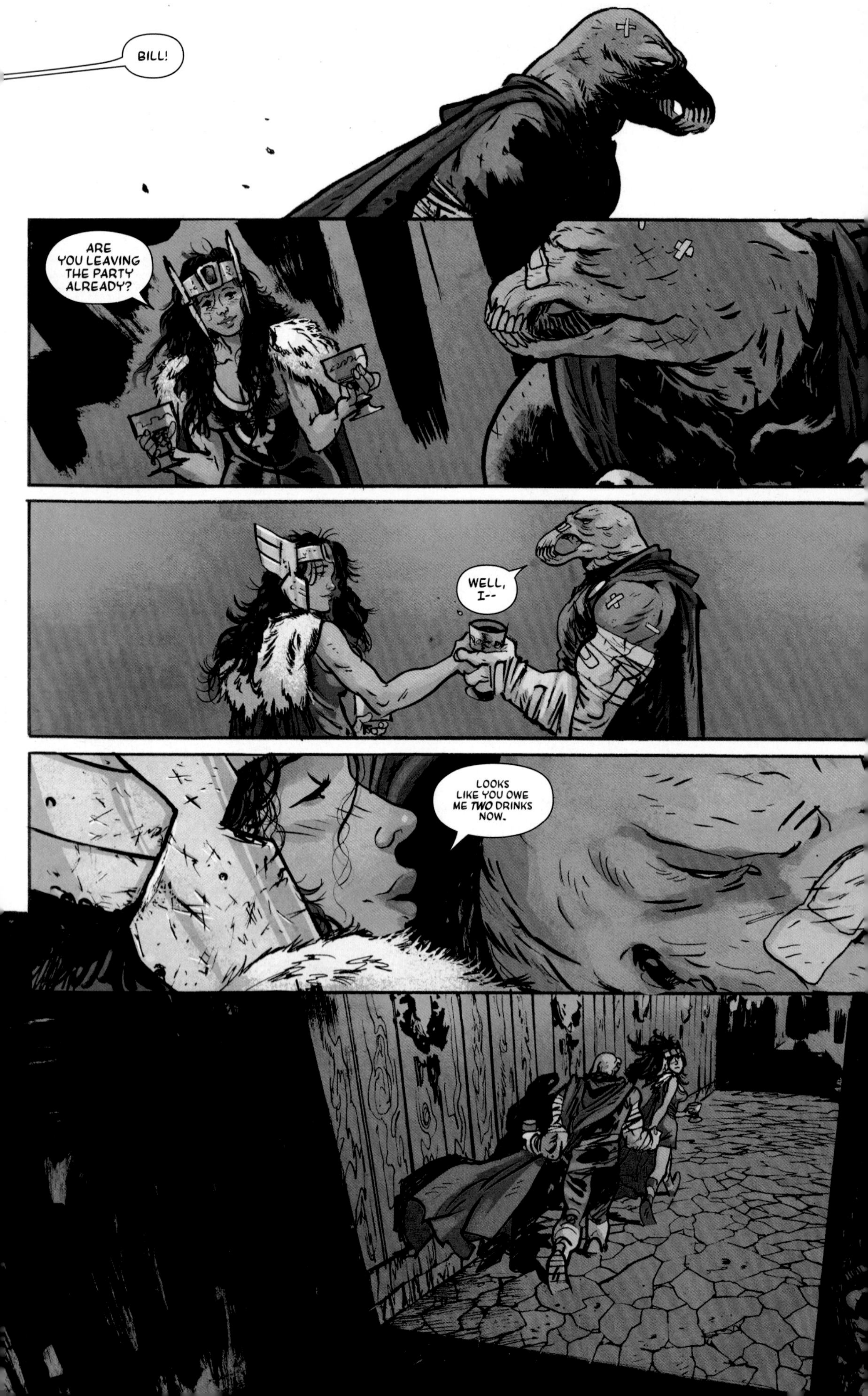
BILL!
ARE YOU LEAVING THE PARTY ALREADY?
WELL, I--
LOOKS LIKE YOU OWE ME *TWO* DRINKS NOW.

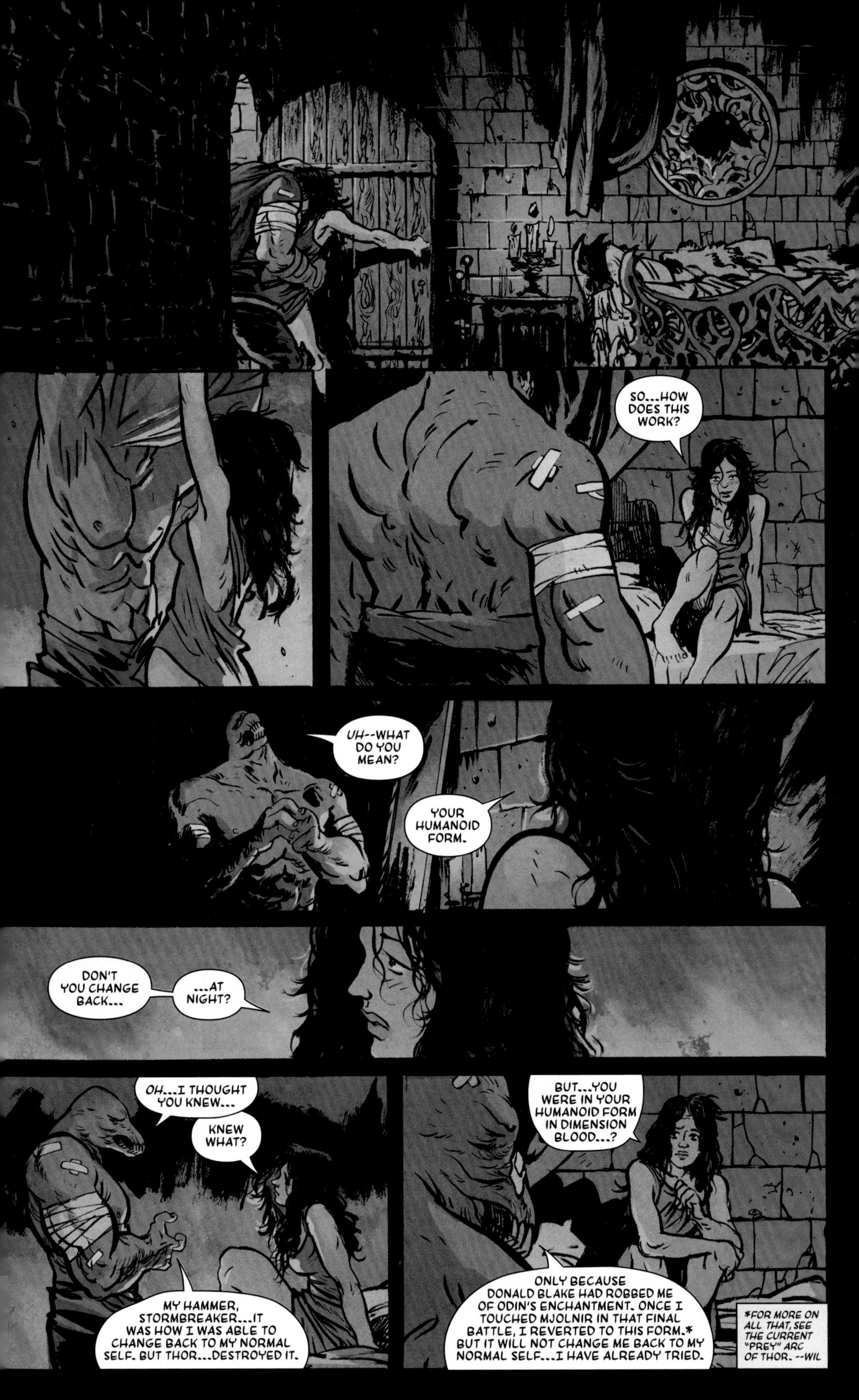
SO...HOW DOES THIS WORK?
UH--WHAT DO YOU MEAN?
YOUR HUMANOID FORM.
DON'T YOU CHANGE BACK...
...AT NIGHT?
OH...I THOUGHT YOU KNEW...
KNEW WHAT?
MY HAMMER, STORMBREAKER...IT WAS HOW I WAS ABLE TO CHANGE BACK TO MY NORMAL SELF. BUT THOR...DESTROYED IT.
BUT...YOU WERE IN YOUR HUMANOID FORM IN DIMENSION BLOOD...?
ONLY BECAUSE DONALD BLAKE HAD ROBBED ME OF ODIN'S ENCHANTMENT. ONCE I TOUCHED MJOLNIR IN THAT FINAL BATTLE, I REVERTED TO THIS FORM.* BUT IT WILL NOT CHANGE ME BACK TO MY NORMAL SELF...I HAVE ALREADY TRIED.
*FOR MORE ON ALL THAT, SEE THE CURRENT "PREY" ARC OF THOR. --WIL

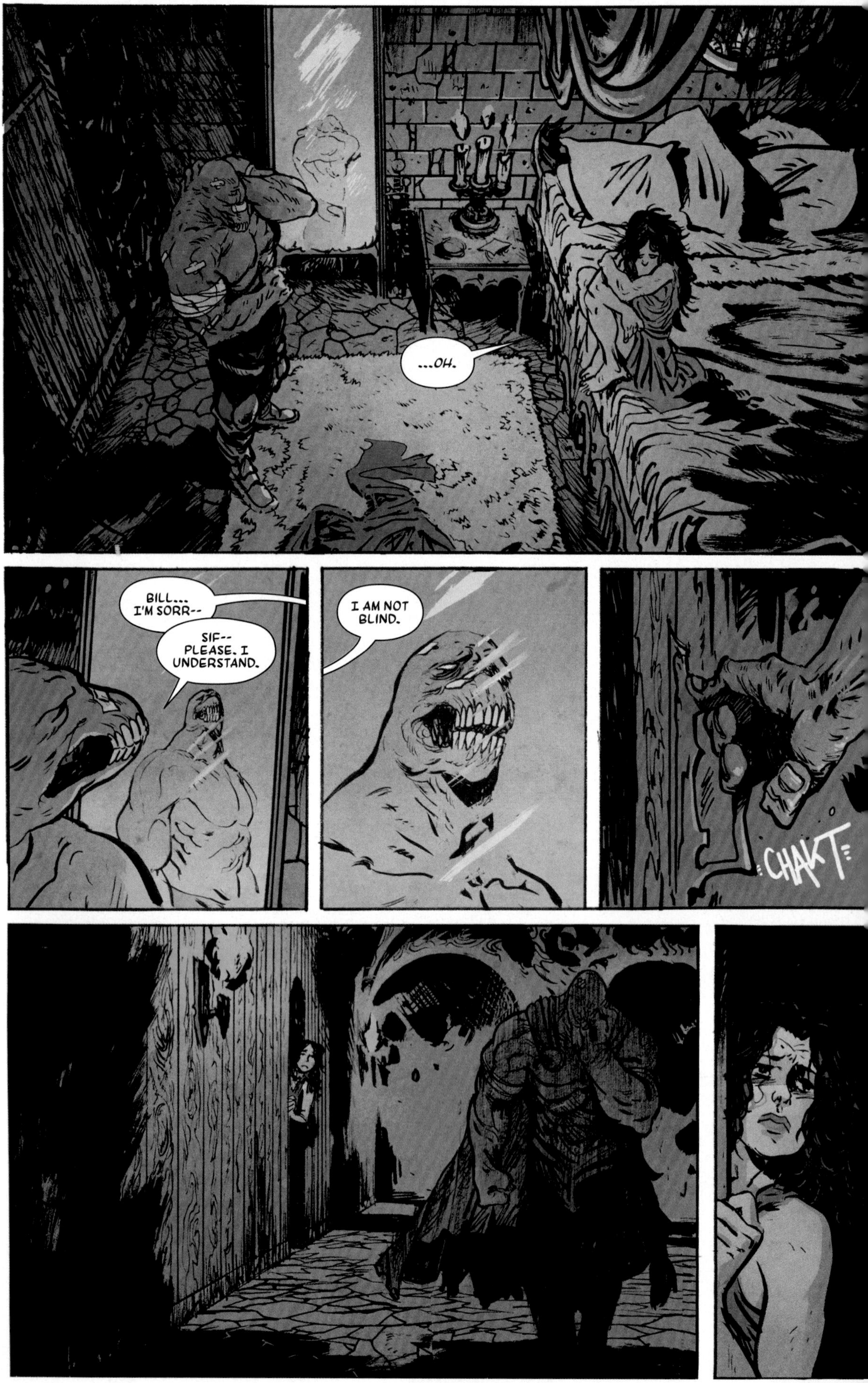
...OH.
BILL... I'M SORR--
SIF-- PLEASE. I UNDERSTAND.
I AM NOT BLIND.
CHAKT

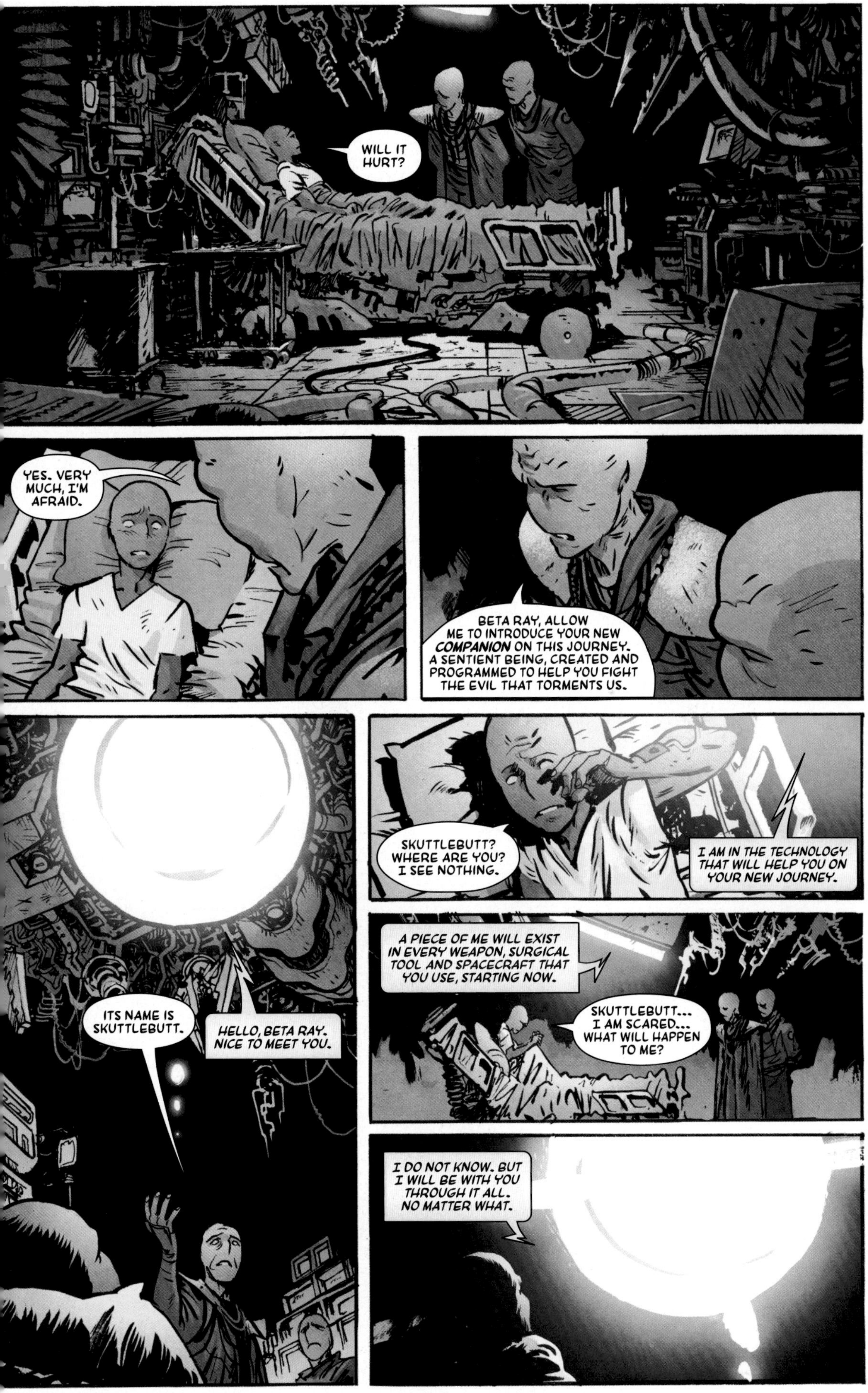
WILL IT HURT?
YES. VERY MUCH, I'M AFRAID.
BETA RAY, ALLOW ME TO INTRODUCE YOUR NEW COMPANION ON THIS JOURNEY. A SENTIENT BEING, CREATED AND PROGRAMMED TO HELP YOU FIGHT THE EVIL THAT TORMENTS US.
ITS NAME IS SKUTTLEBUTT.
HELLO, BETA RAY. NICE TO MEET YOU.
SKUTTLEBUTT? WHERE ARE YOU? I SEE NOTHING.
I AM IN THE TECHNOLOGY THAT WILL HELP YOU ON YOUR NEW JOURNEY.
A PIECE OF ME WILL EXIST IN EVERY WEAPON, SURGICAL TOOL AND SPACECRAFT THAT YOU USE, STARTING NOW.
SKUTTLEBUTT... I AM SCARED... WHAT WILL HAPPEN TO ME?
I DO NOT KNOW. BUT I WILL BE WITH YOU THROUGH IT ALL. NO MATTER WHAT.

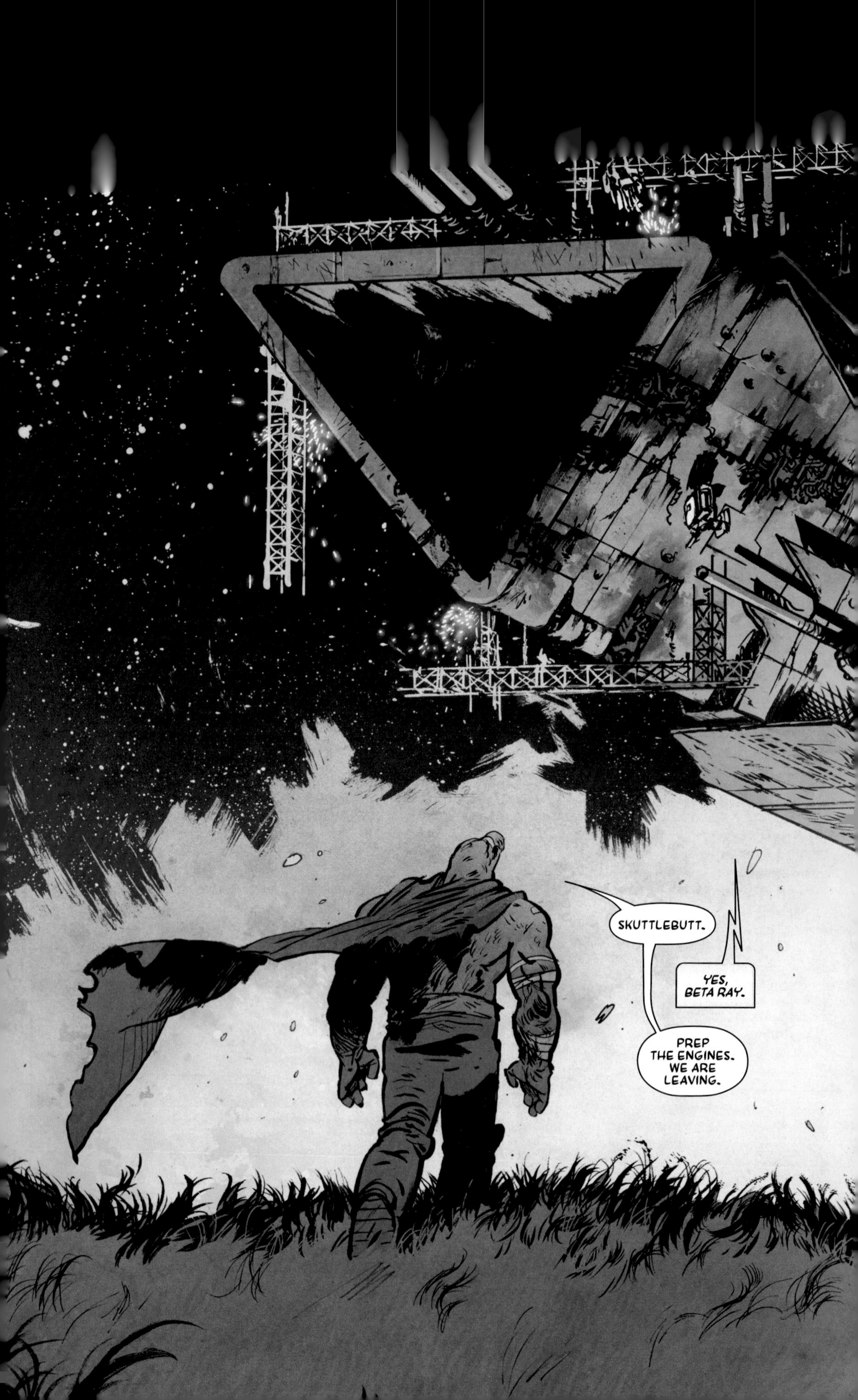
SKUTTLEBUTT.
YES, BETA RAY.
PREP THE ENGINES. WE ARE LEAVING.

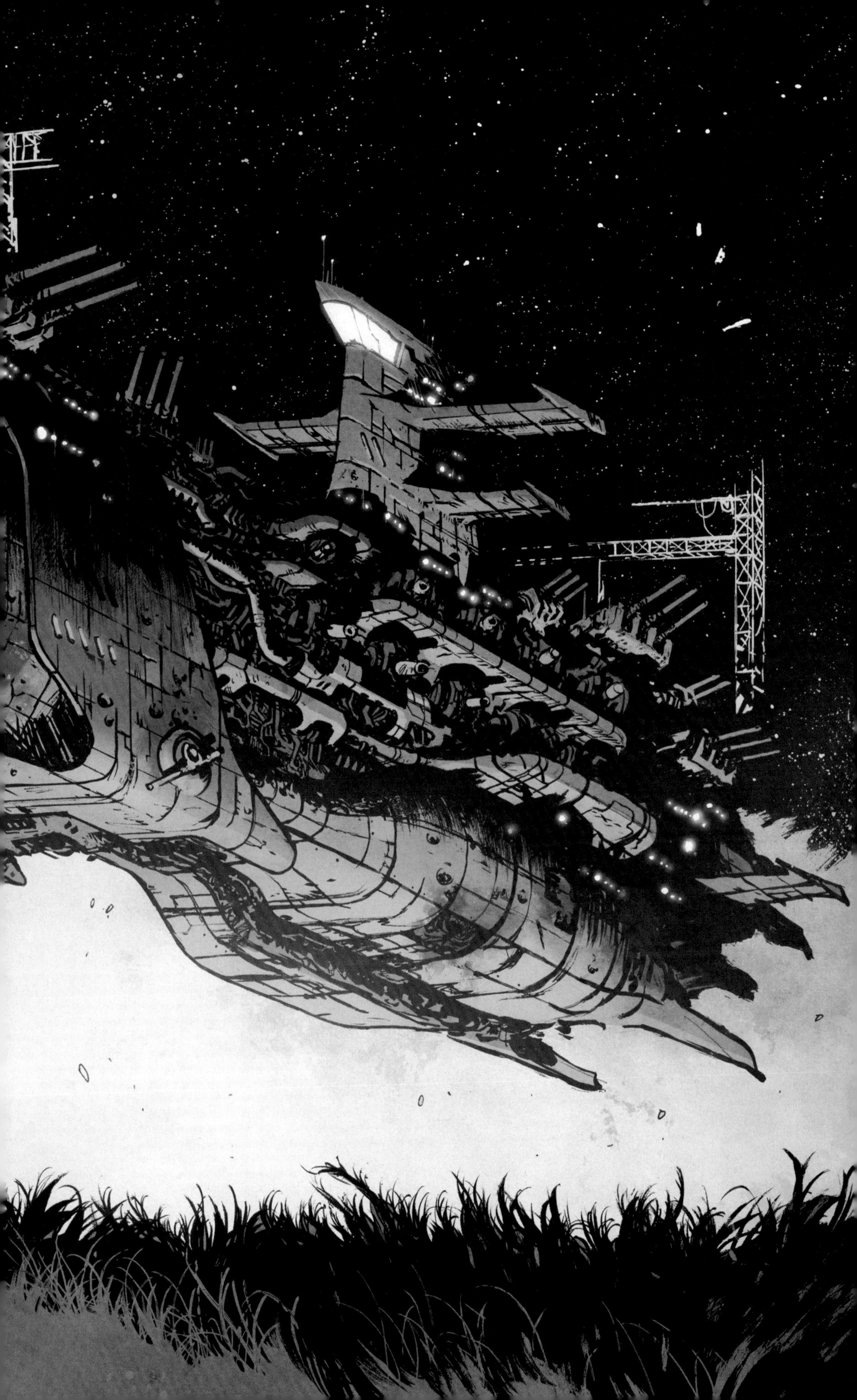

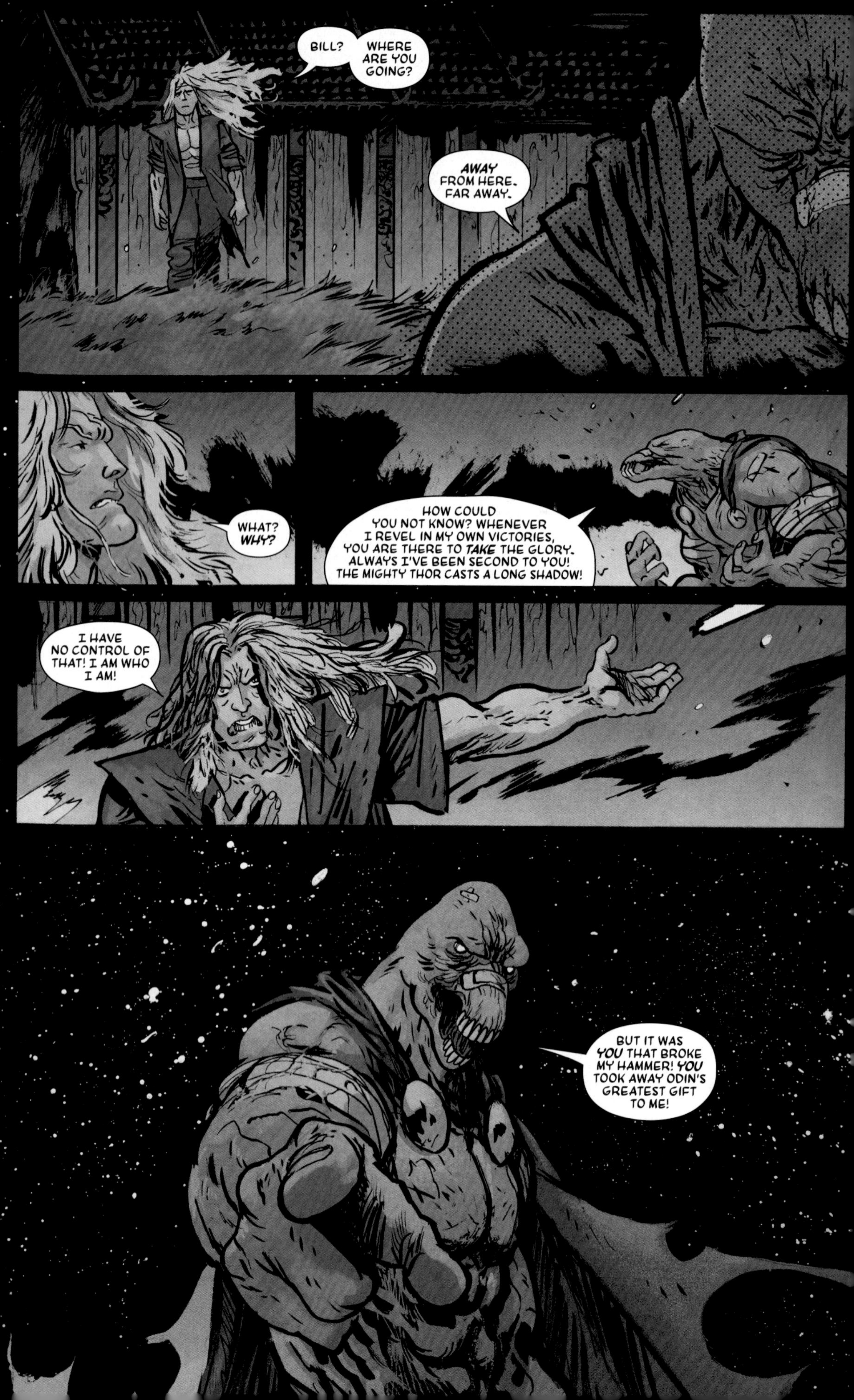
BILL?
WHERE ARE YOU GOING?
AWAY FROM HERE. FAR AWAY.
WHAT? WHY?
HOW COULD YOU NOT KNOW? WHENEVER I REVEL IN MY OWN VICTORIES, YOU ARE THERE TO TAKE THE GLORY. ALWAYS I'VE BEEN SECOND TO YOU! THE MIGHTY THOR CASTS A LONG SHADOW!
I HAVE NO CONTROL OF THAT! I AM WHO I AM!
BUT IT WAS YOU THAT BROKE MY HAMMER! YOU TOOK AWAY ODIN'S GREATEST GIFT TO ME!

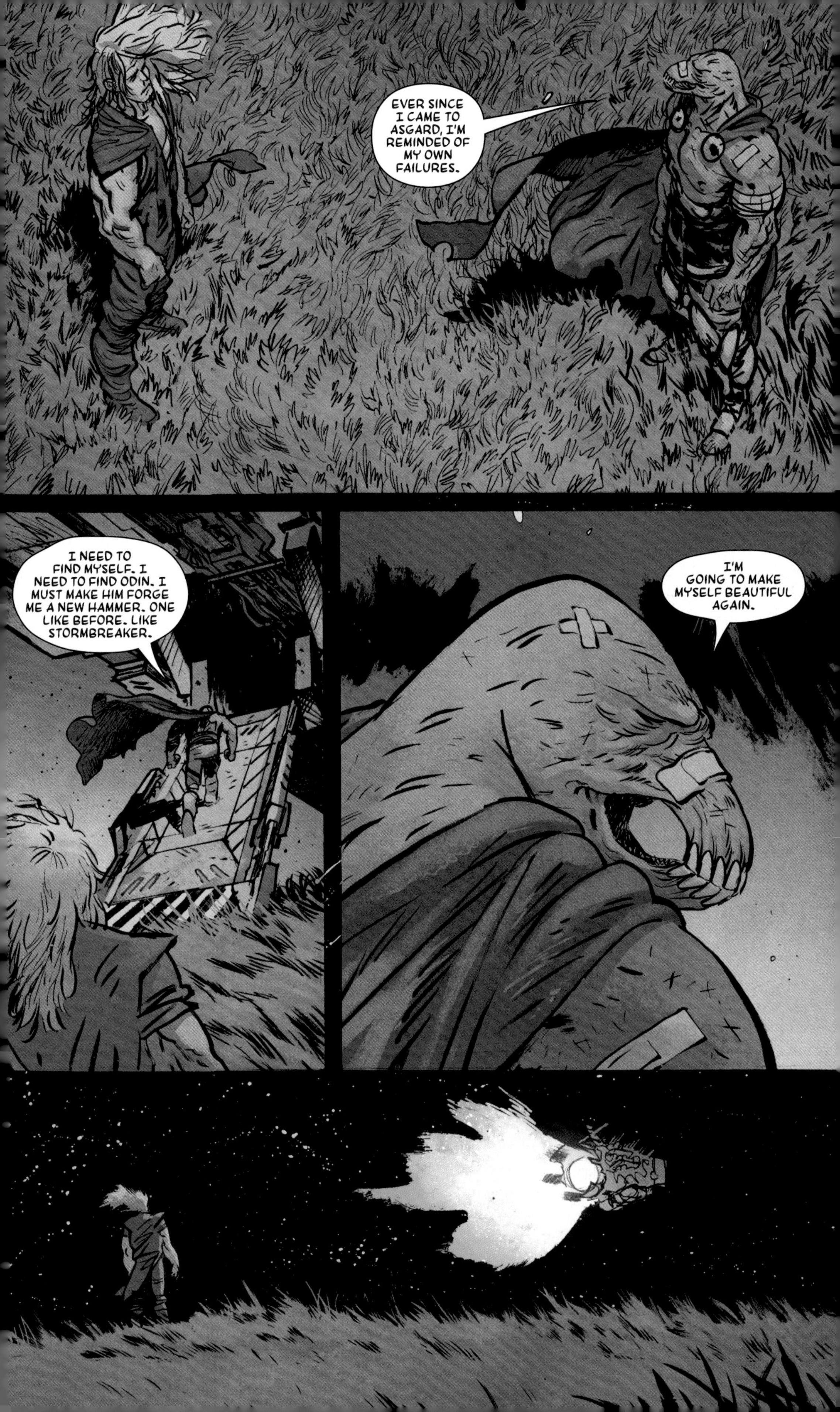
EVER SINCE I CAME TO ASGARD, I'M REMINDED OF MY OWN FAILURES.
I NEED TO FIND MYSELF. I NEED TO FIND ODIN. I MUST MAKE HIM FORGE ME A NEW HAMMER. ONE LIKE BEFORE. LIKE STORMBREAKER.
I'M GOING TO MAKE MYSELF BEAUTIFUL AGAIN.

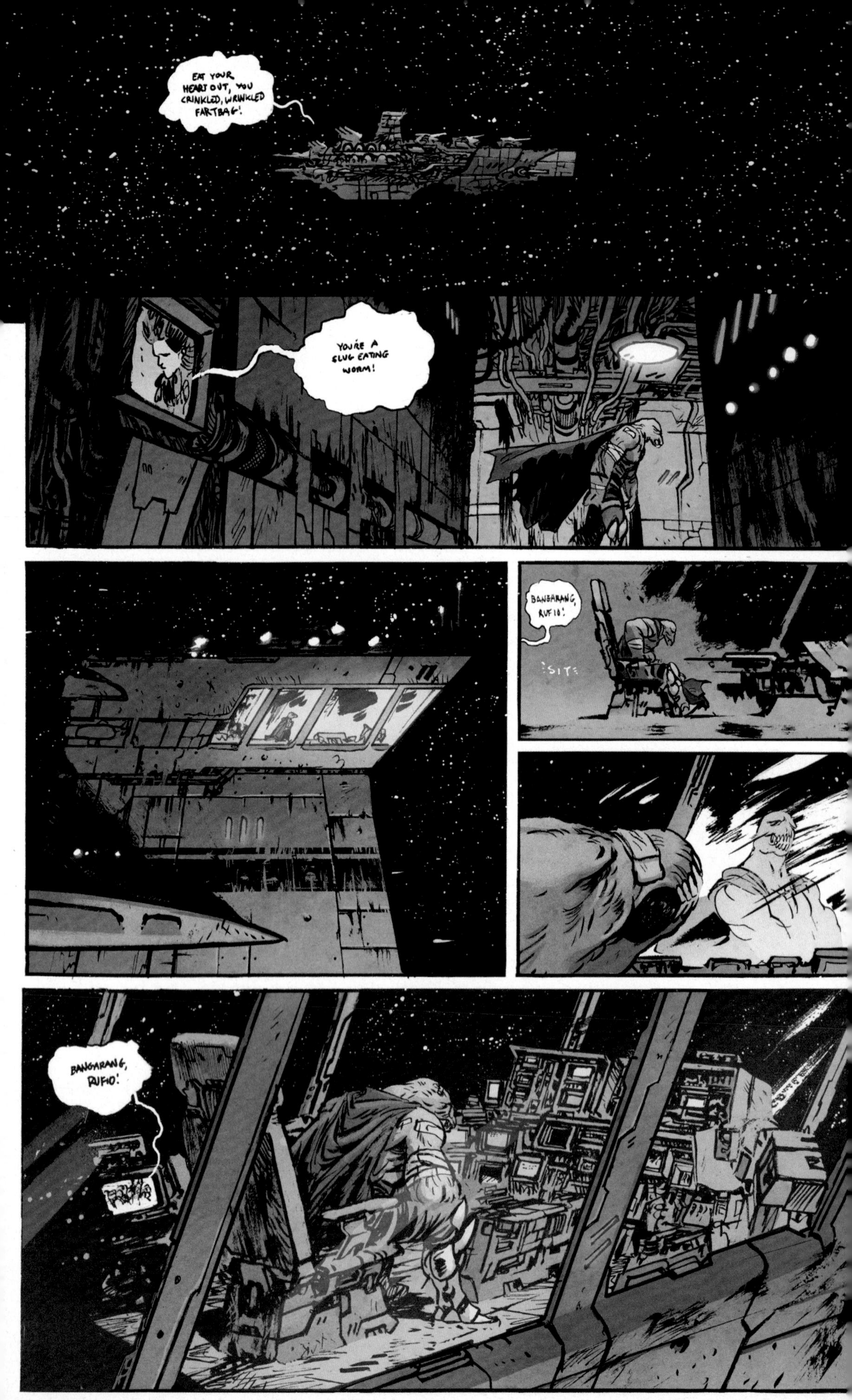
EAT YOUR HEART OUT, YOU CRINKLED, WRINKLED FARTBAG!
YOU'RE A SLUG EATING WORM!
BANGARANG, RUFIO!
SIT
BANGARANG, RUFIO!

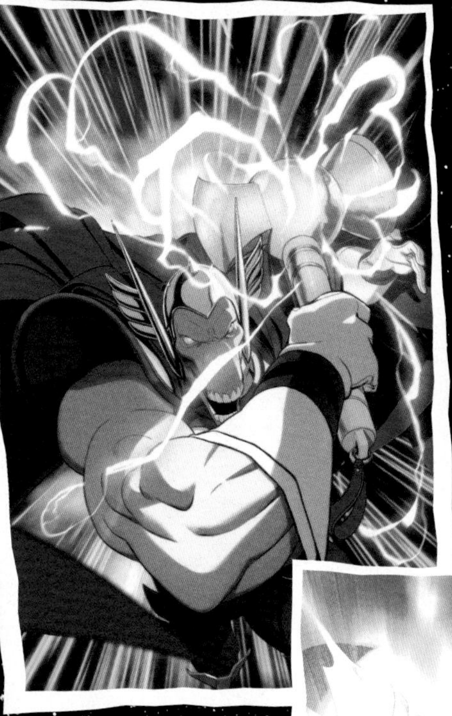

#1 VARIANT BY CHASE CONLEY

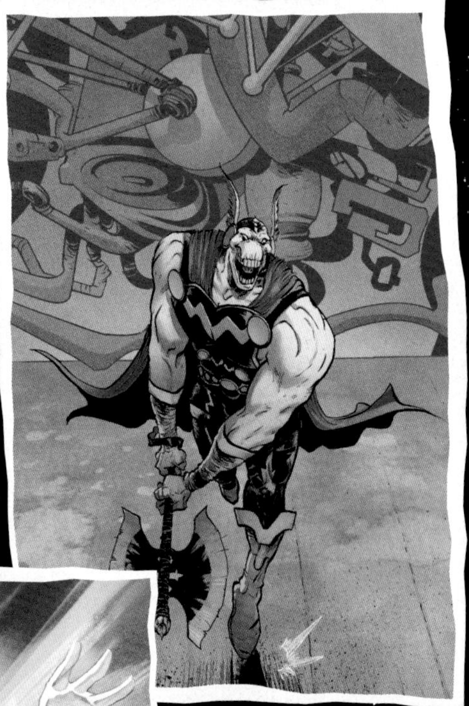

#2 VARIANT BY PAUL POPE & MIKE SPICER

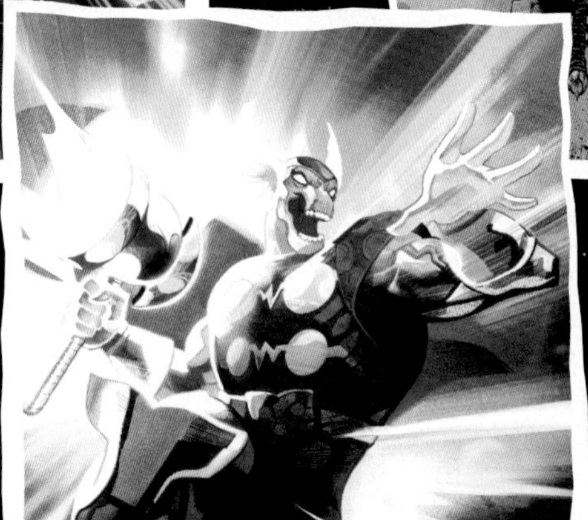

#3 VARIANT BY MIKE DEL MUNDO

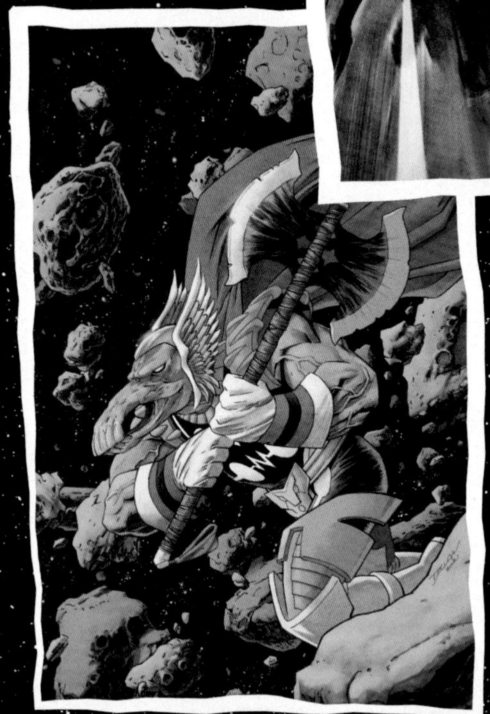

#4 VARIANT BY DECLAN SHALVEY

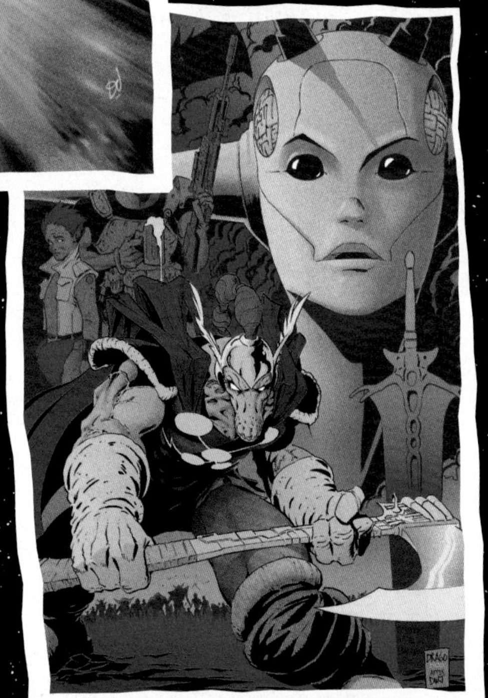

#5 VARIANT BY NICK DRAGOTTA & RICO RENZI

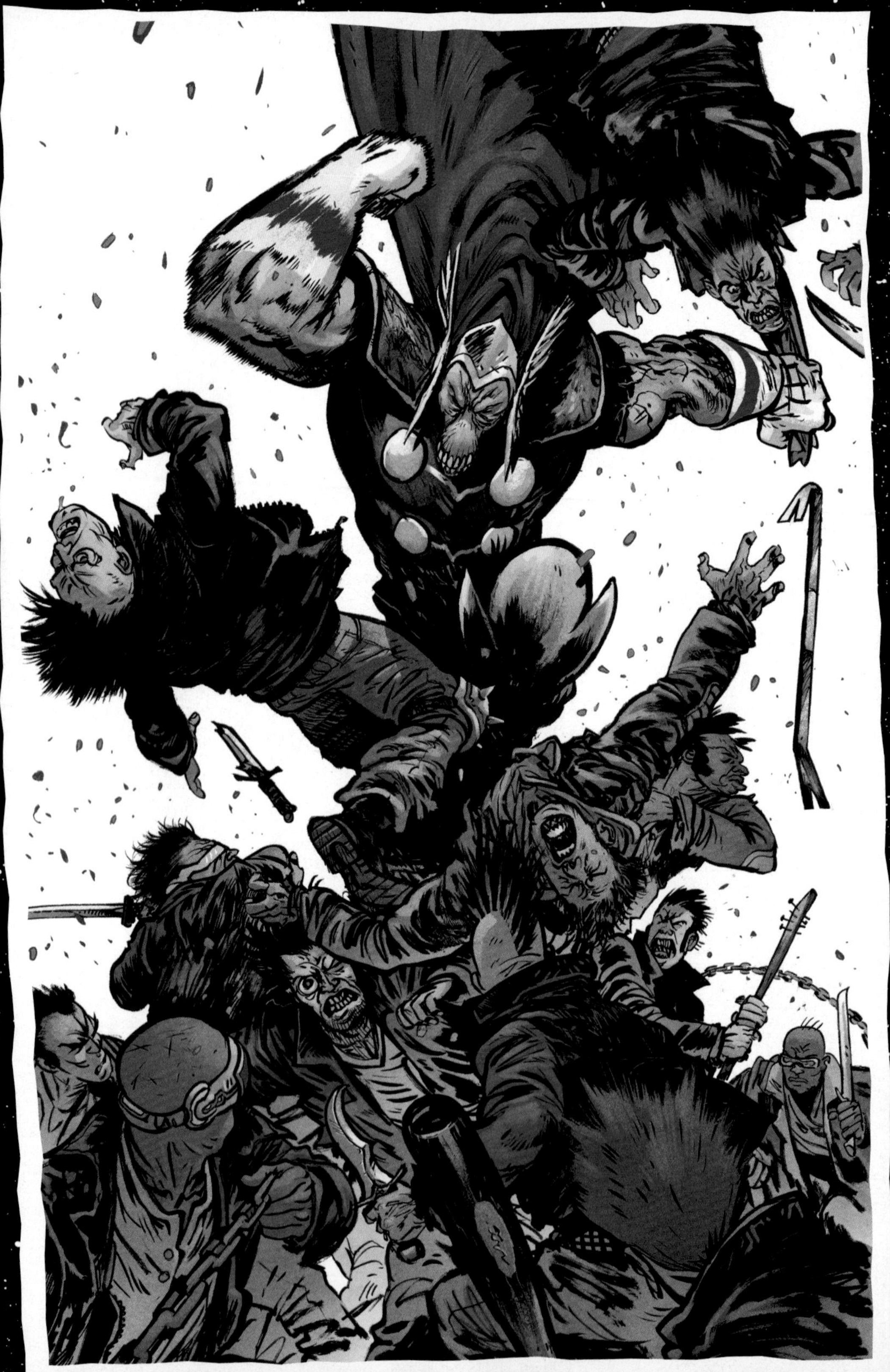

2

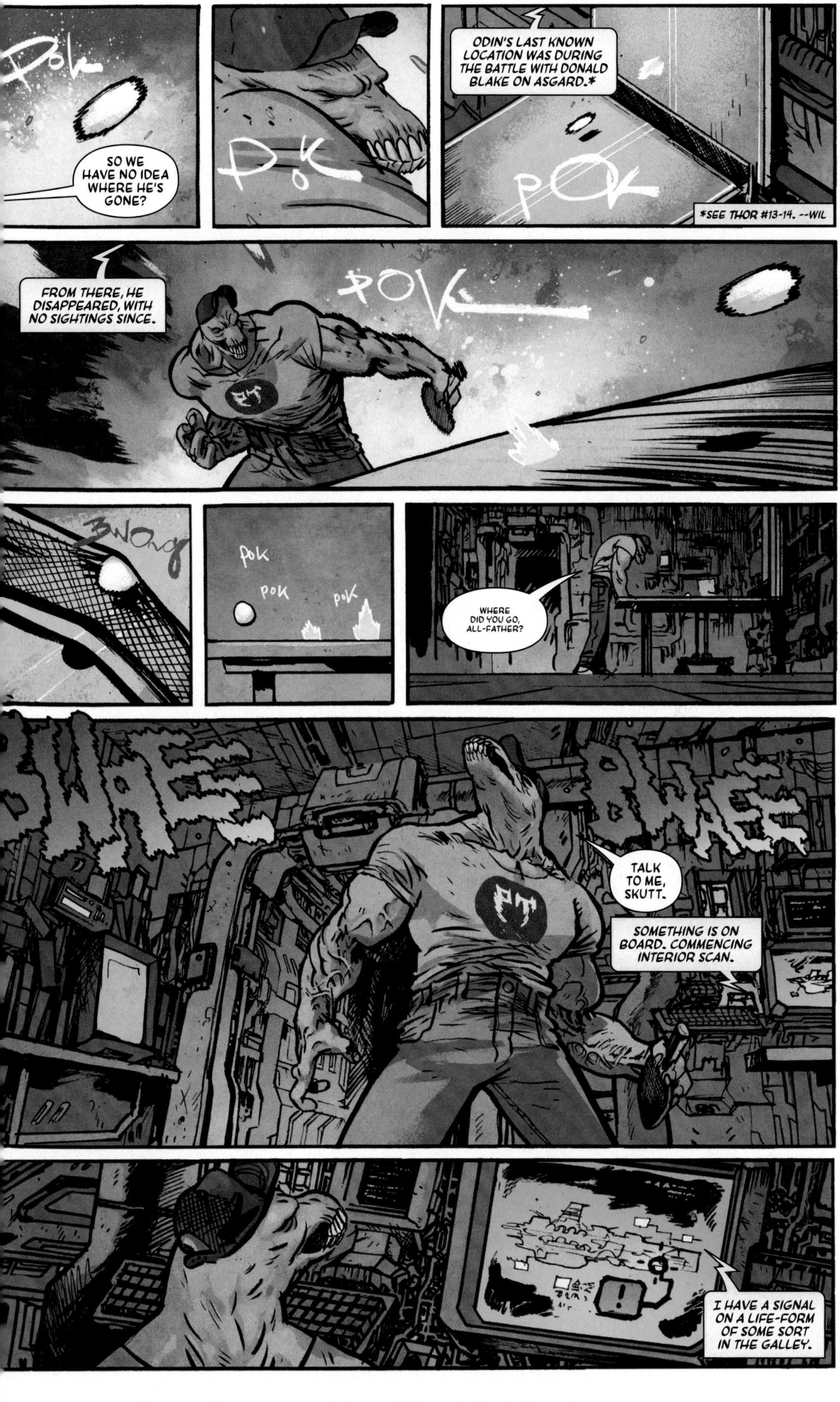
POK
SO WE HAVE NO IDEA WHERE HE'S GONE?
POK
ODIN'S LAST KNOWN LOCATION WAS DURING THE BATTLE WITH DONALD BLAKE ON ASGARD.*
POK
*SEE THOR #13-14. --WIL
FROM THERE, HE DISAPPEARED, WITH NO SIGHTINGS SINCE.
POK
BWONG
POK
POK
POK
WHERE DID YOU GO, ALL-FATHER?
TALK TO ME, SKUTT.
SOMETHING IS ON BOARD. COMMENCING INTERIOR SCAN.
I HAVE A SIGNAL ON A LIFE-FORM OF SOME SORT IN THE GALLEY.

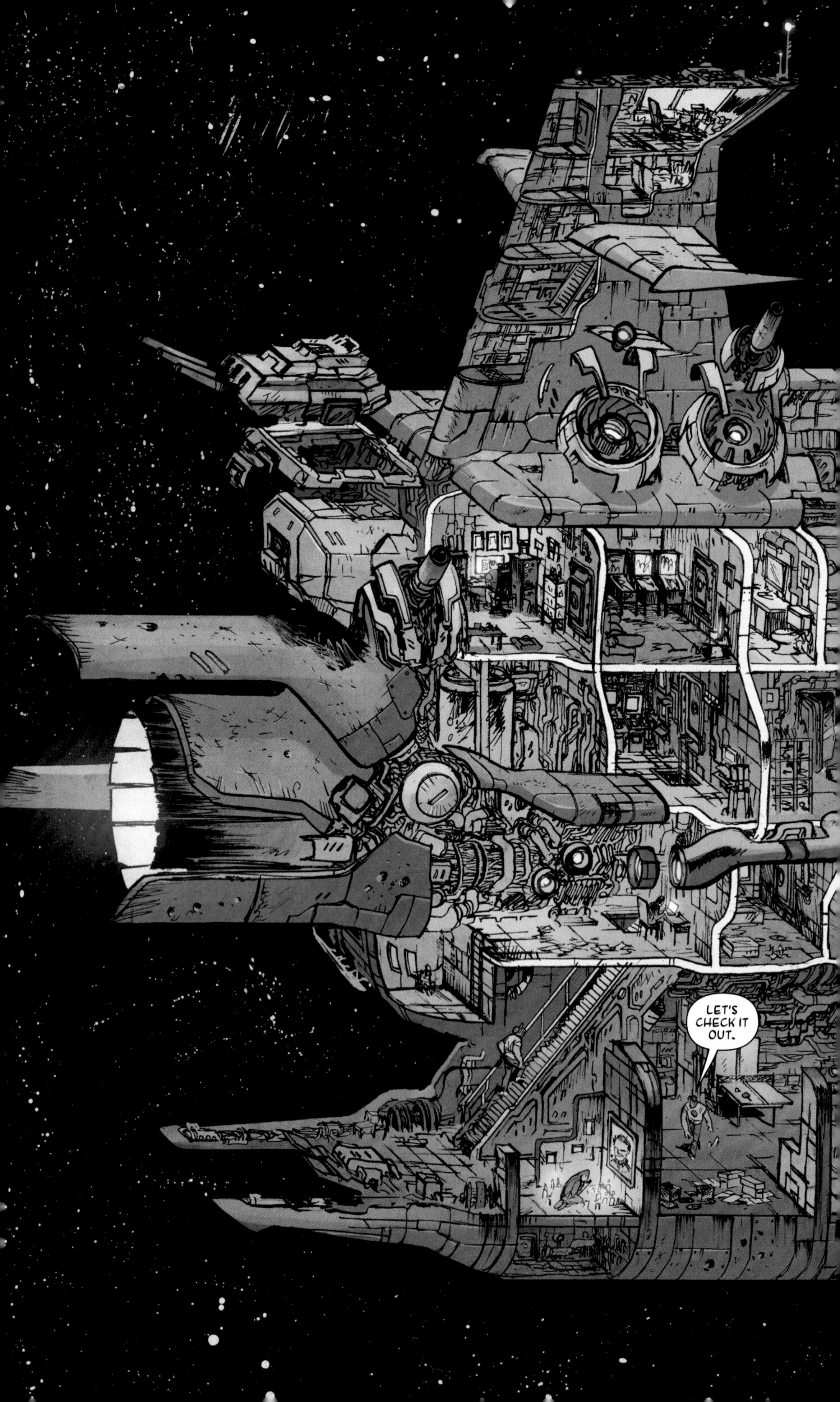
LET'S CHECK IT OUT.

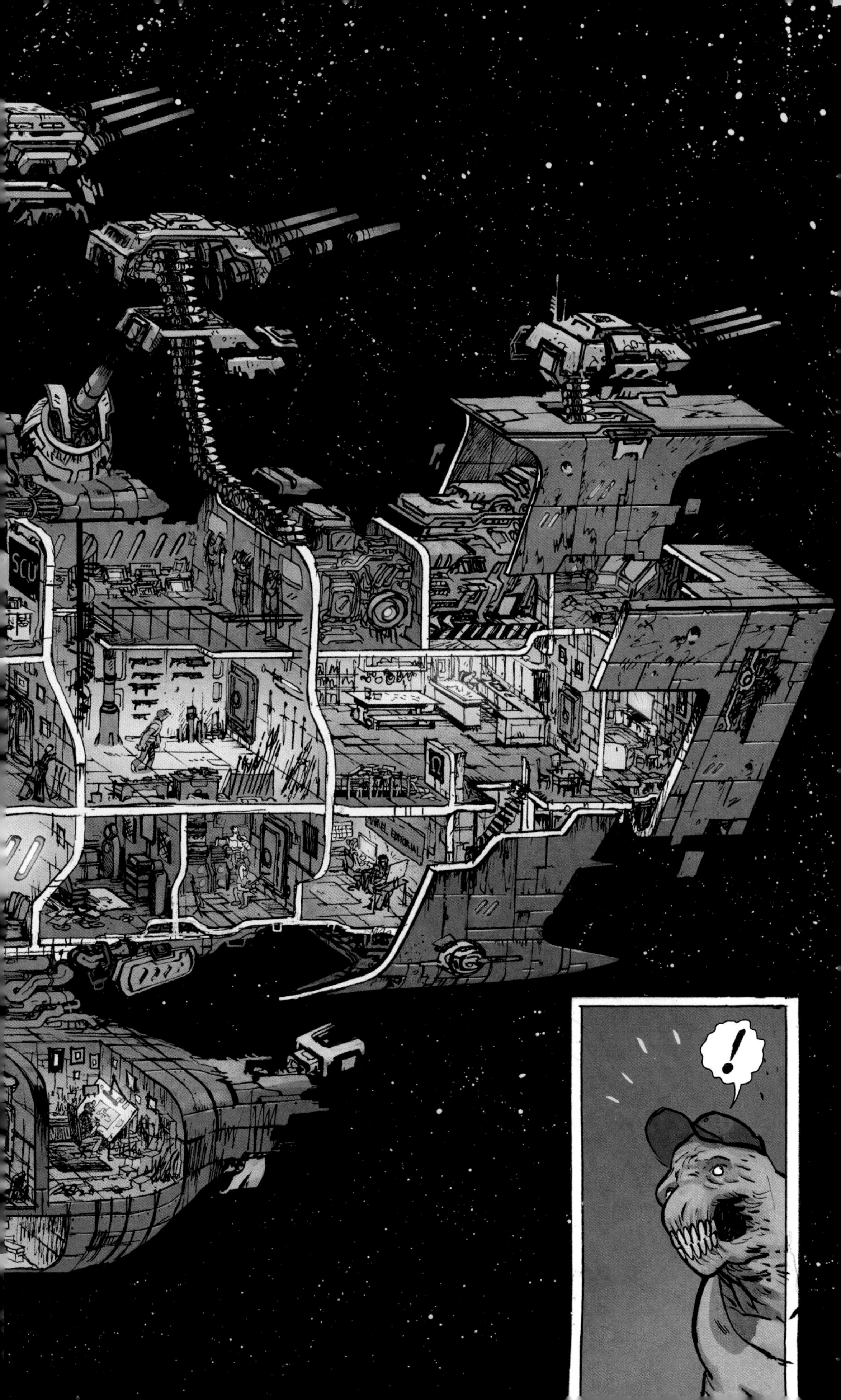
SCU
MARVEL EDITORIAL
!

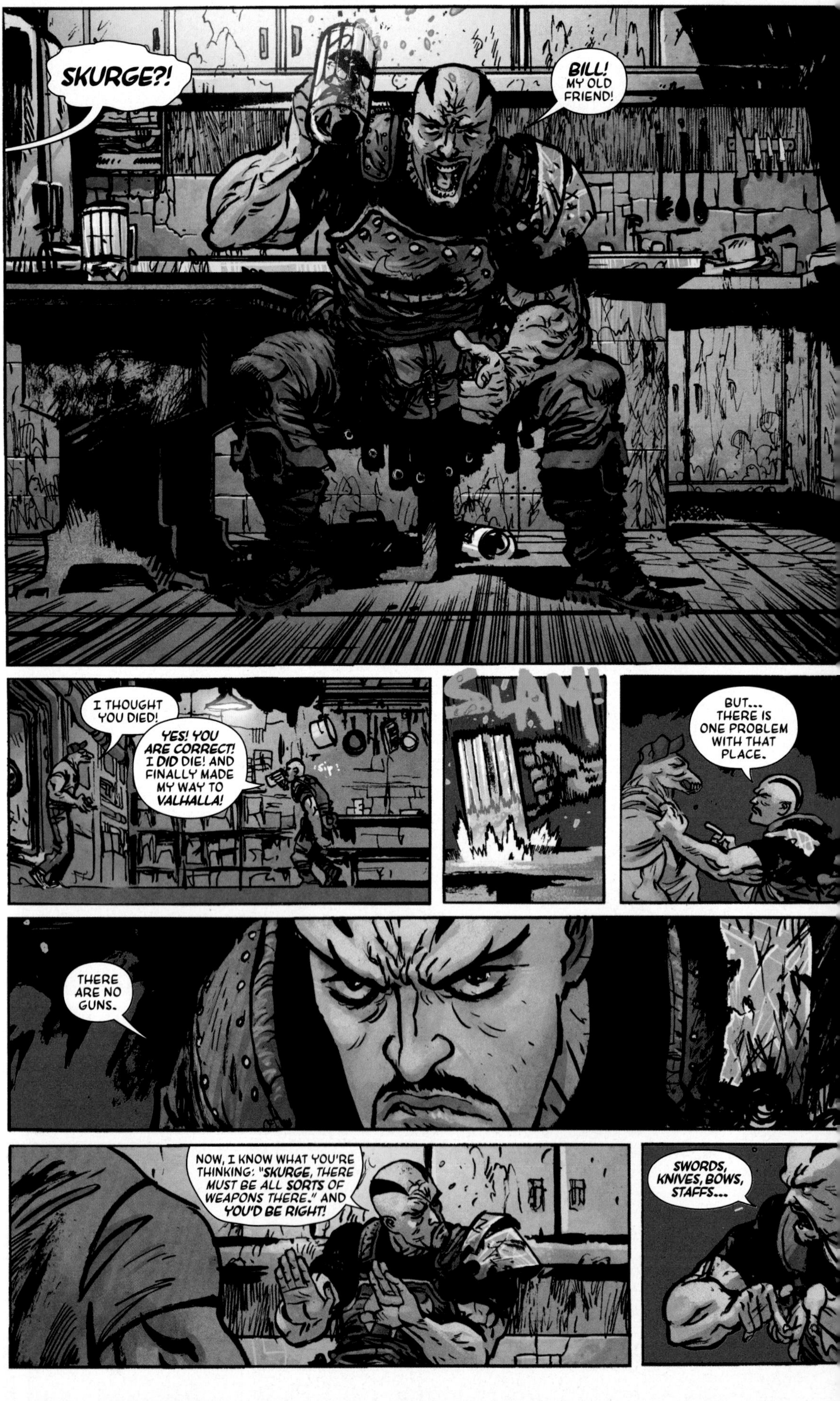
SKURGE?!
BILL! MY OLD FRIEND!
I THOUGHT YOU DIED!
YES! YOU ARE CORRECT! I DID DIE! AND FINALLY MADE MY WAY TO VALHALLA!
SIP
SLAM!
BUT... THERE IS ONE PROBLEM WITH THAT PLACE.
THERE ARE NO GUNS.
NOW, I KNOW WHAT YOU'RE THINKING: "SKURGE, THERE MUST BE ALL SORTS OF WEAPONS THERE." AND YOU'D BE RIGHT!
SWORDS, KNIVES, BOWS, STAFFS...

BUT NO *GUNS!* HOW CAN A HEAVENLY PLACE BE *HEAVENLY* WITHOUT *GUNS?!*

I-- WHAT IS IT?

BUT THAT'S NOT WHY I AM HERE. BILL... I MUST BE HONEST...

I SAW WHAT HAPPENED TO YOU ON ASGARD. WITH SIF.

WHAT?! HOW--?

AS I SAID! VALHALLA IS *BORING!* SOMETIMES I CANNOT HELP BUT VISIT MY OLD HOME IN ETHEREAL FORM. AND IT WAS DURING THIS LATEST VISIT...

...THAT I WITNESSED YOUR *REJECTION.*

HUG

BROTHER...MY SOUL CRIED OUT FOR YOU. AND I *DEMANDED* THE VALKYRIES GIVE ME TEMPORARY LEAVE SO I COULD COME *HELP* YOU ON YOUR QUEST. I WANT TO BE YOUR... AH, WHAT DO THOSE HUMANS CALL IT--?

AH, YES! WINGMAN! THAT'S IT!

SKURGE. I APPRECIATE YOUR CANDOR. HOWEVER, THIS IS A MISSION THAT I MUST DO ALO--

NONSENSE! WHO ELSE IS GOING TO HELP YOU BECOME YOUR OLD SELF AGAIN?! DO ME A FAVOR AND LET ME JOIN YOU. I CAN BE USEFUL!

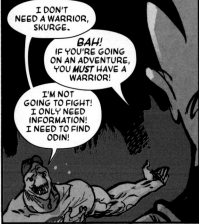
I DON'T NEED A WARRIOR, SKURGE.

BAH! IF YOU'RE GOING ON AN ADVENTURE, YOU *MUST* HAVE A WARRIOR!

I'M NOT GOING TO FIGHT! I ONLY NEED INFORMATION! I NEED TO FIND ODIN!

AND I KNOW WHERE HE IS.

SEE? *USEFUL.*

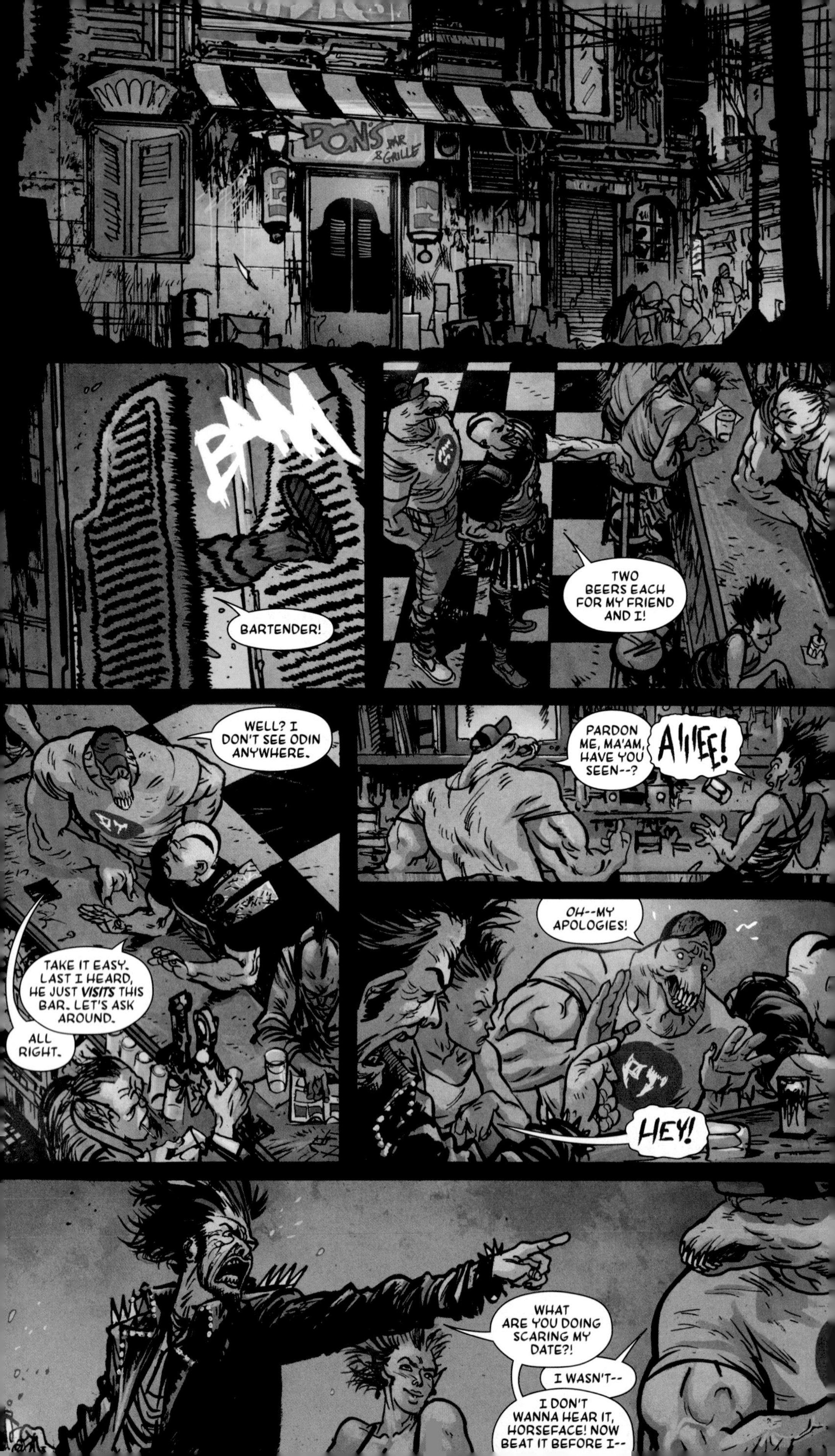
DON'S BAR & GRILLE
BAM
BARTENDER!
TWO BEERS EACH FOR MY FRIEND AND I!
WELL? I DON'T SEE ODIN ANYWHERE.
TAKE IT EASY. LAST I HEARD, HE JUST *VISITS* THIS BAR. LET'S ASK AROUND.
ALL RIGHT.
PARDON ME, MA'AM, HAVE YOU SEEN--?
AIIEEE!
OH--MY APOLOGIES!
HEY!
WHAT ARE YOU DOING SCARING MY DATE?!
I WASN'T--
I DON'T WANNA HEAR IT, HORSEFACE! NOW BEAT IT BEFORE I--

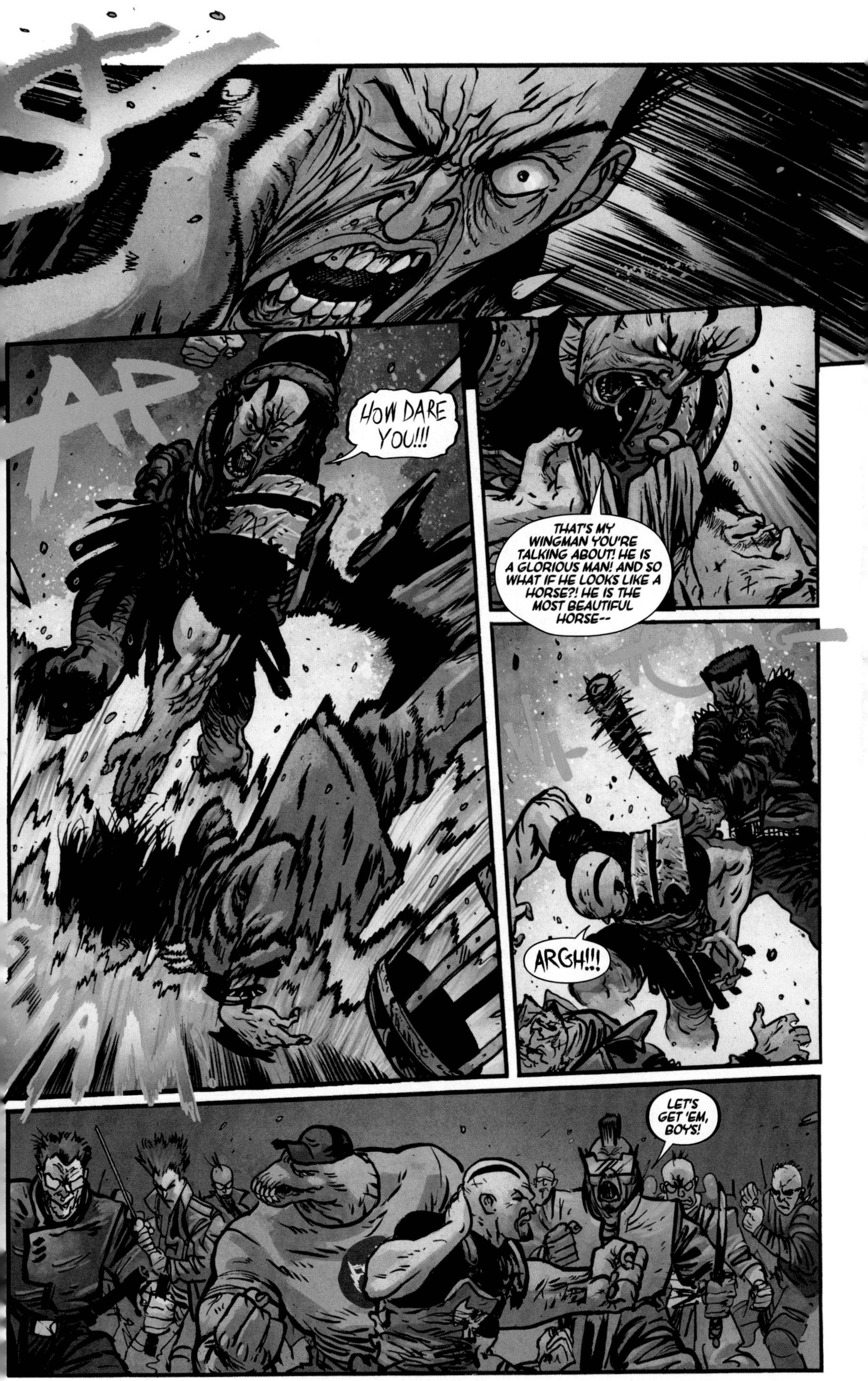
HOW DARE YOU!!!
THAT'S MY WINGMAN YOU'RE TALKING ABOUT! HE IS A GLORIOUS MAN! AND SO WHAT IF HE LOOKS LIKE A HORSE?! HE IS THE MOST BEAUTIFUL HORSE--
ARGH!!!
LET'S GET 'EM, BOYS!

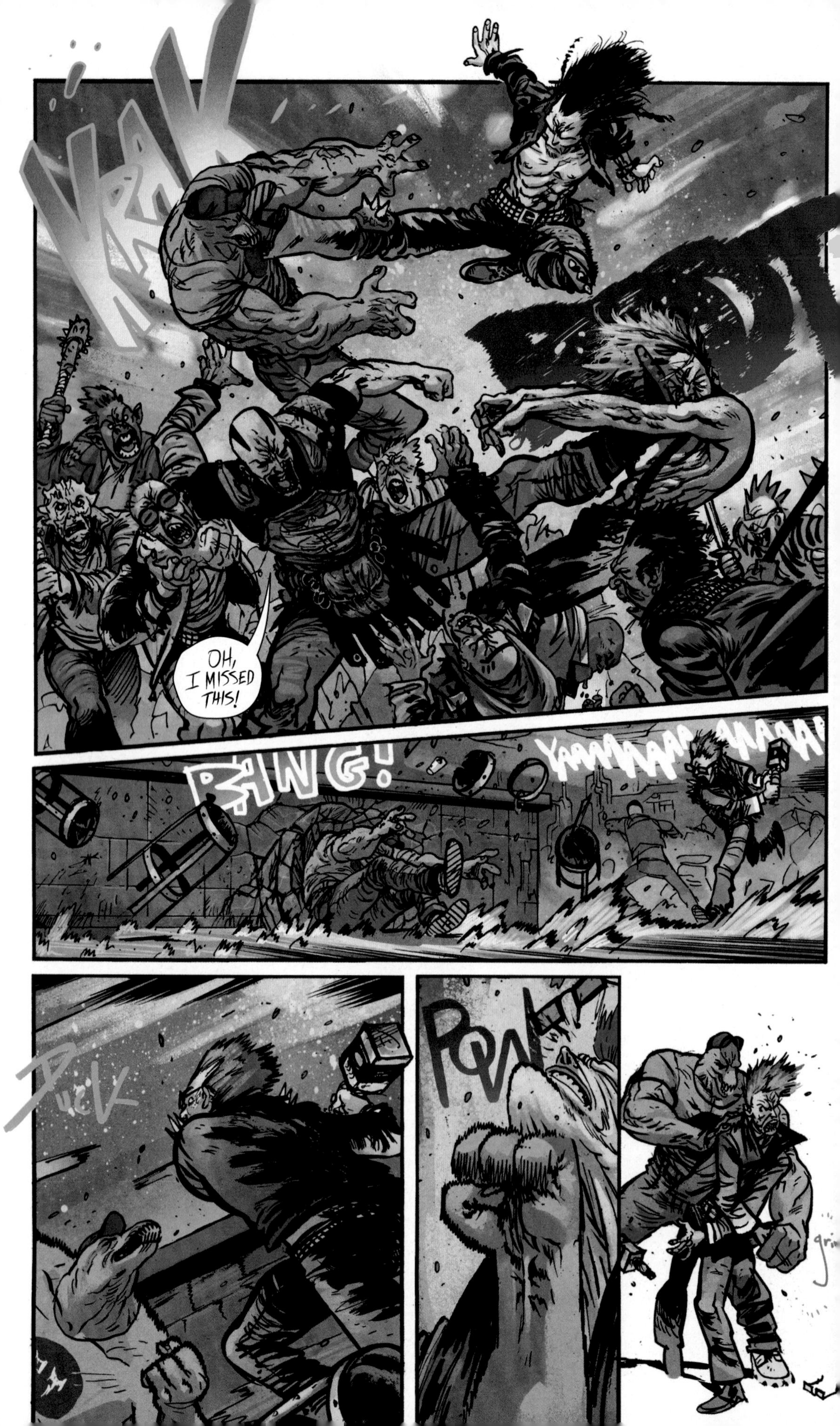
OH, I MISSED THIS!
BANG!
POW

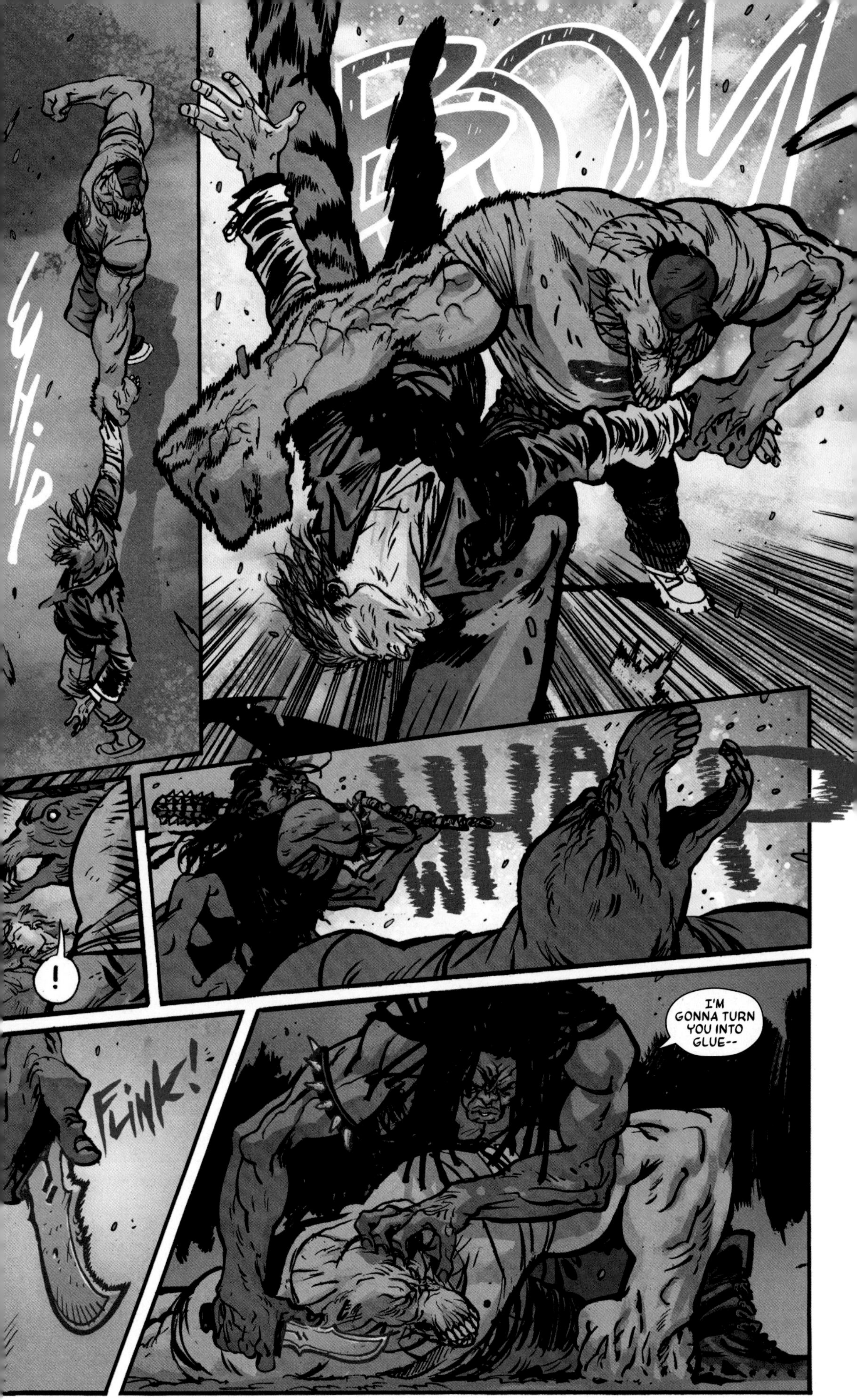

WHIP
BOOM
WHAP
!
FLINK!
I'M GONNA TURN YOU INTO GLUE--

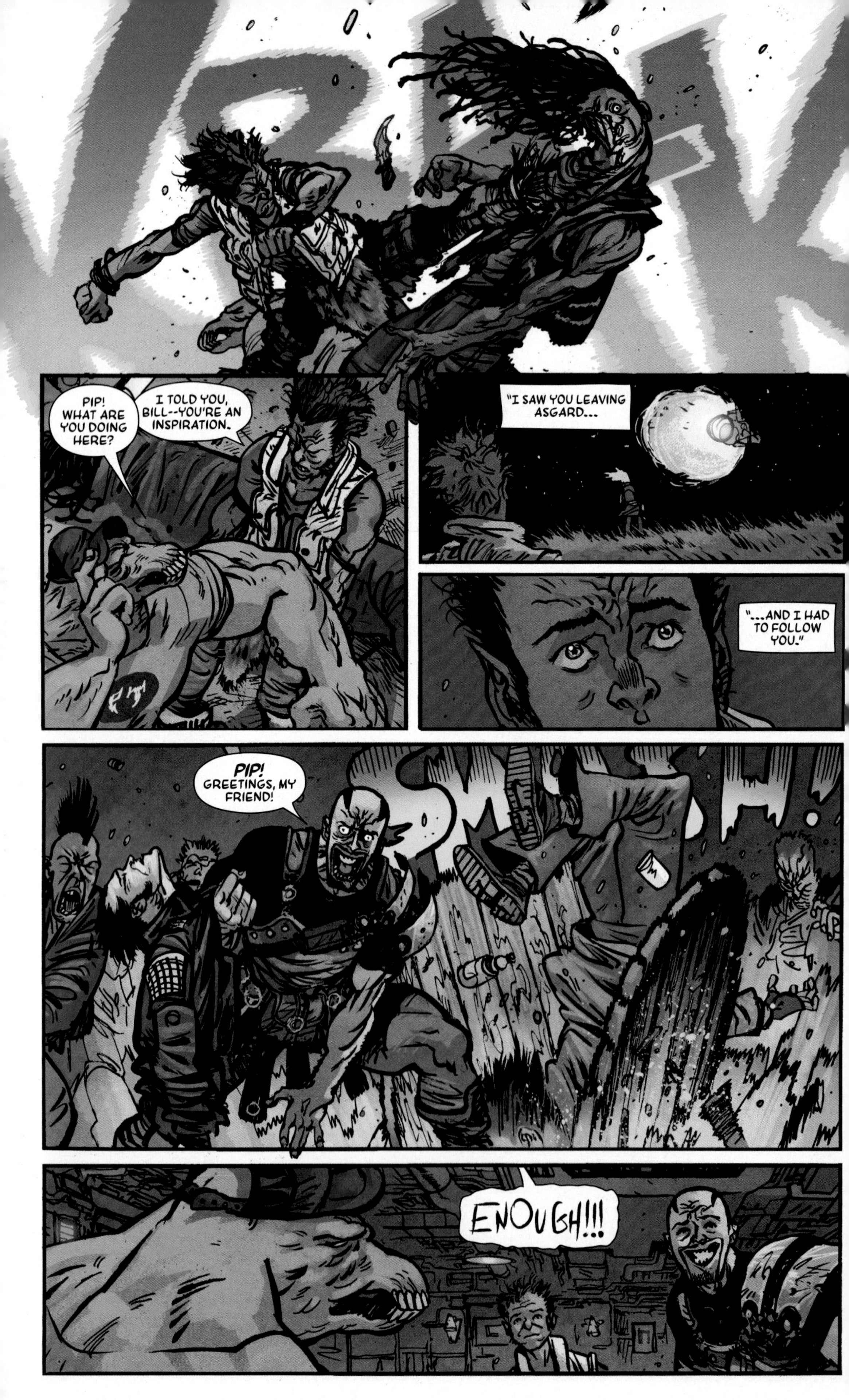

PIP! WHAT ARE YOU DOING HERE?
I TOLD YOU, BILL--YOU'RE AN INSPIRATION.
"I SAW YOU LEAVING ASGARD...
"...AND I HAD TO FOLLOW YOU."
PIP! GREETINGS, MY FRIEND!
ENOUGH!!!

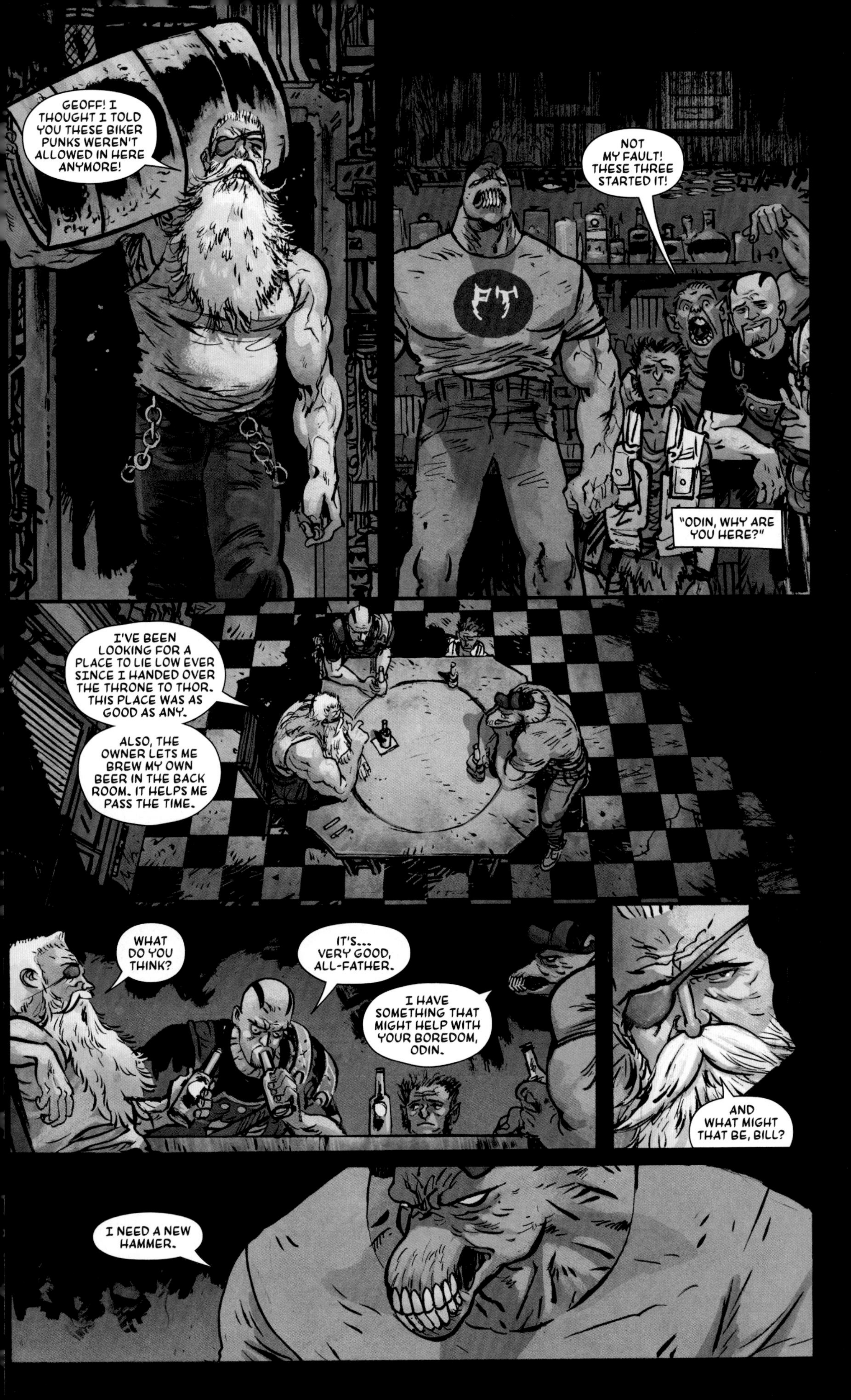
GEOFF! I THOUGHT I TOLD YOU THESE BIKER PUNKS WEREN'T ALLOWED IN HERE ANYMORE!
NOT MY FAULT! THESE THREE STARTED IT!
"ODIN, WHY ARE YOU HERE?"
I'VE BEEN LOOKING FOR A PLACE TO LIE LOW EVER SINCE I HANDED OVER THE THRONE TO THOR. THIS PLACE WAS AS GOOD AS ANY.
ALSO, THE OWNER LETS ME BREW MY OWN BEER IN THE BACK ROOM. IT HELPS ME PASS THE TIME.
WHAT DO YOU THINK?
IT'S... VERY GOOD, ALL-FATHER.
I HAVE SOMETHING THAT MIGHT HELP WITH YOUR BOREDOM, ODIN.
AND WHAT MIGHT THAT BE, BILL?
I NEED A NEW HAMMER.

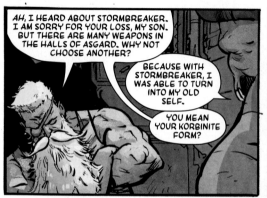

AH, I HEARD ABOUT STORMBREAKER. I AM SORRY FOR YOUR LOSS, MY SON. BUT THERE ARE MANY WEAPONS IN THE HALLS OF ASGARD. WHY NOT CHOOSE ANOTHER?

BECAUSE WITH STORMBREAKER, I WAS ABLE TO TURN INTO MY OLD SELF.

YOU MEAN YOUR KORBINITE FORM?

YES! I WANT THAT POWER BACK. AND THAT'S WHY I'M HERE. YEARS AGO, YOU WERE ABLE TO HELP MAKE ME WHOLE. CAN YOU DO IT AGAIN?

OH, BILL. LOOK AT ME! I AM OLD, BEAT DOWN. I DO NOT HAVE THE POWER OR INFLUENCE TO HELP YOU ANYMORE. I AM NOT THE GOD I USED TO BE.

BUT...WHAT OF THE DWARVES OF NIDAVELLIR? COULD THEY NOT MAKE ME A NEW WEAPON?

THEIR WEAPONS ARE LEGENDARY AND NEARLY UNBREAKABLE, IT IS TRUE. BUT IT IS NOT THE WEAPON THAT WOULD GIVE YOU THE POWER YOU SEEK. IT IS THE MAGIC THAT IS IMBUED WITHIN IT. AND I NO LONGER HAVE THAT POWER.

IT LEFT ME A LONG TIME AGO.

I'M SORRY, WINGMAN.

IS THERE NO OTHER WAY?

I KNOW THIS IS OF LITTLE COMFORT, BUT...I HAVE KNOWN YOU A LONG TIME, BILL. AND EVER SINCE YOU RESCUED MY SON DURING YOUR FIRST GREAT BATTLE, I KNEW YOU WERE SOMEONE SPECIAL. YOUR BEAUTY SHINES FROM THE INSI--

SPARE ME THE PLATITUDES, ALL-FATHER!

I HAVE BEEN FIGHTING BY YOUR AND YOUR SONS' SIDES FOR YEARS.

NEVER HAVE I ASKED YOU FOR ANYTHING. AND NOW, AFTER YOUR OWN KIN DESTROYS WHAT IS MOST PRECIOUS TO ME, A GIFT YOU BESTOWED, YOU WOULD SEND ME AWAY WITH NOTHING?

...I KNOW WHAT IT FEELS LIKE TO HATE WHO YOU ARE ON THE OUTSIDE.

THERE IS ONE OTHER WAY FOR YOU TO GET WHAT YOU SEEK.

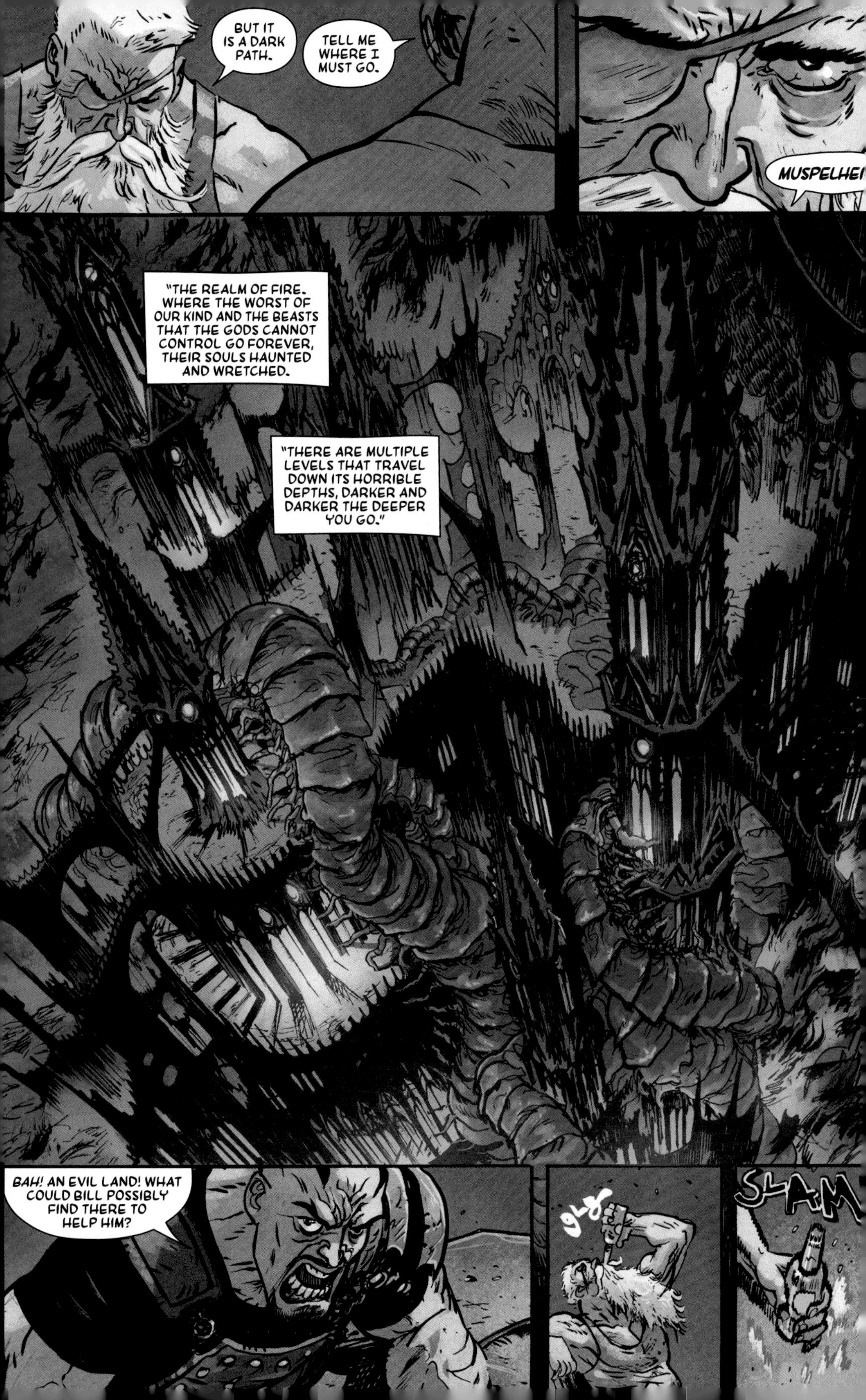
BUT IT IS A DARK PATH.
TELL ME WHERE I MUST GO.
MUSPELHEI
"THE REALM OF FIRE. WHERE THE WORST OF OUR KIND AND THE BEASTS THAT THE GODS CANNOT CONTROL GO FOREVER, THEIR SOULS HAUNTED AND WRETCHED.
"THERE ARE MULTIPLE LEVELS THAT TRAVEL DOWN ITS HORRIBLE DEPTHS, DARKER AND DARKER THE DEEPER YOU GO."
BAH! AN EVIL LAND! WHAT COULD BILL POSSIBLY FIND THERE TO HELP HIM?
SLAM

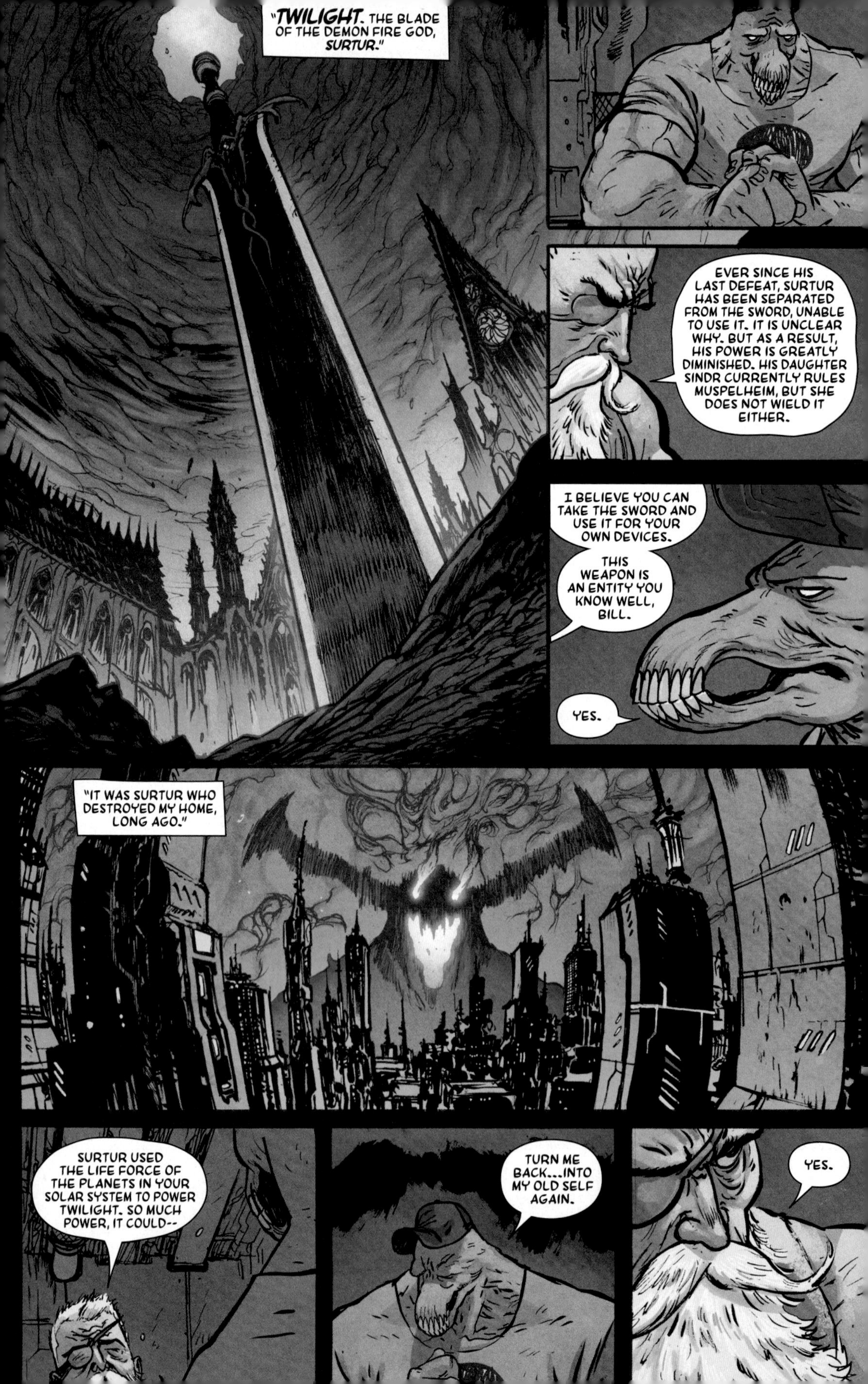
"TWILIGHT. THE BLADE OF THE DEMON FIRE GOD, SURTUR."
EVER SINCE HIS LAST DEFEAT, SURTUR HAS BEEN SEPARATED FROM THE SWORD, UNABLE TO USE IT. IT IS UNCLEAR WHY. BUT AS A RESULT, HIS POWER IS GREATLY DIMINISHED. HIS DAUGHTER SINDR CURRENTLY RULES MUSPELHEIM, BUT SHE DOES NOT WIELD IT EITHER.
I BELIEVE YOU CAN TAKE THE SWORD AND USE IT FOR YOUR OWN DEVICES.
THIS WEAPON IS AN ENTITY YOU KNOW WELL, BILL.
YES.
"IT WAS SURTUR WHO DESTROYED MY HOME, LONG AGO."
SURTUR USED THE LIFE FORCE OF THE PLANETS IN YOUR SOLAR SYSTEM TO POWER TWILIGHT. SO MUCH POWER, IT COULD--
TURN ME BACK...INTO MY OLD SELF AGAIN.
YES.

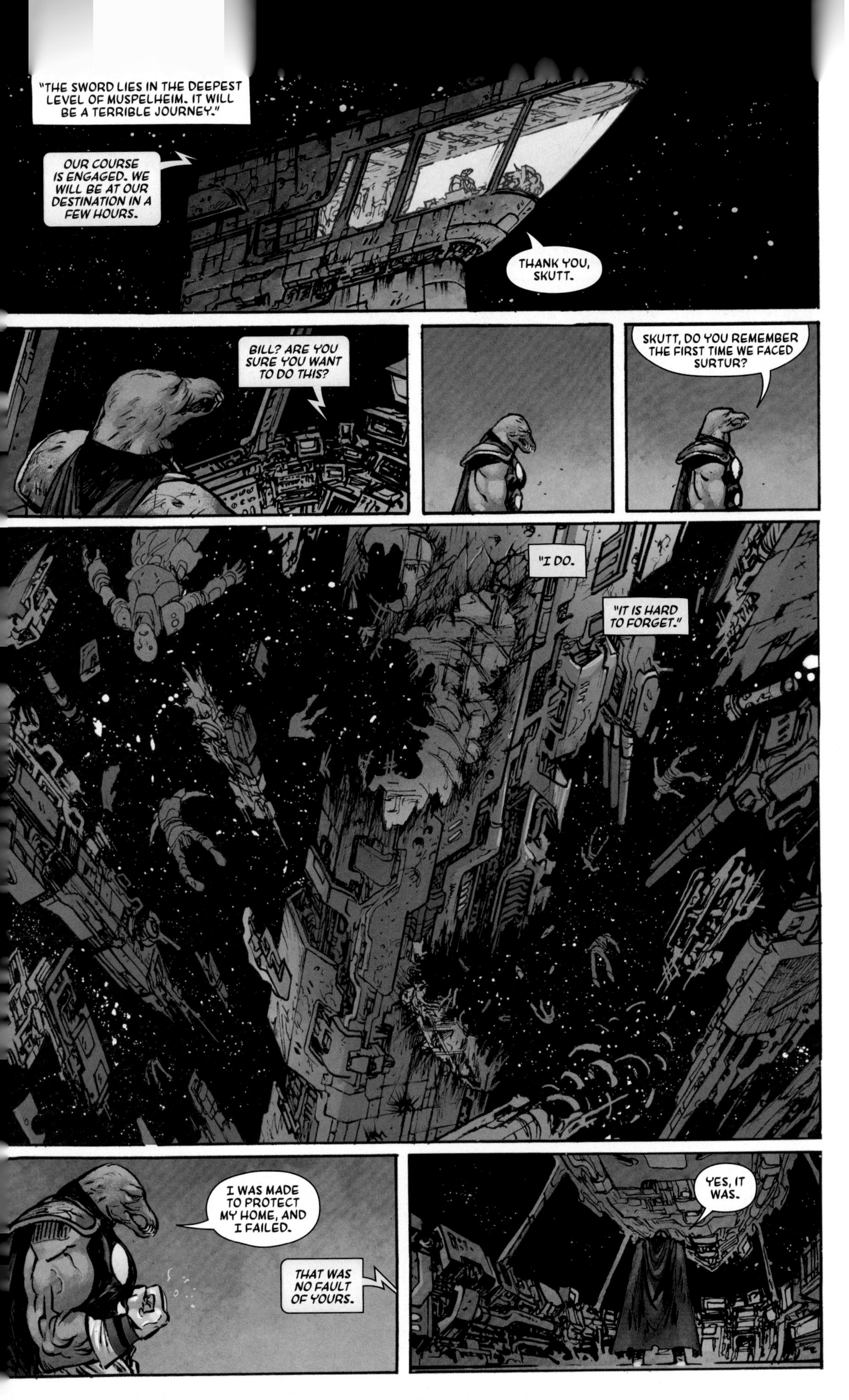
"THE SWORD LIES IN THE DEEPEST LEVEL OF MUSPELHEIM. IT WILL BE A TERRIBLE JOURNEY."
OUR COURSE IS ENGAGED. WE WILL BE AT OUR DESTINATION IN A FEW HOURS.
THANK YOU, SKUTT.
BILL? ARE YOU SURE YOU WANT TO DO THIS?
SKUTT, DO YOU REMEMBER THE FIRST TIME WE FACED SURTUR?
"I DO.
"IT IS HARD TO FORGET."
I WAS MADE TO PROTECT MY HOME, AND I FAILED.
THAT WAS NO FAULT OF YOURS.
YES, IT WAS.

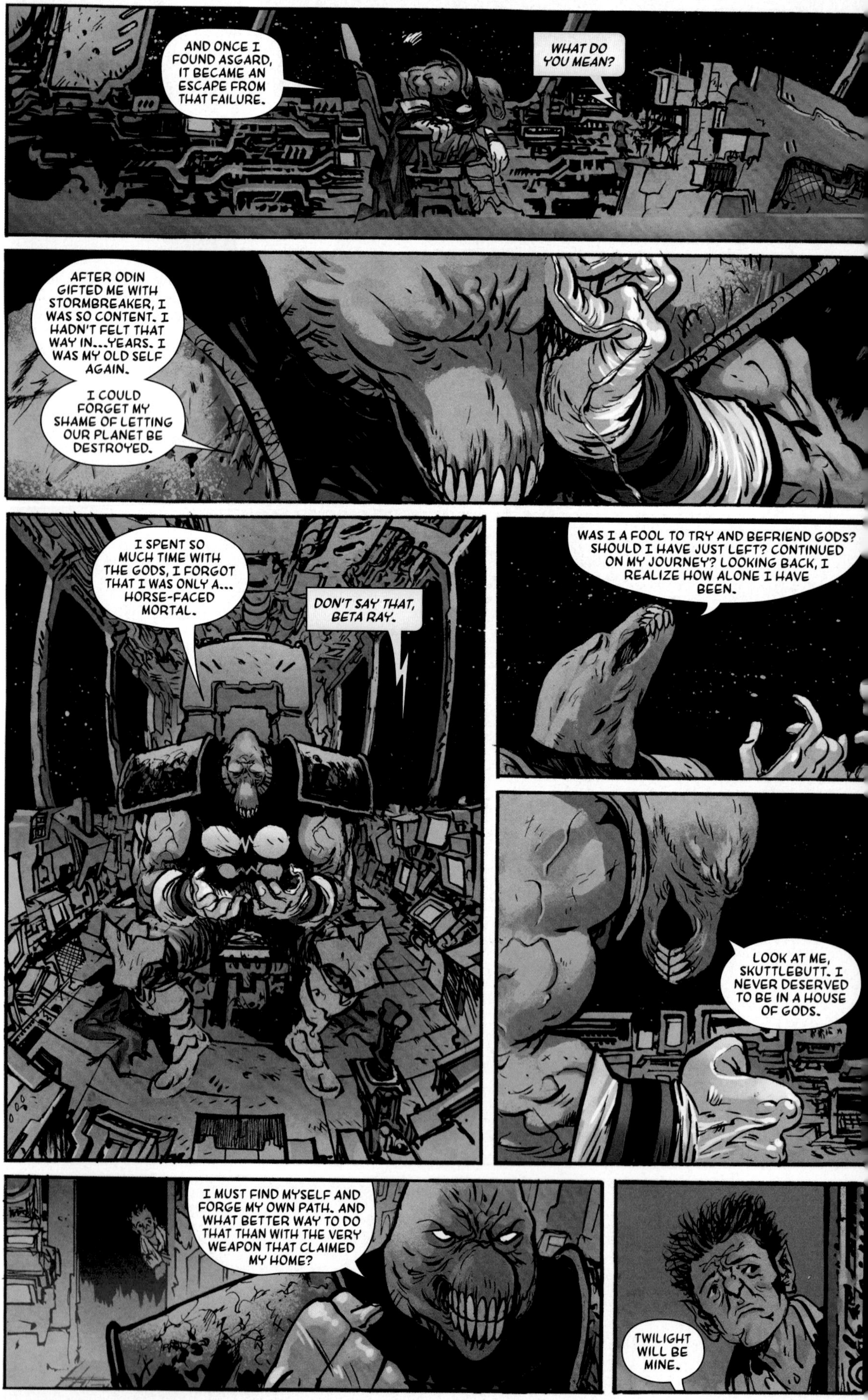
AND ONCE I FOUND ASGARD, IT BECAME AN ESCAPE FROM THAT FAILURE.
WHAT DO YOU MEAN?
AFTER ODIN GIFTED ME WITH STORMBREAKER, I WAS SO CONTENT. I HADN'T FELT THAT WAY IN...YEARS. I WAS MY OLD SELF AGAIN.
I COULD FORGET MY SHAME OF LETTING OUR PLANET BE DESTROYED.
I SPENT SO MUCH TIME WITH THE GODS, I FORGOT THAT I WAS ONLY A... HORSE-FACED MORTAL.
DON'T SAY THAT, BETA RAY.
WAS I A FOOL TO TRY AND BEFRIEND GODS? SHOULD I HAVE JUST LEFT? CONTINUED ON MY JOURNEY? LOOKING BACK, I REALIZE HOW ALONE I HAVE BEEN.
LOOK AT ME, SKUTTLEBUTT. I NEVER DESERVED TO BE IN A HOUSE OF GODS.
I MUST FIND MYSELF AND FORGE MY OWN PATH. AND WHAT BETTER WAY TO DO THAT THAN WITH THE VERY WEAPON THAT CLAIMED MY HOME?
TWILIGHT WILL BE MINE.

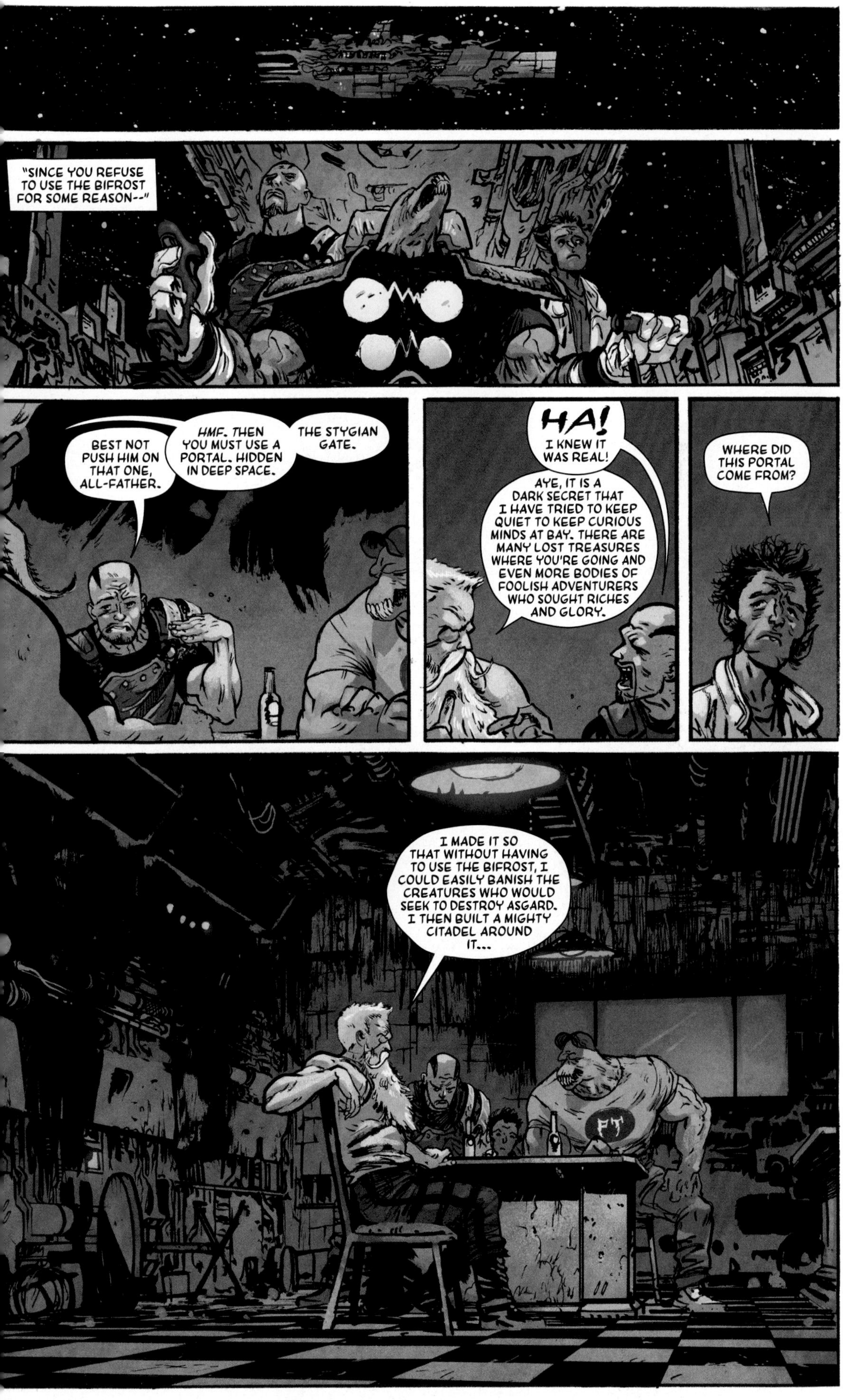

"SINCE YOU REFUSE TO USE THE BIFROST FOR SOME REASON--"
BEST NOT PUSH HIM ON THAT ONE, ALL-FATHER.
HMF. THEN YOU MUST USE A PORTAL. HIDDEN IN DEEP SPACE.
THE STYGIAN GATE.
HA! I KNEW IT WAS REAL!
AYE, IT IS A DARK SECRET THAT I HAVE TRIED TO KEEP QUIET TO KEEP CURIOUS MINDS AT BAY. THERE ARE MANY LOST TREASURES WHERE YOU'RE GOING AND EVEN MORE BODIES OF FOOLISH ADVENTURERS WHO SOUGHT RICHES AND GLORY.
WHERE DID THIS PORTAL COME FROM?
I MADE IT SO THAT WITHOUT HAVING TO USE THE BIFROST, I COULD EASILY BANISH THE CREATURES WHO WOULD SEEK TO DESTROY ASGARD. I THEN BUILT A MIGHTY CITADEL AROUND IT...

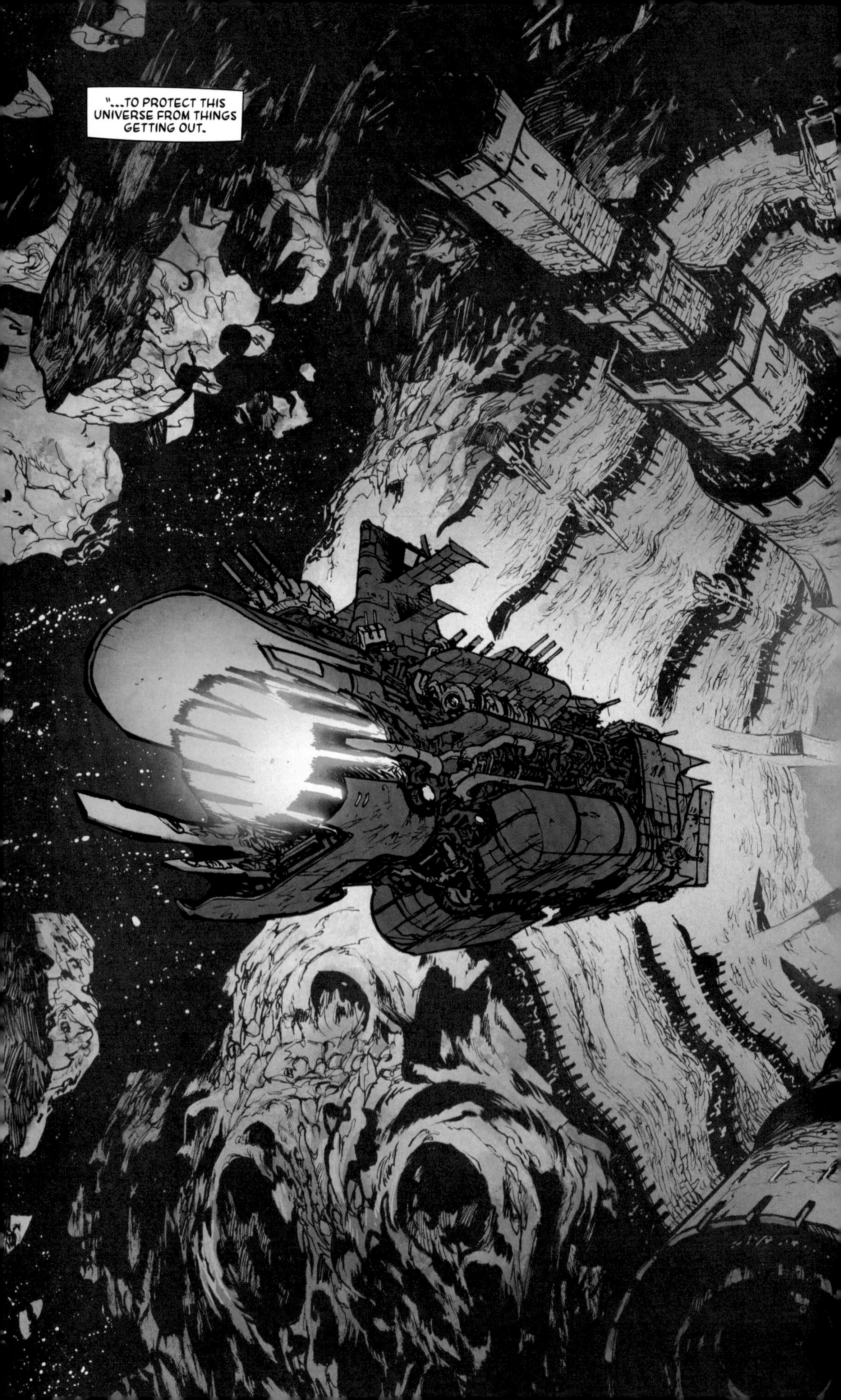
"...TO PROTECT THIS UNIVERSE FROM THINGS GETTING OUT.

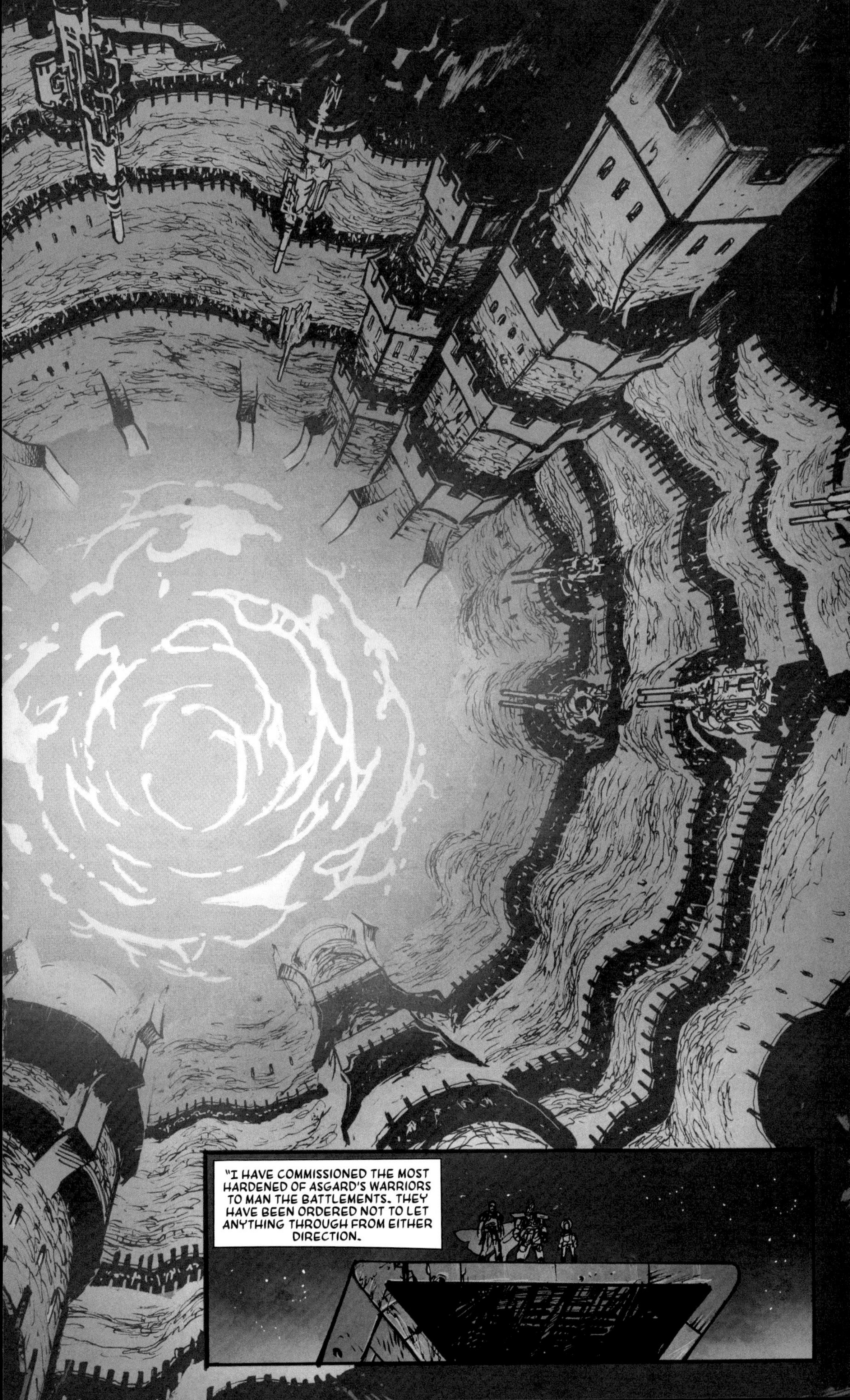
"I HAVE COMMISSIONED THE MOST HARDENED OF ASGARD'S WARRIORS TO MAN THE BATTLEMENTS. THEY HAVE BEEN ORDERED NOT TO LET ANYTHING THROUGH FROM EITHER DIRECTION.

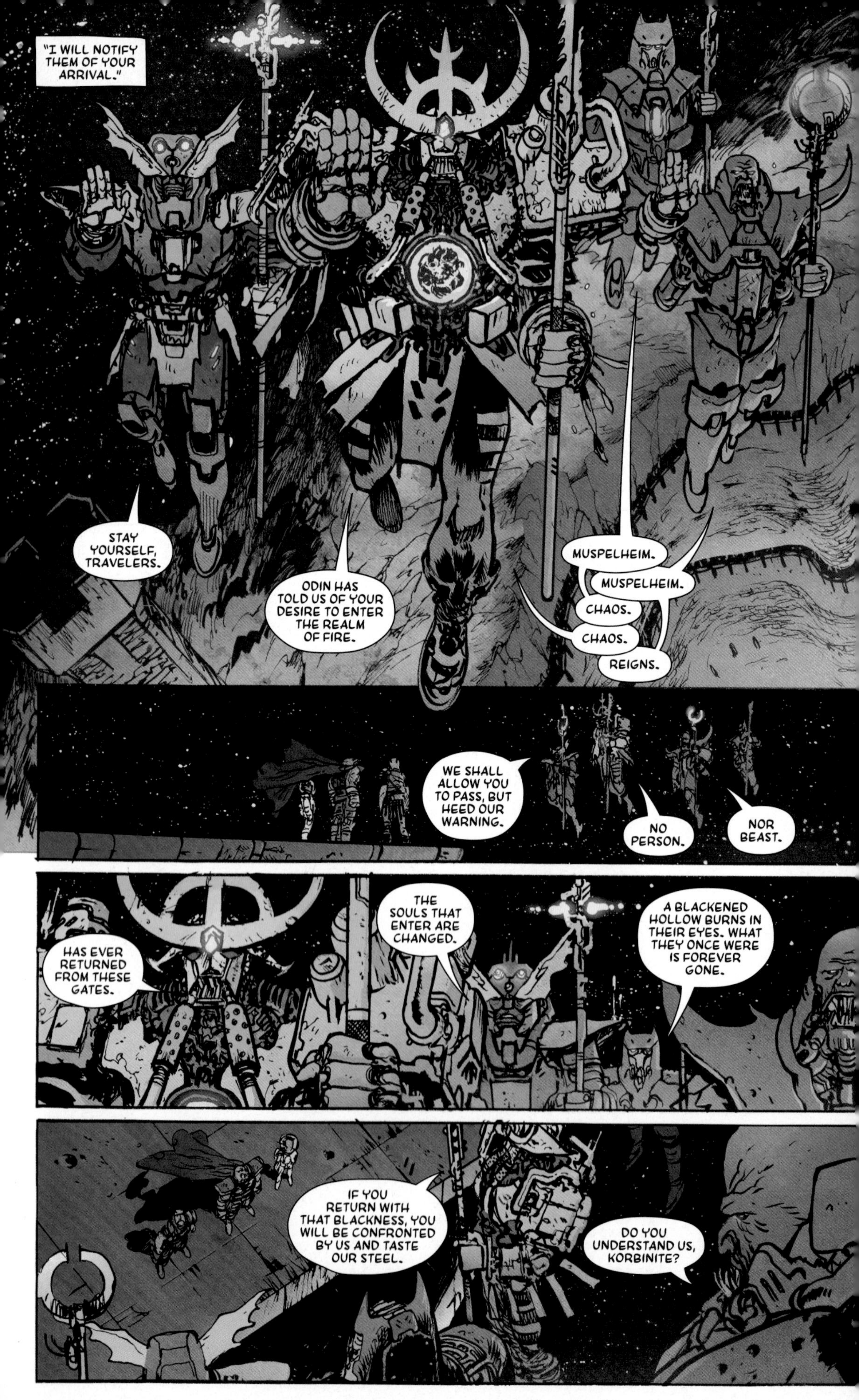
"I WILL NOTIFY THEM OF YOUR ARRIVAL."
STAY YOURSELF, TRAVELERS.
ODIN HAS TOLD US OF YOUR DESIRE TO ENTER THE REALM OF FIRE.
MUSPELHEIM.
MUSPELHEIM.
CHAOS.
CHAOS.
REIGNS.
WE SHALL ALLOW YOU TO PASS, BUT HEED OUR WARNING.
NO PERSON.
NOR BEAST.
HAS EVER RETURNED FROM THESE GATES.
THE SOULS THAT ENTER ARE CHANGED.
A BLACKENED HOLLOW BURNS IN THEIR EYES. WHAT THEY ONCE WERE IS FOREVER GONE.
IF YOU RETURN WITH THAT BLACKNESS, YOU WILL BE CONFRONTED BY US AND TASTE OUR STEEL.
DO YOU UNDERSTAND US, KORBINITE?

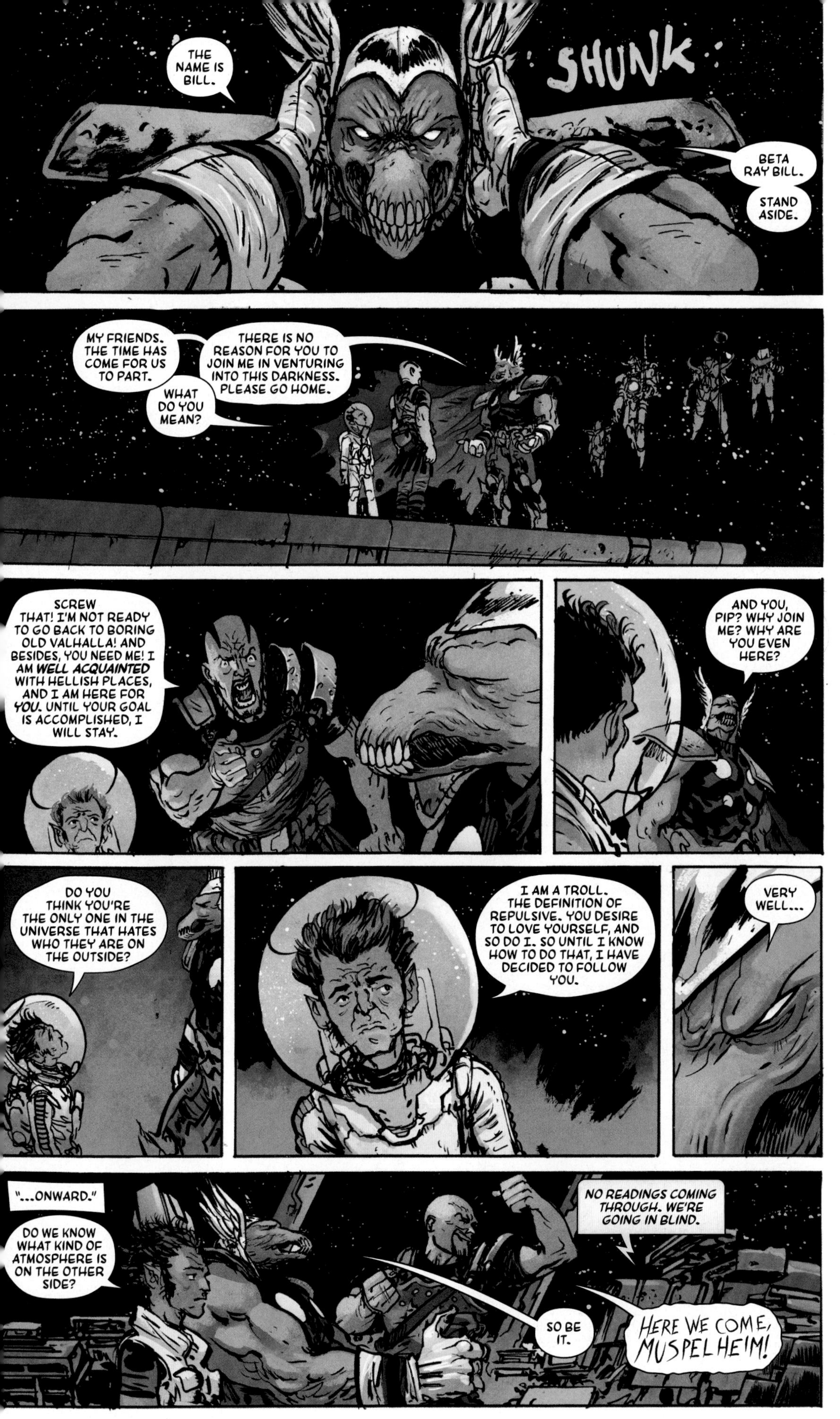
THE NAME IS BILL.
SHUNK
BETA RAY BILL.
STAND ASIDE.
MY FRIENDS. THE TIME HAS COME FOR US TO PART.
THERE IS NO REASON FOR YOU TO JOIN ME IN VENTURING INTO THIS DARKNESS. PLEASE GO HOME.
WHAT DO YOU MEAN?
SCREW THAT! I'M NOT READY TO GO BACK TO BORING OLD VALHALLA! AND BESIDES, YOU NEED ME! I AM WELL ACQUAINTED WITH HELLISH PLACES, AND I AM HERE FOR YOU. UNTIL YOUR GOAL IS ACCOMPLISHED, I WILL STAY.
AND YOU, PIP? WHY JOIN ME? WHY ARE YOU EVEN HERE?
DO YOU THINK YOU'RE THE ONLY ONE IN THE UNIVERSE THAT HATES WHO THEY ARE ON THE OUTSIDE?
I AM A TROLL. THE DEFINITION OF REPULSIVE. YOU DESIRE TO LOVE YOURSELF, AND SO DO I. SO UNTIL I KNOW HOW TO DO THAT, I HAVE DECIDED TO FOLLOW YOU.
VERY WELL...
"...ONWARD."
DO WE KNOW WHAT KIND OF ATMOSPHERE IS ON THE OTHER SIDE?
NO READINGS COMING THROUGH. WE'RE GOING IN BLIND.
SO BE IT.
HERE WE COME, MUSPELHEIM!

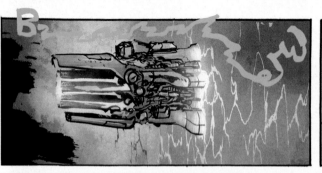

BY THE
GODS...

LOOK
AT THIS
PLACE.

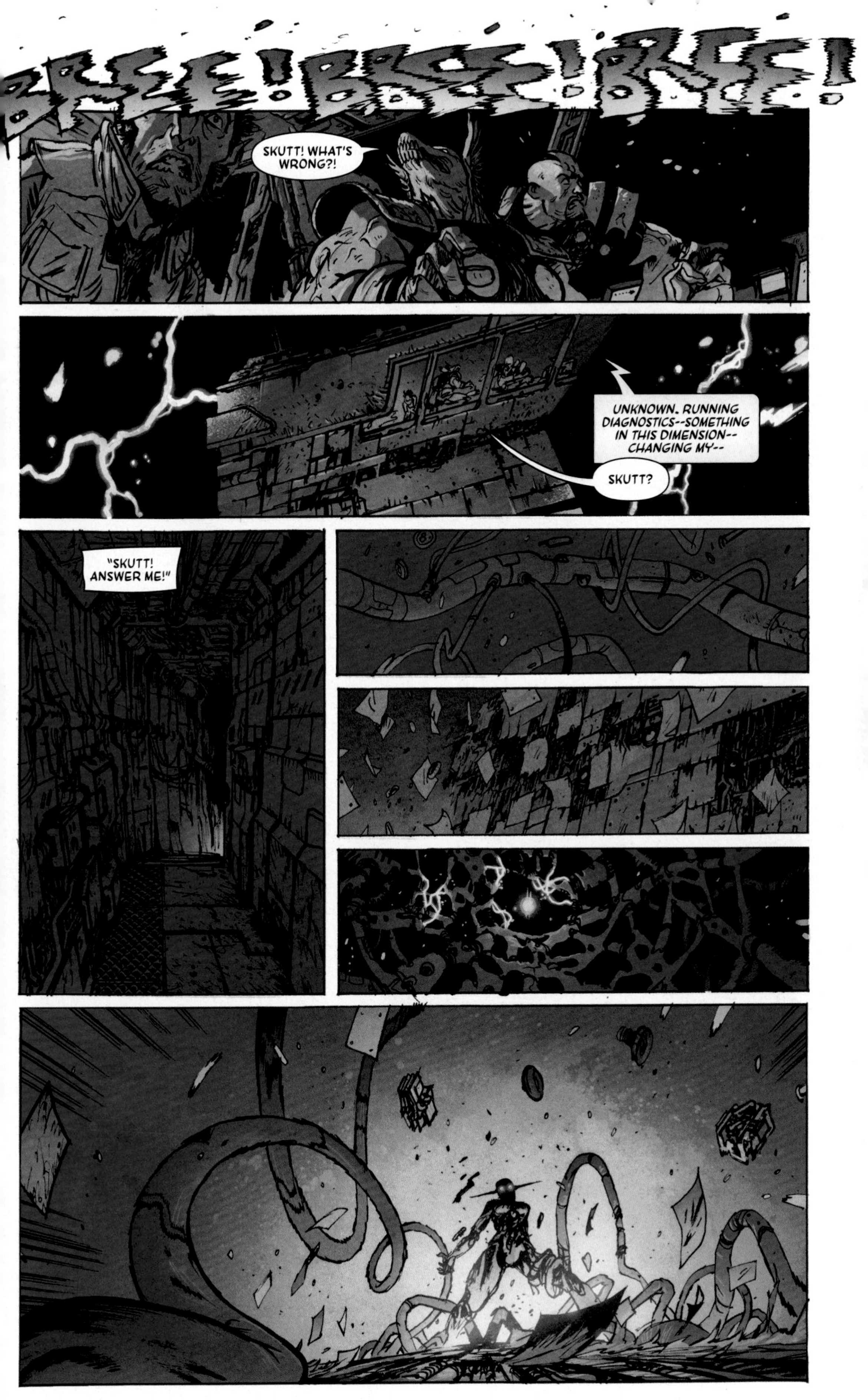

SKUTT! WHAT'S WRONG?!
UNKNOWN. RUNNING DIAGNOSTICS--SOMETHING IN THIS DIMENSION--CHANGING MY--
SKUTT?
"SKUTT! ANSWER ME!"

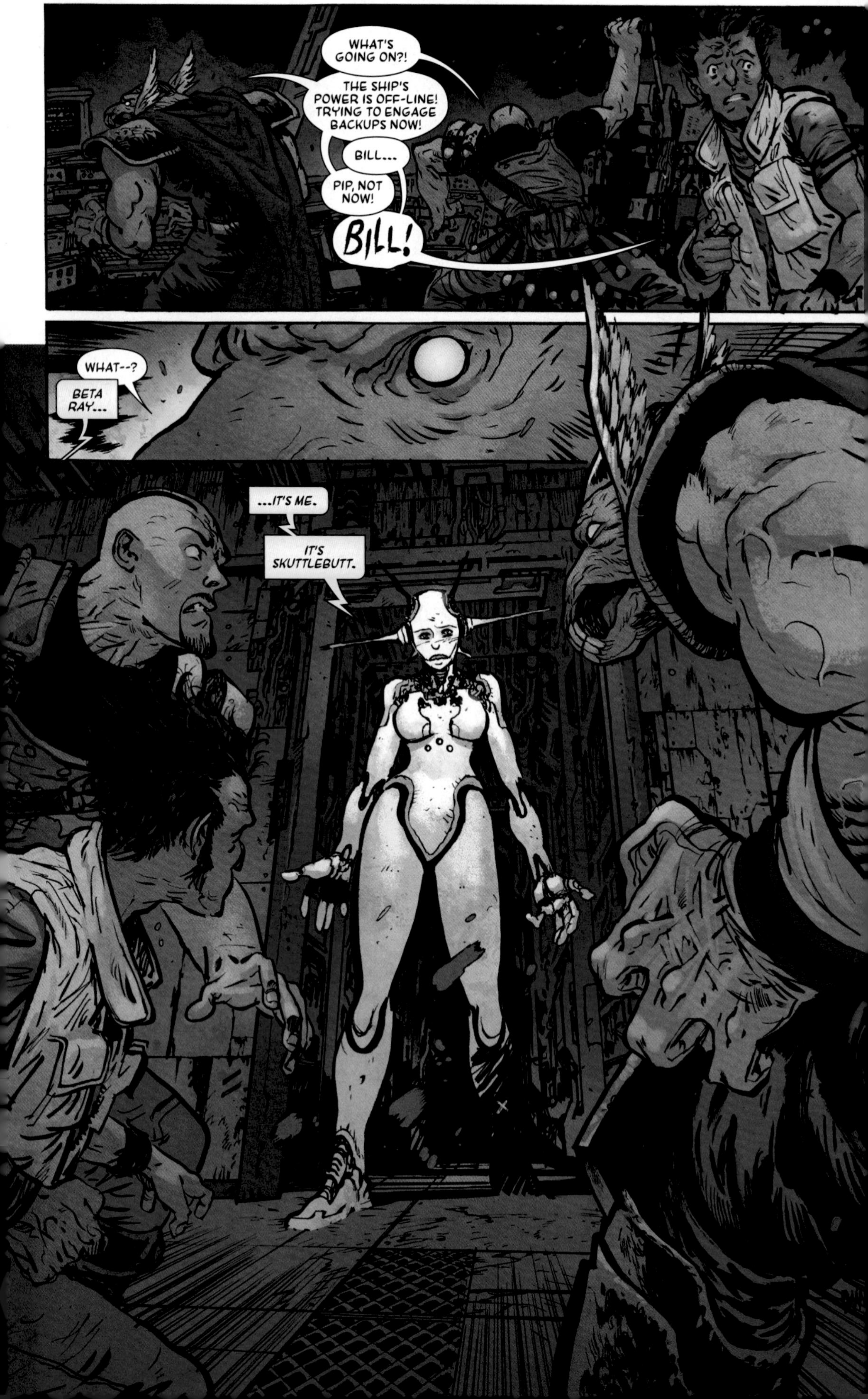
WHAT'S GOING ON?!
THE SHIP'S POWER IS OFF-LINE! TRYING TO ENGAGE BACKUPS NOW!
BILL...
PIP, NOT NOW!
BILL!
WHAT--?
BETA RAY...
...IT'S ME.
IT'S SKUTTLEBUTT.

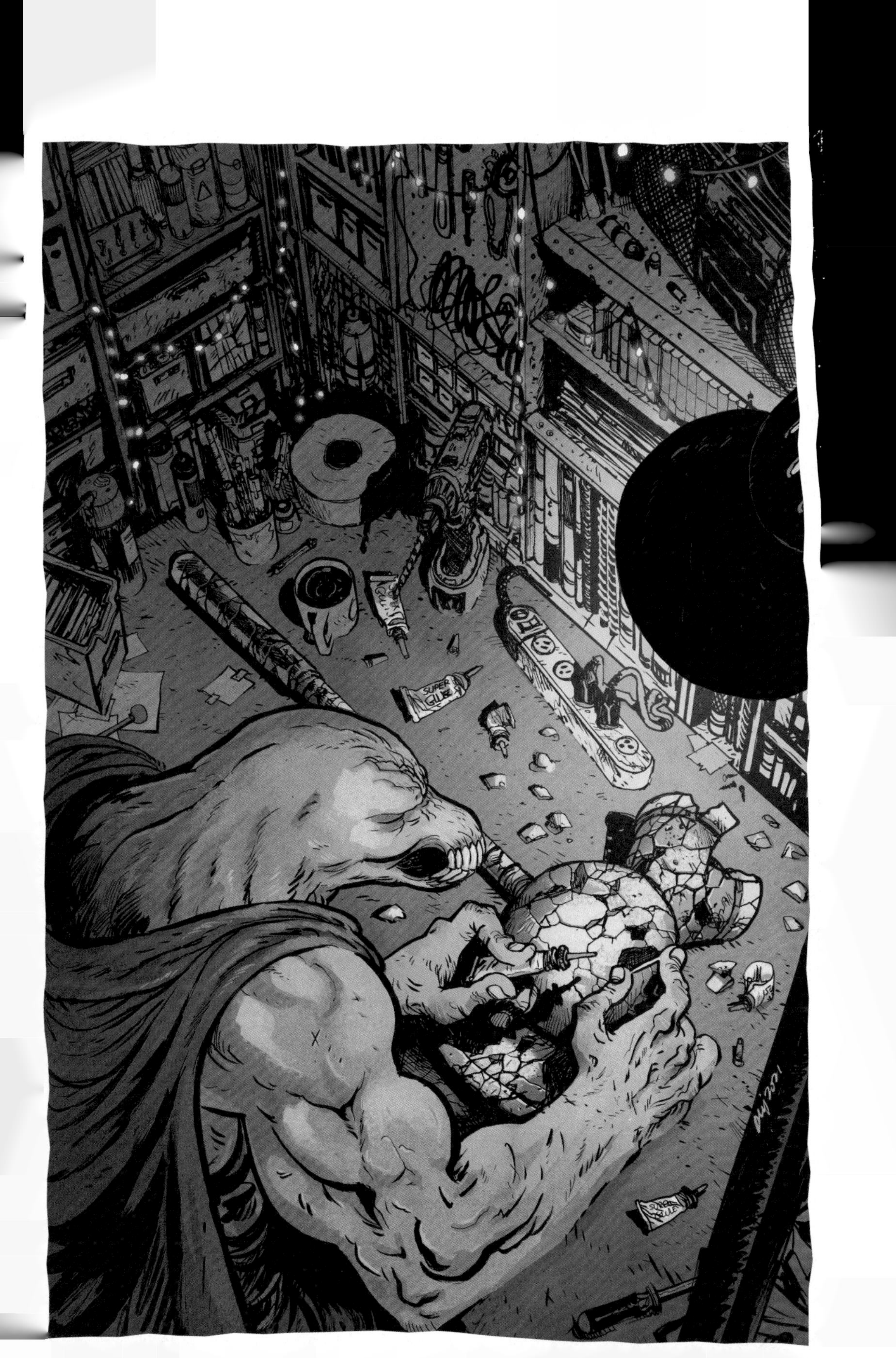
SUPER GLUE

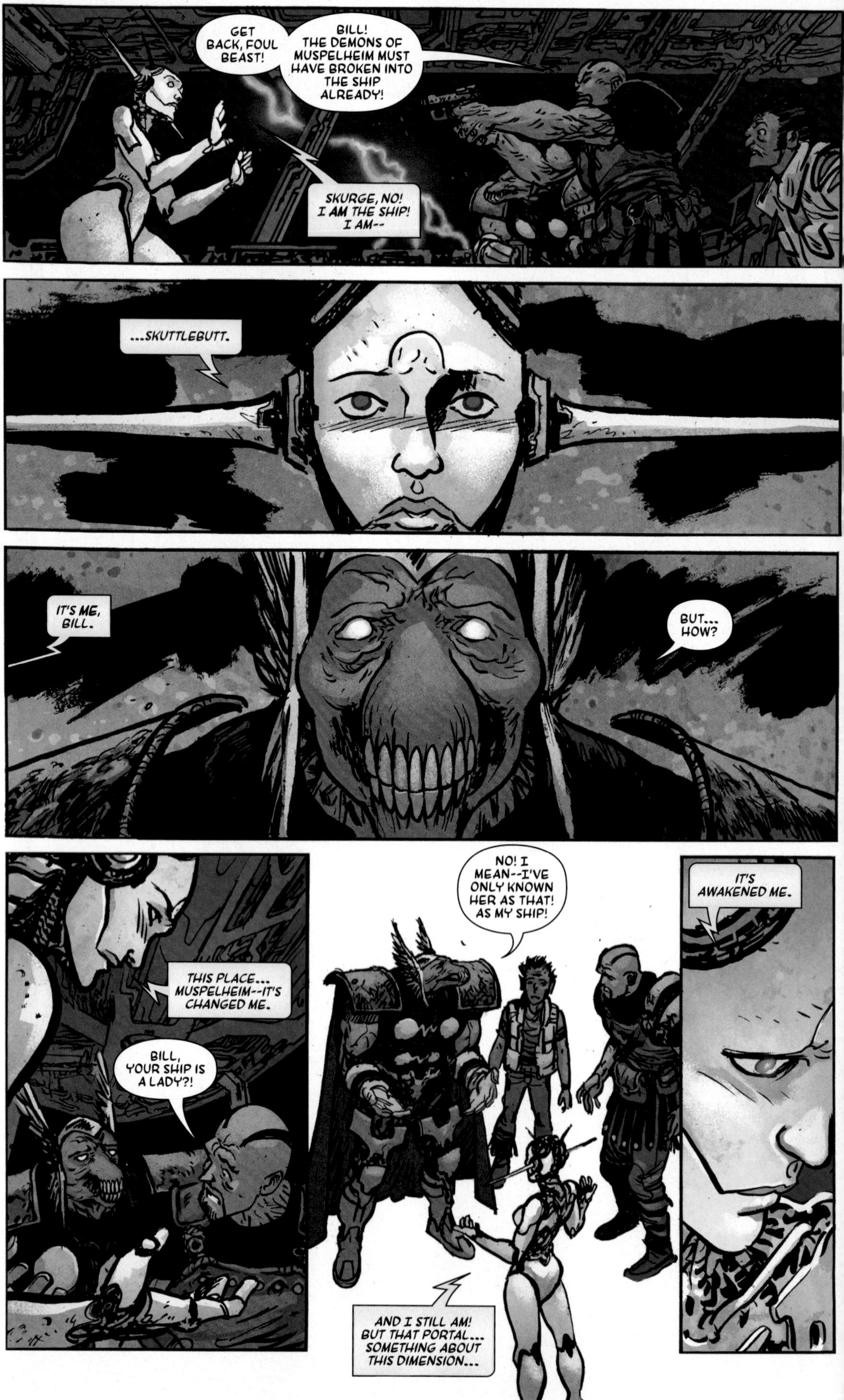

GET BACK, FOUL BEAST!
BILL! THE DEMONS OF MUSPELHEIM MUST HAVE BROKEN INTO THE SHIP ALREADY!
SKURGE, NO! I AM THE SHIP! I AM--
...SKUTTLEBUTT.
IT'S ME, BILL.
BUT... HOW?
THIS PLACE... MUSPELHEIM--IT'S CHANGED ME.
BILL, YOUR SHIP IS A LADY?!
NO! I MEAN--I'VE ONLY KNOWN HER AS THAT! AS MY SHIP!
AND I STILL AM! BUT THAT PORTAL... SOMETHING ABOUT THIS DIMENSION...
IT'S AWAKENED ME.

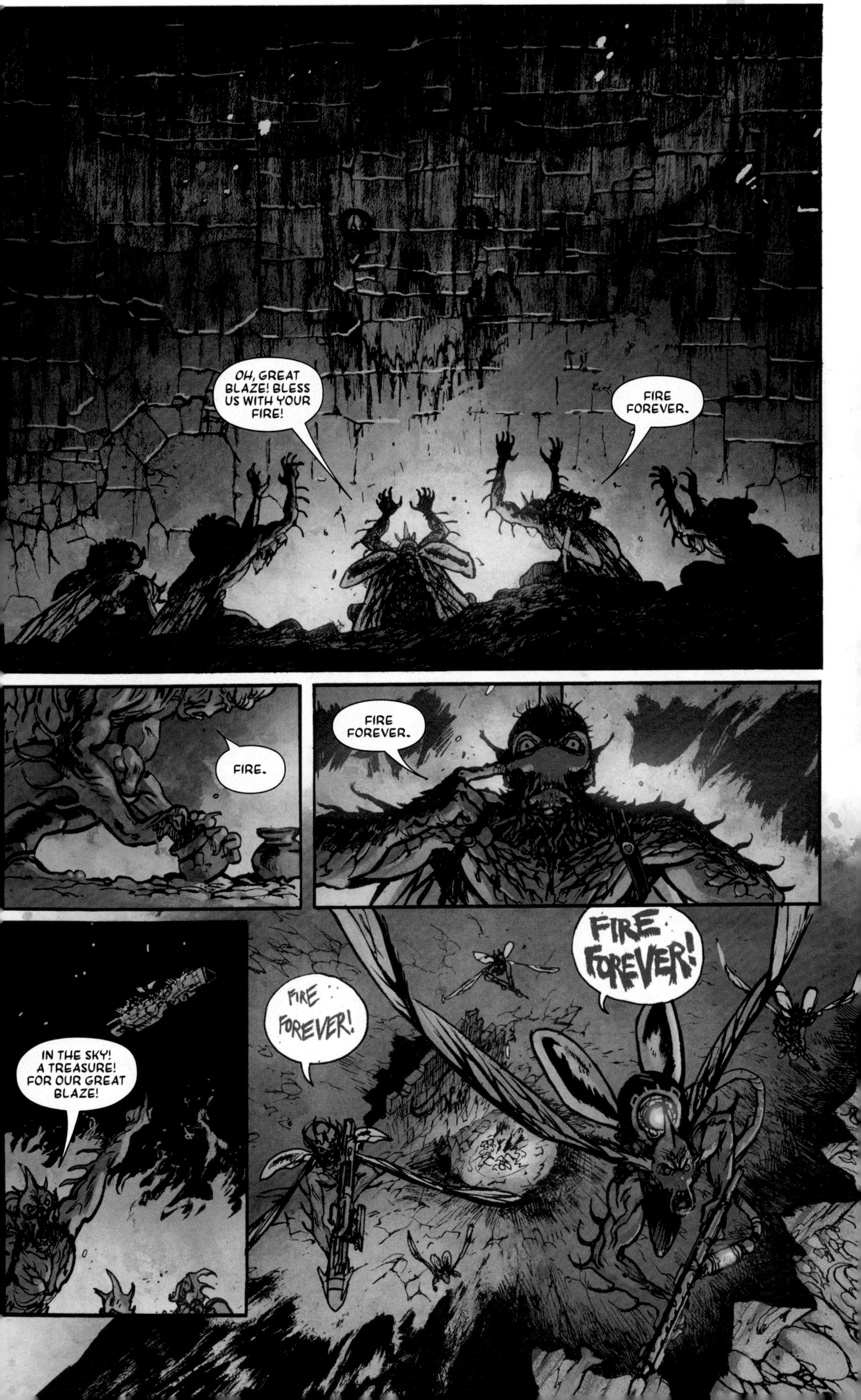
OH, GREAT BLAZE! BLESS US WITH YOUR FIRE!
FIRE FOREVER.
FIRE.
FIRE FOREVER.
IN THE SKY! A TREASURE! FOR OUR GREAT BLAZE!
FIRE FOREVER!
FIRE FOREVER!

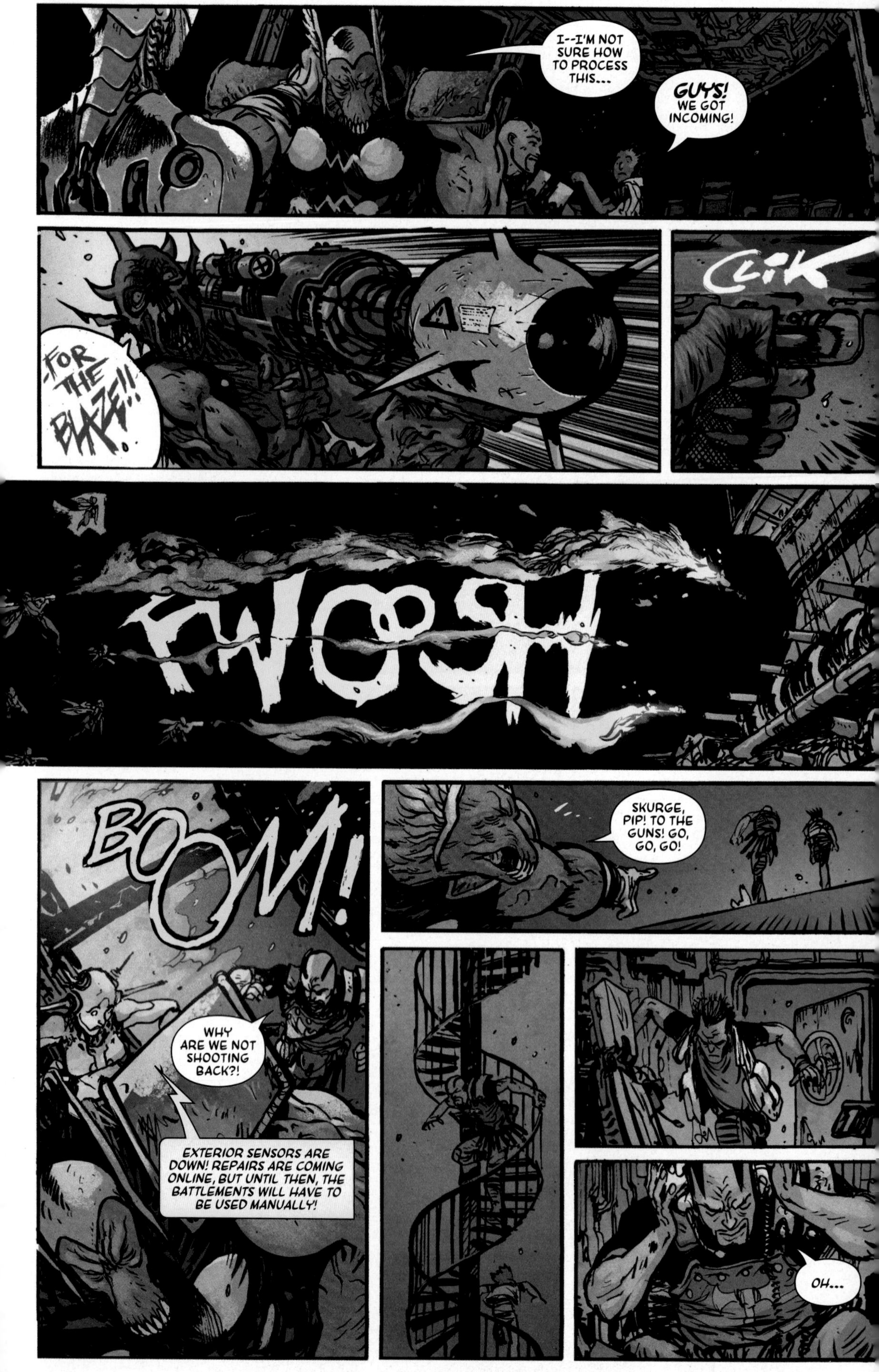

I--I'M NOT SURE HOW TO PROCESS THIS...
GUYS! WE GOT INCOMING!
FOR THE BLAZE!!
CLIK
FWOOSH
BOOM!
SKURGE, PIP! TO THE GUNS! GO, GO, GO!
WHY ARE WE NOT SHOOTING BACK?!
EXTERIOR SENSORS ARE DOWN! REPAIRS ARE COMING ONLINE, BUT UNTIL THEN, THE BATTLEMENTS WILL HAVE TO BE USED MANUALLY!
OH...

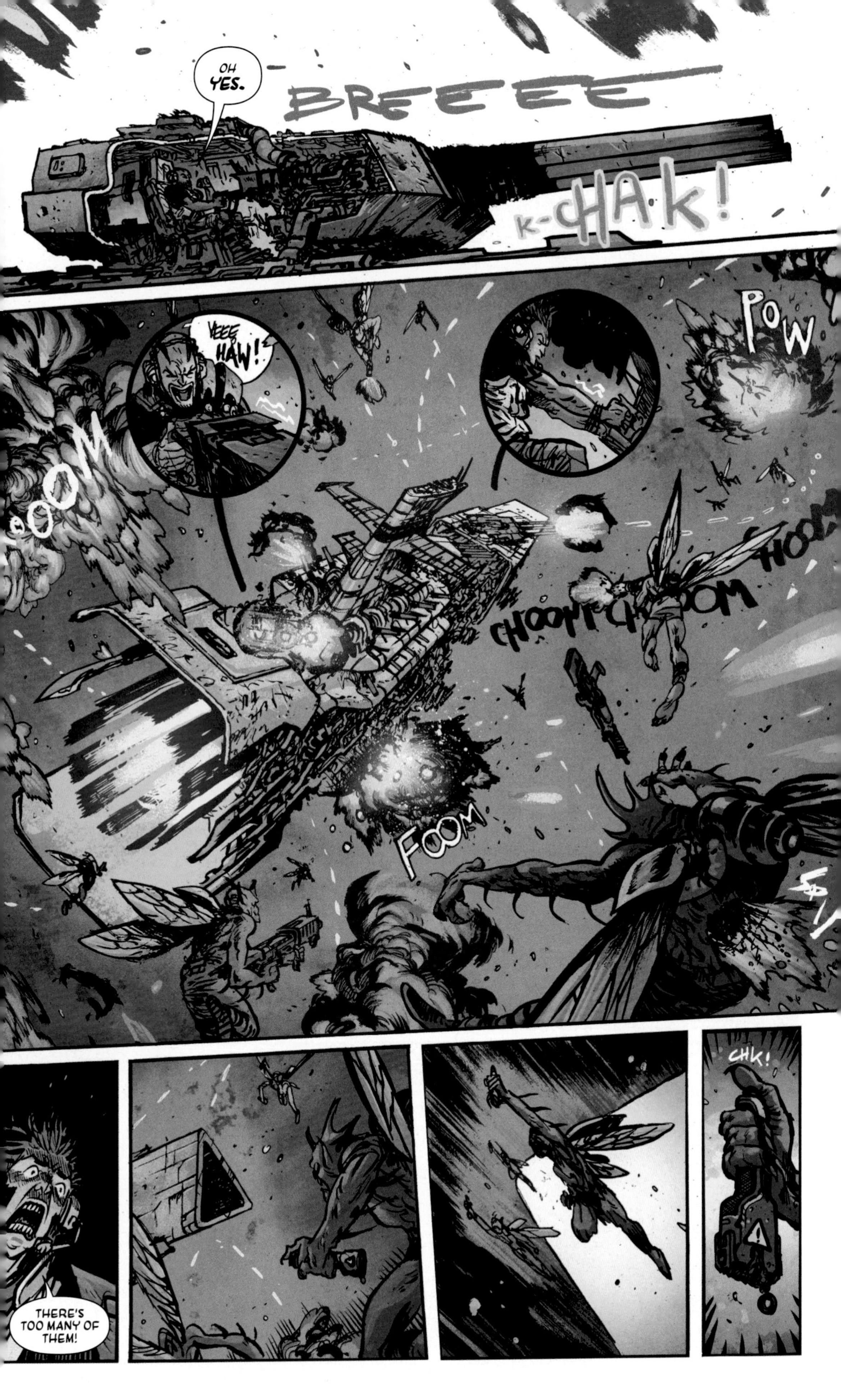
OH YES.
BREEEEE
K-CHAK!
YEEE HAW!
POW
BOOOM
CHOOM CHOOM CHOOM
FOOM
CHK!
THERE'S TOO MANY OF THEM!

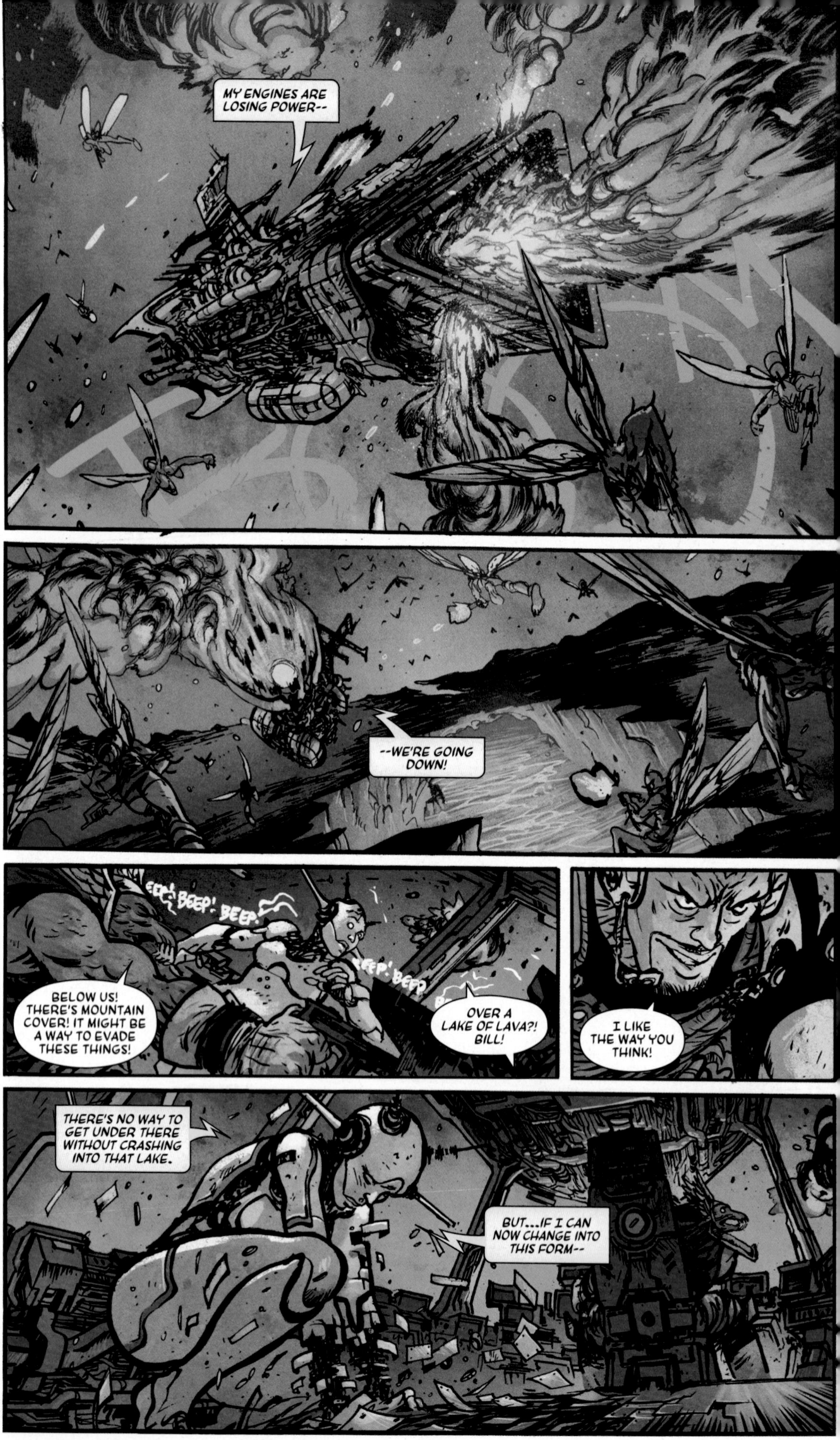
MY ENGINES ARE LOSING POWER--
--WE'RE GOING DOWN!
BEEP! BEEP!
BEEP! BEEP!
BELOW US! THERE'S MOUNTAIN COVER! IT MIGHT BE A WAY TO EVADE THESE THINGS!
OVER A LAKE OF LAVA?! BILL!
I LIKE THE WAY YOU THINK!
THERE'S NO WAY TO GET UNDER THERE WITHOUT CRASHING INTO THAT LAKE.
BUT...IF I CAN NOW CHANGE INTO THIS FORM--

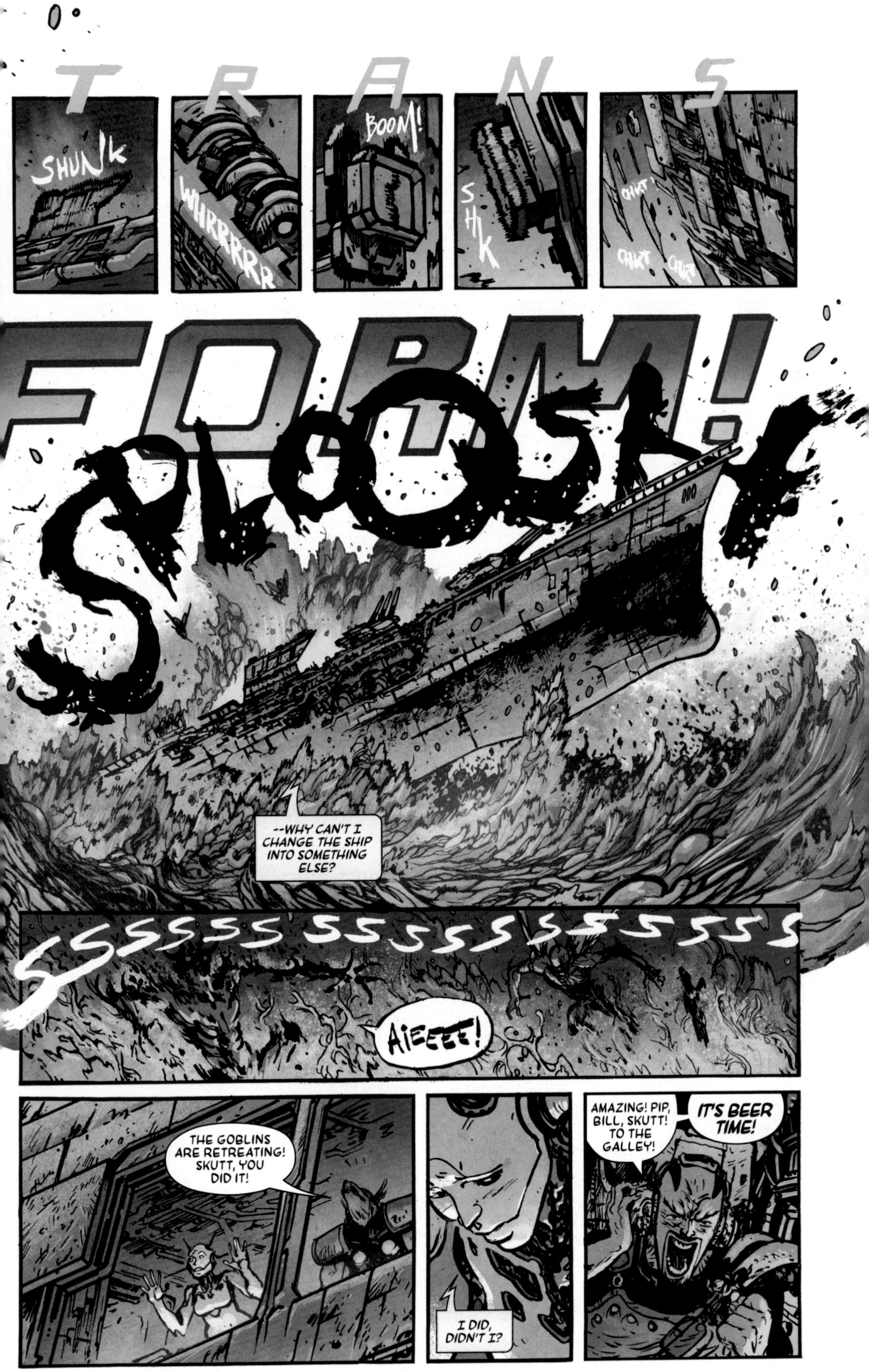
TRANS
SHUNK
WHRRRRRR
BOOM!
SHK
CHKT! CHKT CHKT
FORM!
SPLOOSH!
--WHY CAN'T I CHANGE THE SHIP INTO SOMETHING ELSE?
SSSSSSSSSSSSSSS
AIEEEE!
THE GOBLINS ARE RETREATING! SKUTT, YOU DID IT!
I DID, DIDN'T I?
AMAZING! PIP, BILL, SKUTT! TO THE GALLEY!
IT'S BEER TIME!

WE DON'T HAVE MUCH TIME. WHATEVER BEINGS ATTACKED US, THERE ARE MORE OUT THERE.

AND IT LOOKS LIKE THEY WORSHIP THIS.

SURTUR.

THEY MUST BE HIS FOLLOWERS. WHICH MAKES OUR JOB HARDER.

HOW IS THE SH--I MEAN... HOW ARE YOU? AFTER OUR BATTLE?

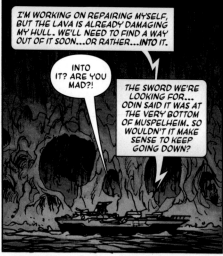

I'M WORKING ON REPAIRING MYSELF, BUT THE LAVA IS ALREADY DAMAGING MY HULL. WE'LL NEED TO FIND A WAY OUT OF IT SOON...OR RATHER...INTO IT.

INTO IT? ARE YOU MAD?!

THE SWORD WE'RE LOOKING FOR... ODIN SAID IT WAS AT THE VERY BOTTOM OF MUSPELHEIM. SO WOULDN'T IT MAKE SENSE TO KEEP GOING DOWN?

I'VE BEEN SCANNING THE BOTTOM OF THIS BURNING SEA. THE CURRENT SEEMS TO FLOW THIS WAY, LIKE THE DRAINING OF A TUB. I THINK THERE'S A LAYER OF THIS PLACE THAT GOES DEEPER THAN ANYONE HAS GONE BEFORE.

HOW DO WE KNOW ANYTHING IS EVEN DOWN THERE?

BECAUSE THERE'S A READING OF SOMETHING VERY POWERFUL UNDERNEATH. IT'S THE STRONGEST POWER SOURCE IN THIS ENTIRE PLACE.

IT CAN ONLY BE ONE THING.

TWILIGHT.

I'M REARRANGING MY HULL STRUCTURE AS FAST AS I CAN TO COMPENSATE FOR THE INTENSE HEAT.

I WAS PLANNING TO CONTINUE TRAVELING ON THE SURFACE OF THE BURNING SEA UNTIL WE ARE DIRECTLY OVER THE OPENING. THIS WAY I CAN SPEND AS LITTLE TIME AS POSSIBLE SUBMERGED.

BILL, WHAT DO YOU THINK?

...WHATEVER GETS ME TO THAT SWORD THE FASTEST.

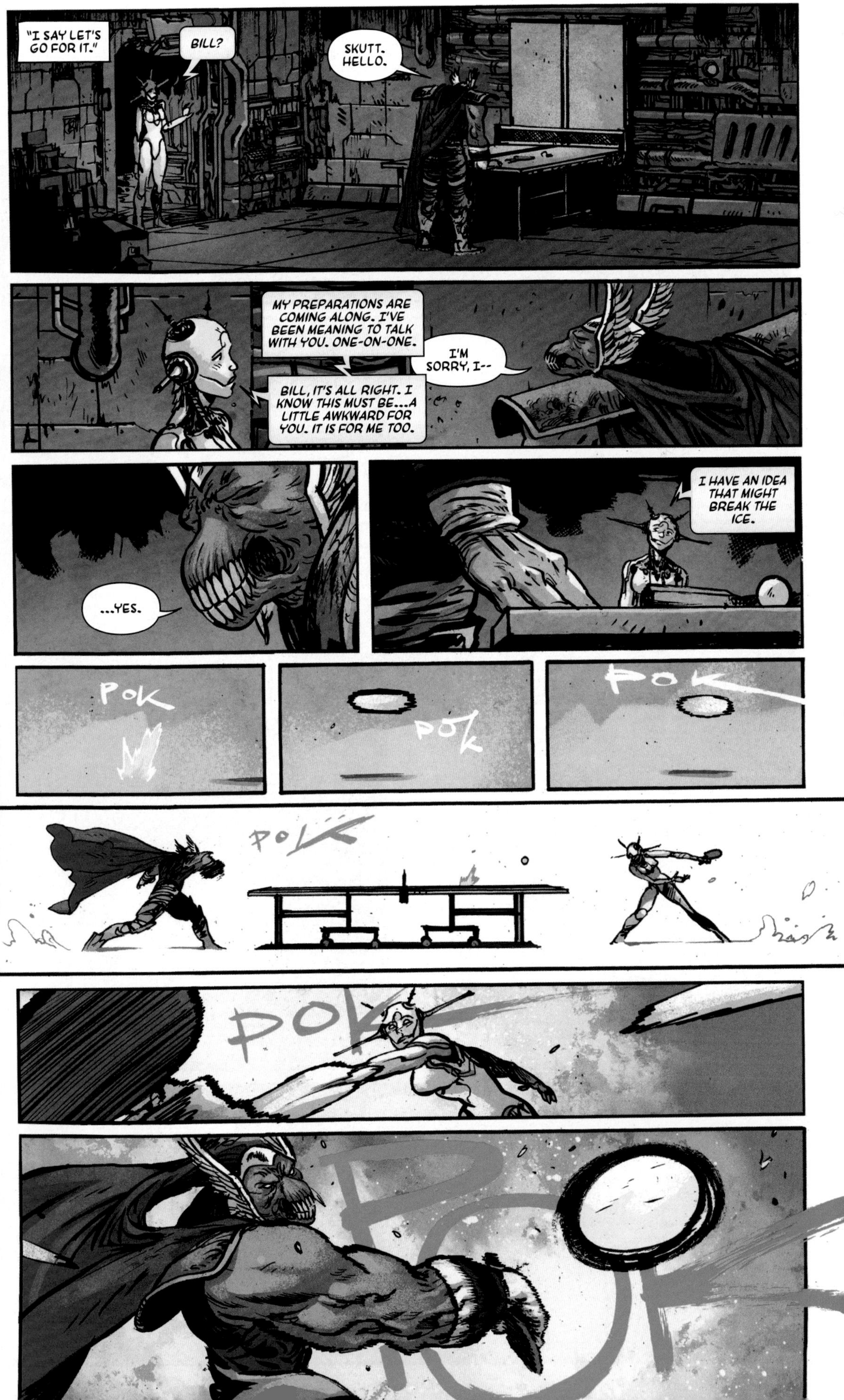
"I SAY LET'S GO FOR IT."
BILL?
SKUTT. HELLO.
MY PREPARATIONS ARE COMING ALONG. I'VE BEEN MEANING TO TALK WITH YOU. ONE-ON-ONE.
BILL, IT'S ALL RIGHT. I KNOW THIS MUST BE...A LITTLE AWKWARD FOR YOU. IT IS FOR ME TOO.
I'M SORRY, I--
...YES.
I HAVE AN IDEA THAT MIGHT BREAK THE ICE.
POK
POK
POK
POK
POK
POK

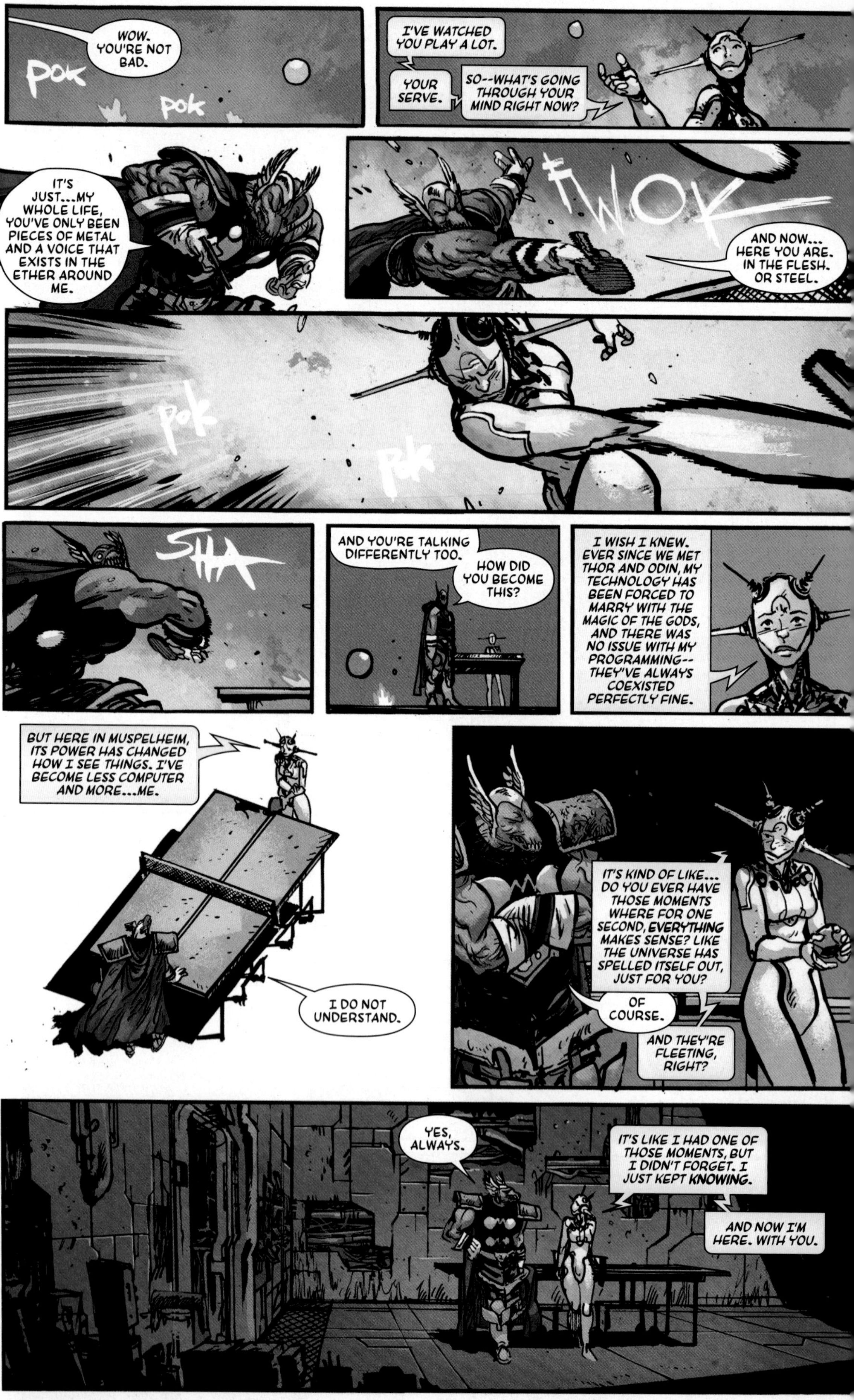

WOW. YOU'RE NOT BAD.
POK
POK
I'VE WATCHED YOU PLAY A LOT.
YOUR SERVE.
SO--WHAT'S GOING THROUGH YOUR MIND RIGHT NOW?
IT'S JUST...MY WHOLE LIFE, YOU'VE ONLY BEEN PIECES OF METAL AND A VOICE THAT EXISTS IN THE ETHER AROUND ME.
TWOK
AND NOW... HERE YOU ARE. IN THE FLESH. OR STEEL.
POK
POK
SHA
AND YOU'RE TALKING DIFFERENTLY TOO.
HOW DID YOU BECOME THIS?
I WISH I KNEW. EVER SINCE WE MET THOR AND ODIN, MY TECHNOLOGY HAS BEEN FORCED TO MARRY WITH THE MAGIC OF THE GODS, AND THERE WAS NO ISSUE WITH MY PROGRAMMING--THEY'VE ALWAYS COEXISTED PERFECTLY FINE.
BUT HERE IN MUSPELHEIM, ITS POWER HAS CHANGED HOW I SEE THINGS. I'VE BECOME LESS COMPUTER AND MORE...ME.
I DO NOT UNDERSTAND.
IT'S KIND OF LIKE... DO YOU EVER HAVE THOSE MOMENTS WHERE FOR ONE SECOND, EVERYTHING MAKES SENSE? LIKE THE UNIVERSE HAS SPELLED ITSELF OUT, JUST FOR YOU?
OF COURSE.
AND THEY'RE FLEETING, RIGHT?
YES, ALWAYS.
IT'S LIKE I HAD ONE OF THOSE MOMENTS, BUT I DIDN'T FORGET. I JUST KEPT KNOWING.
AND NOW I'M HERE. WITH YOU.

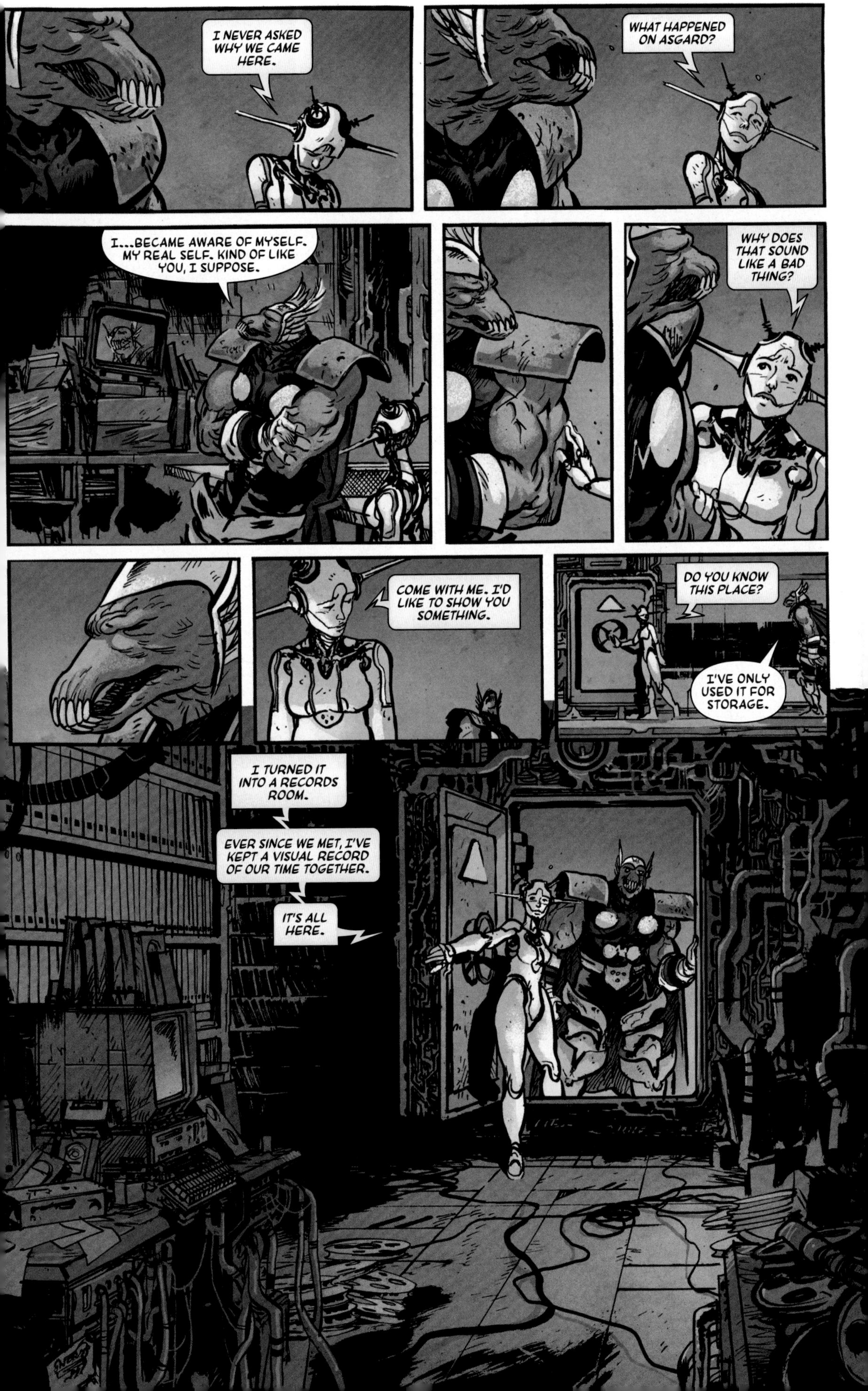
I NEVER ASKED WHY WE CAME HERE.
WHAT HAPPENED ON ASGARD?
I...BECAME AWARE OF MYSELF. MY REAL SELF. KIND OF LIKE YOU, I SUPPOSE.
WHY DOES THAT SOUND LIKE A BAD THING?
COME WITH ME. I'D LIKE TO SHOW YOU SOMETHING.
DO YOU KNOW THIS PLACE?
I'VE ONLY USED IT FOR STORAGE.
I TURNED IT INTO A RECORDS ROOM.
EVER SINCE WE MET, I'VE KEPT A VISUAL RECORD OF OUR TIME TOGETHER.
IT'S ALL HERE.

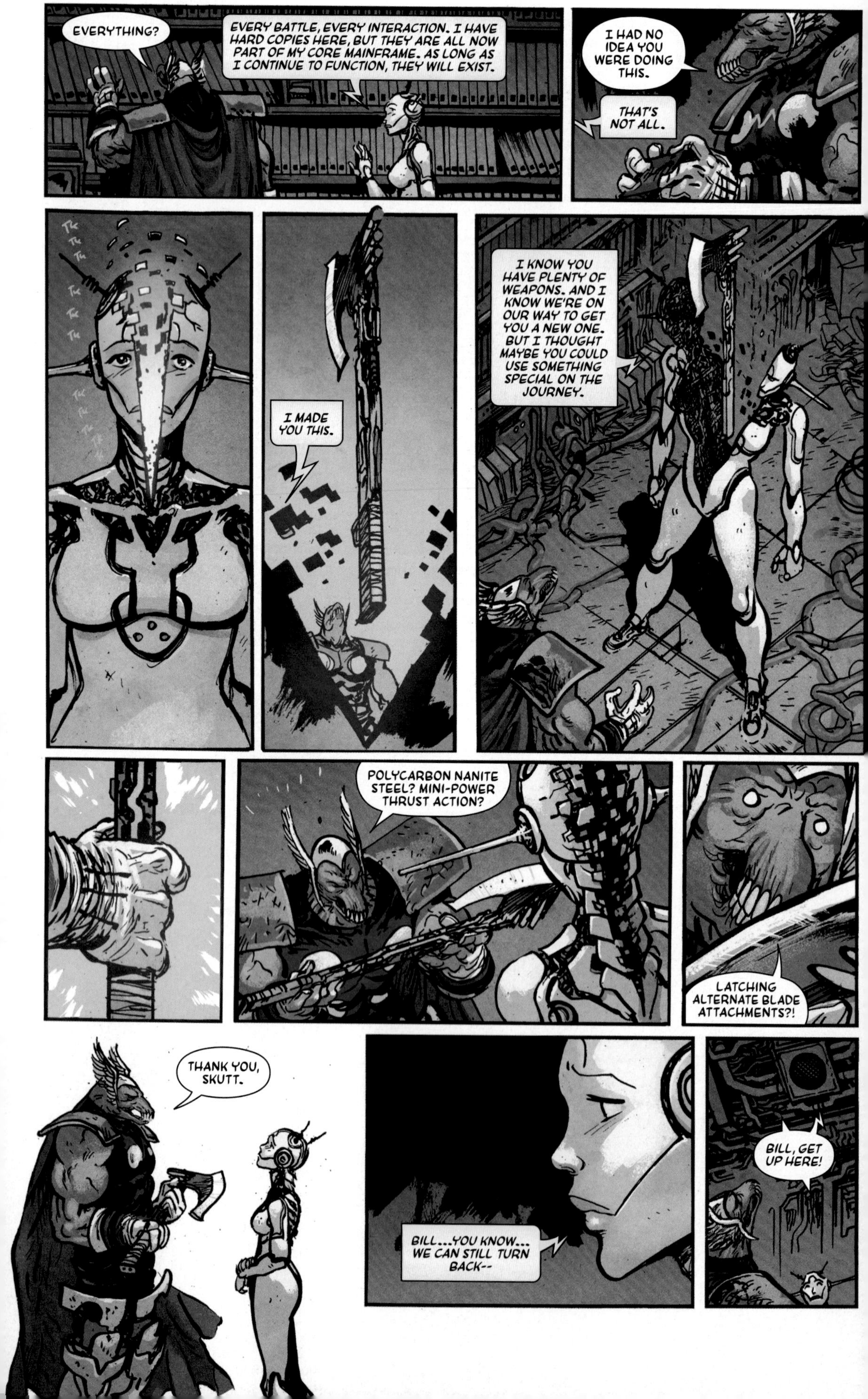
EVERYTHING?
EVERY BATTLE, EVERY INTERACTION. I HAVE HARD COPIES HERE, BUT THEY ARE ALL NOW PART OF MY CORE MAINFRAME. AS LONG AS I CONTINUE TO FUNCTION, THEY WILL EXIST.
I HAD NO IDEA YOU WERE DOING THIS.
THAT'S NOT ALL.
I MADE YOU THIS.
I KNOW YOU HAVE PLENTY OF WEAPONS. AND I KNOW WE'RE ON OUR WAY TO GET YOU A NEW ONE. BUT I THOUGHT MAYBE YOU COULD USE SOMETHING SPECIAL ON THE JOURNEY.
POLYCARBON NANITE STEEL? MINI-POWER THRUST ACTION?
LATCHING ALTERNATE BLADE ATTACHMENTS?!
THANK YOU, SKUTT.
BILL...YOU KNOW... WE CAN STILL TURN BACK--
BILL, GET UP HERE!

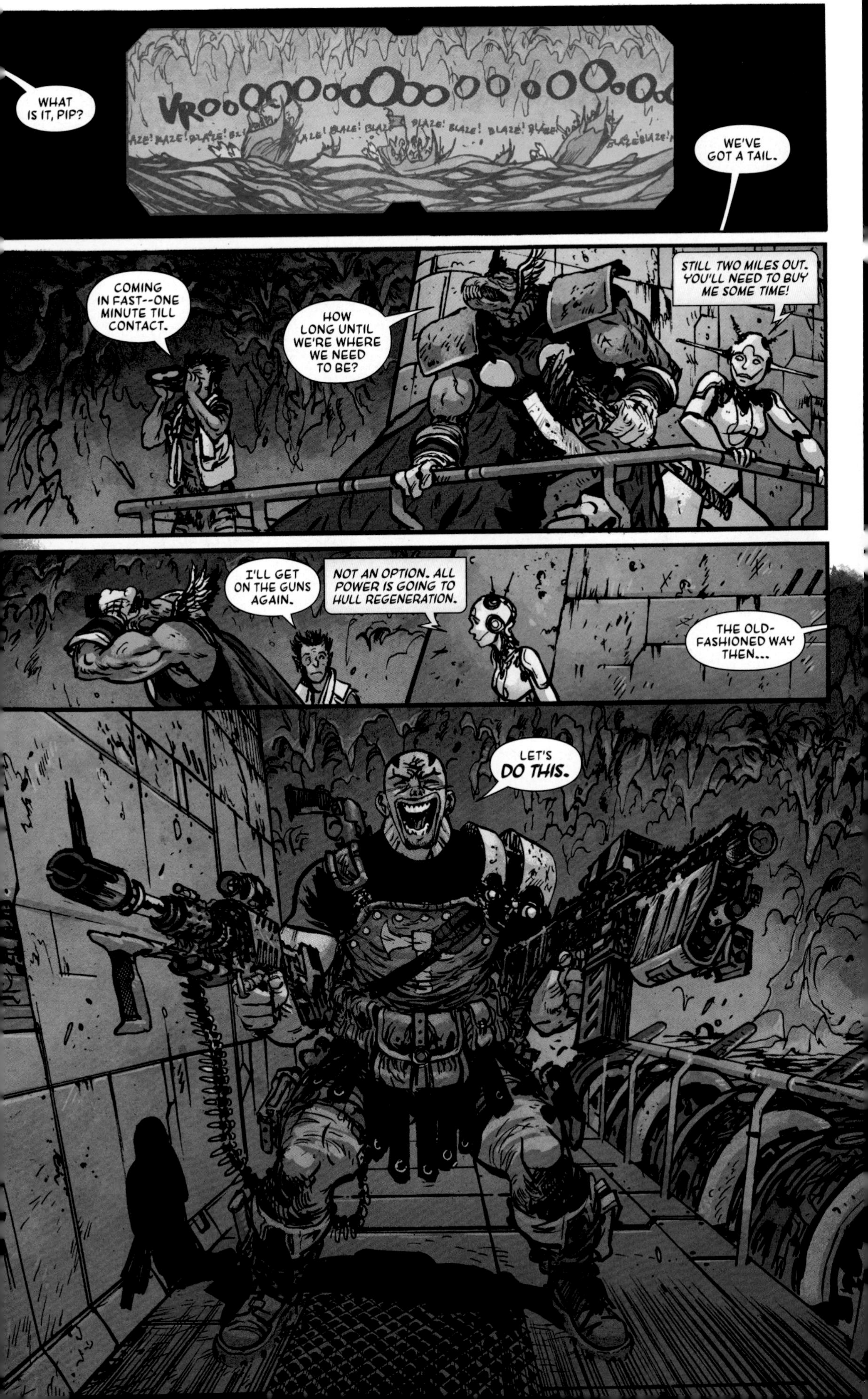
WHAT IS IT, PIP?
WE'VE GOT A TAIL.
COMING IN FAST--ONE MINUTE TILL CONTACT.
HOW LONG UNTIL WE'RE WHERE WE NEED TO BE?
STILL TWO MILES OUT. YOU'LL NEED TO BUY ME SOME TIME!
I'LL GET ON THE GUNS AGAIN.
NOT AN OPTION. ALL POWER IS GOING TO HULL REGENERATION.
THE OLD-FASHIONED WAY THEN...
LET'S DO THIS.

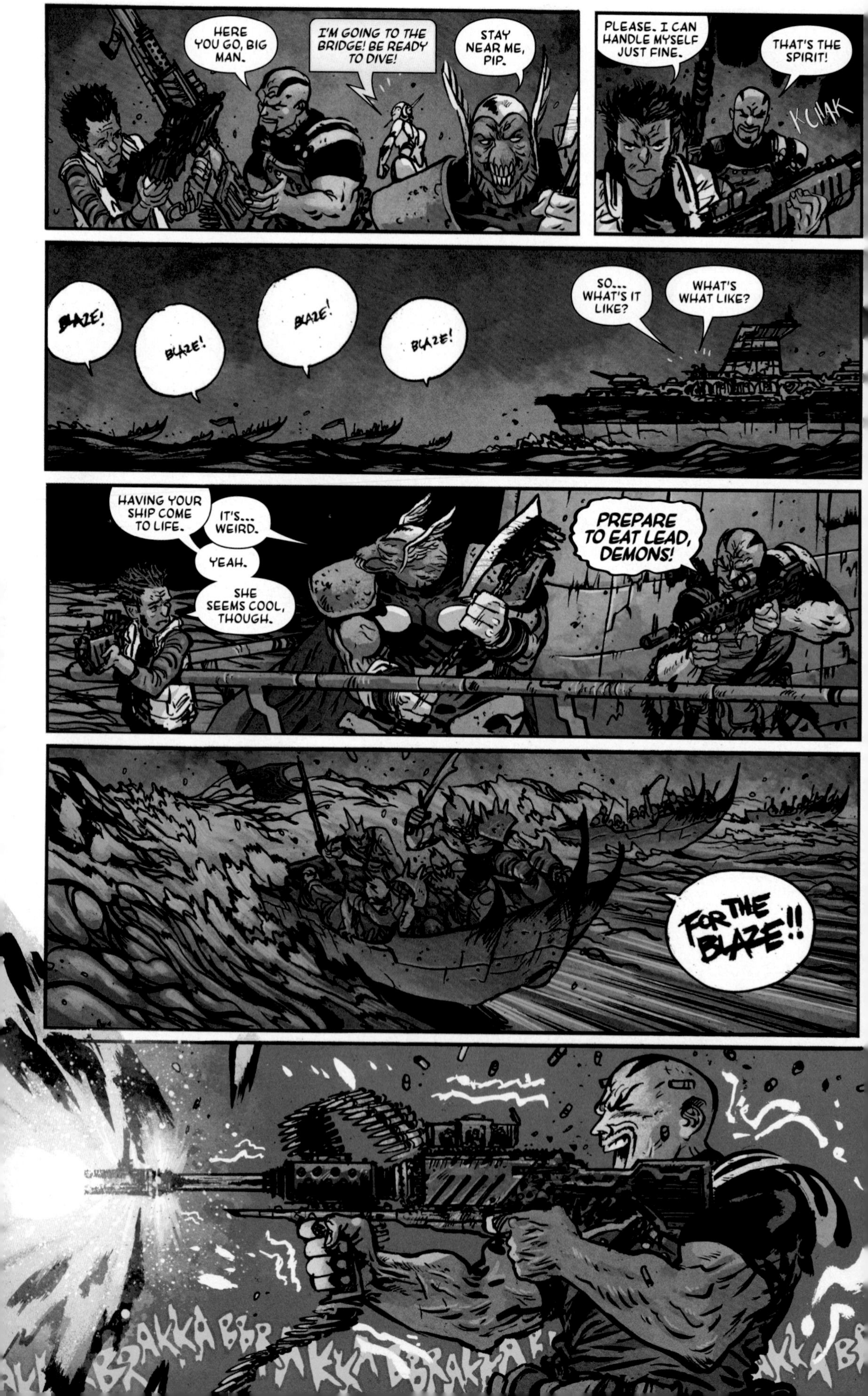
HERE YOU GO, BIG MAN.
I'M GOING TO THE BRIDGE! BE READY TO DIVE!
STAY NEAR ME, PIP.
PLEASE. I CAN HANDLE MYSELF JUST FINE.
THAT'S THE SPIRIT!
KCHAK
BLAZE!
BLAZE!
BLAZE!
BLAZE!
SO... WHAT'S IT LIKE?
WHAT'S WHAT LIKE?
HAVING YOUR SHIP COME TO LIFE.
IT'S... WEIRD.
YEAH.
SHE SEEMS COOL, THOUGH.
PREPARE TO EAT LEAD, DEMONS!
FOR THE BLAZE!!
BRAKKA BRAKKA

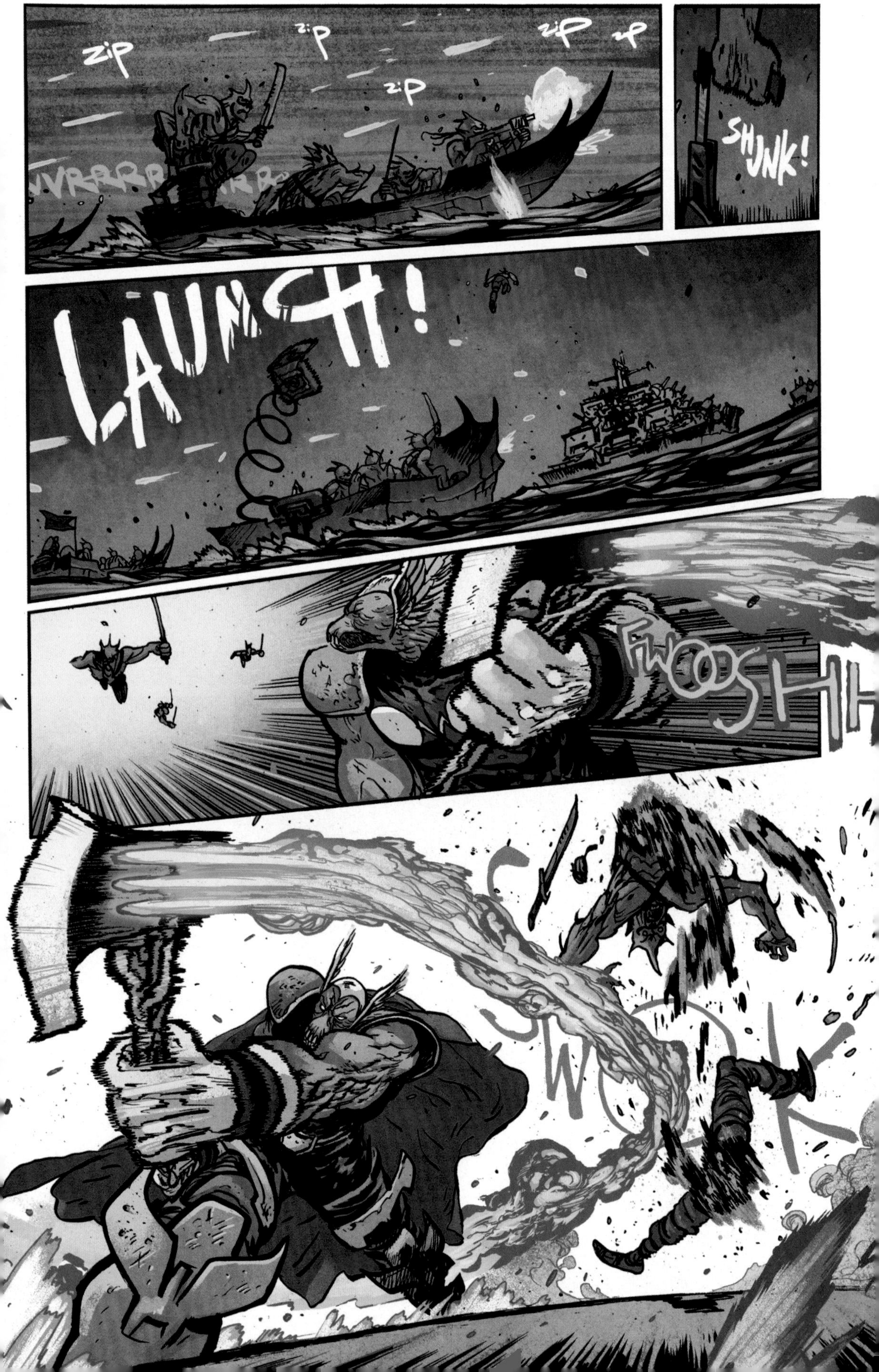
ZIP
ZIP
ZIP
ZIP
ZIP
SHUNK!
LAUNCH!
FWOOSHHH

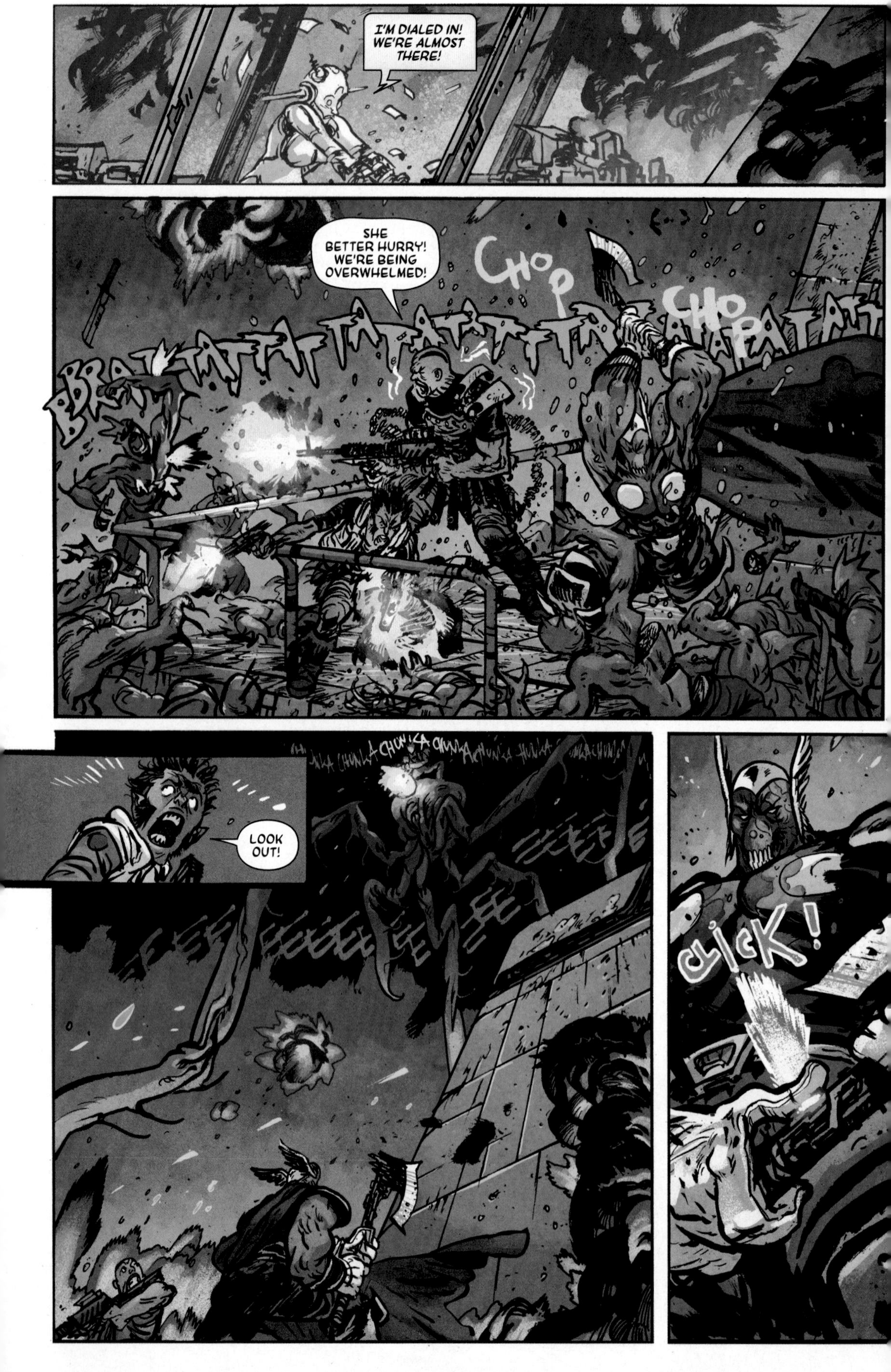
I'M DIALED IN! WE'RE ALMOST THERE!
SHE BETTER HURRY! WE'RE BEING OVERWHELMED!
CHOP
CHOP
LOOK OUT!
CLICK!

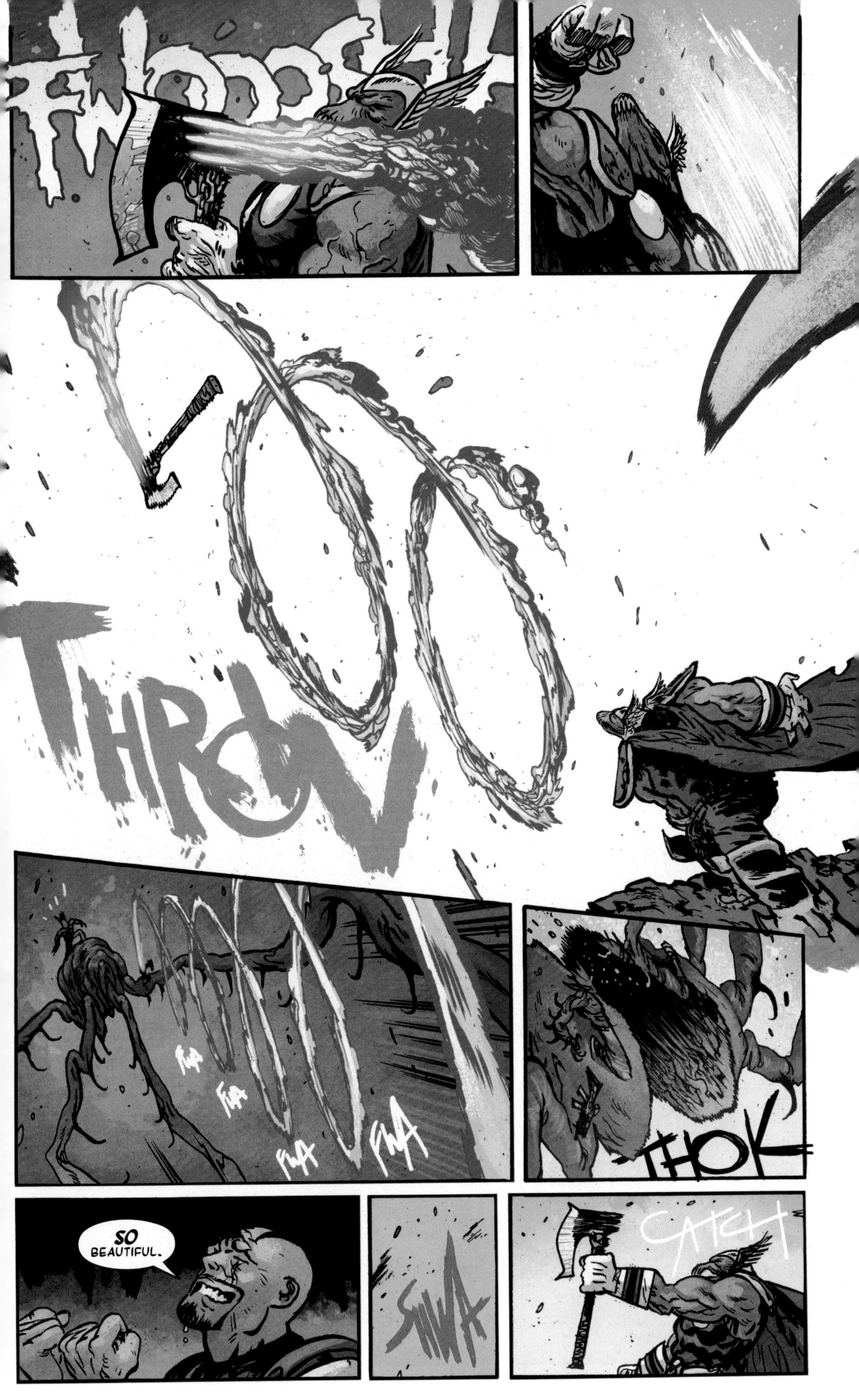
THROW
FWA
FWA
FWA
FWA
THOK
SO BEAUTIFUL.
SHWA
CATCH

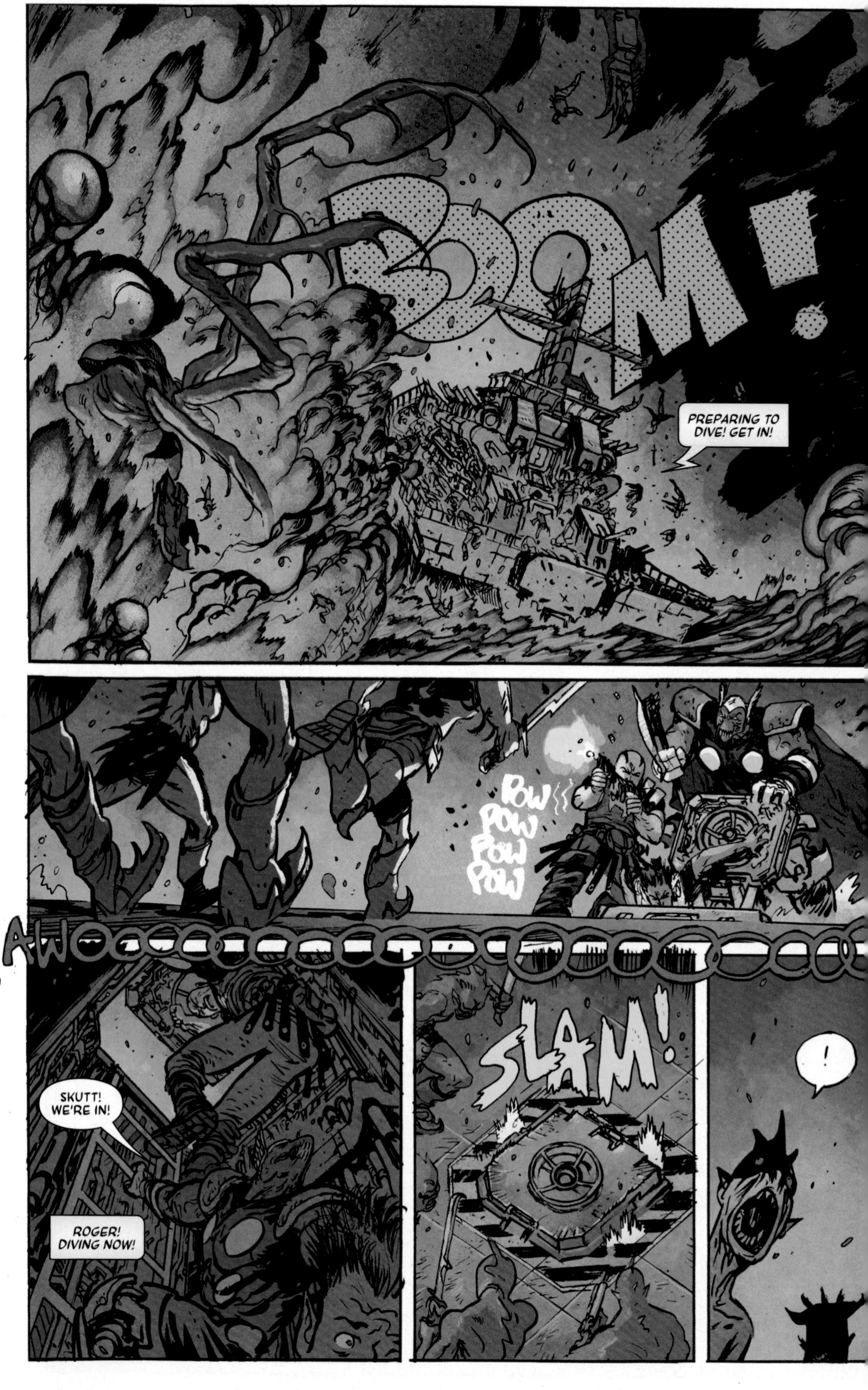
BOOM!
PREPARING TO DIVE! GET IN!
POW POW POW POW
AWOOOOOOOOOOOOOOOOOO
SKUTT! WE'RE IN!
ROGER! DIVING NOW!
SLAM!
!

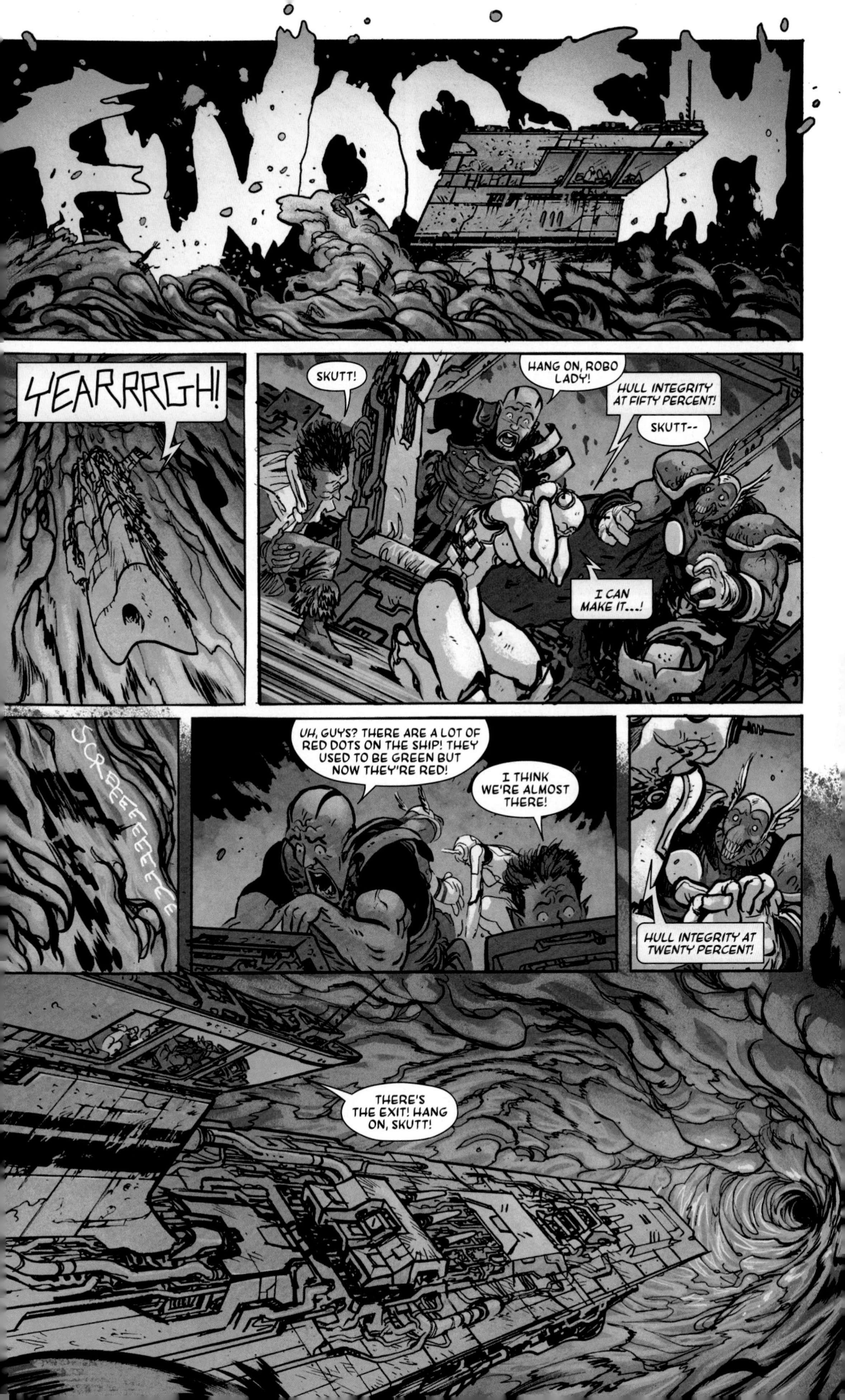
FWOOSH
YEARRRGH!
SKUTT!
HANG ON, ROBO LADY!
HULL INTEGRITY AT FIFTY PERCENT!
SKUTT--
I CAN MAKE IT...!
SCREEEEEEEEEE
UH, GUYS? THERE ARE A LOT OF RED DOTS ON THE SHIP! THEY USED TO BE GREEN BUT NOW THEY'RE RED!
I THINK WE'RE ALMOST THERE!
HULL INTEGRITY AT TWENTY PERCENT!
THERE'S THE EXIT! HANG ON, SKUTT!

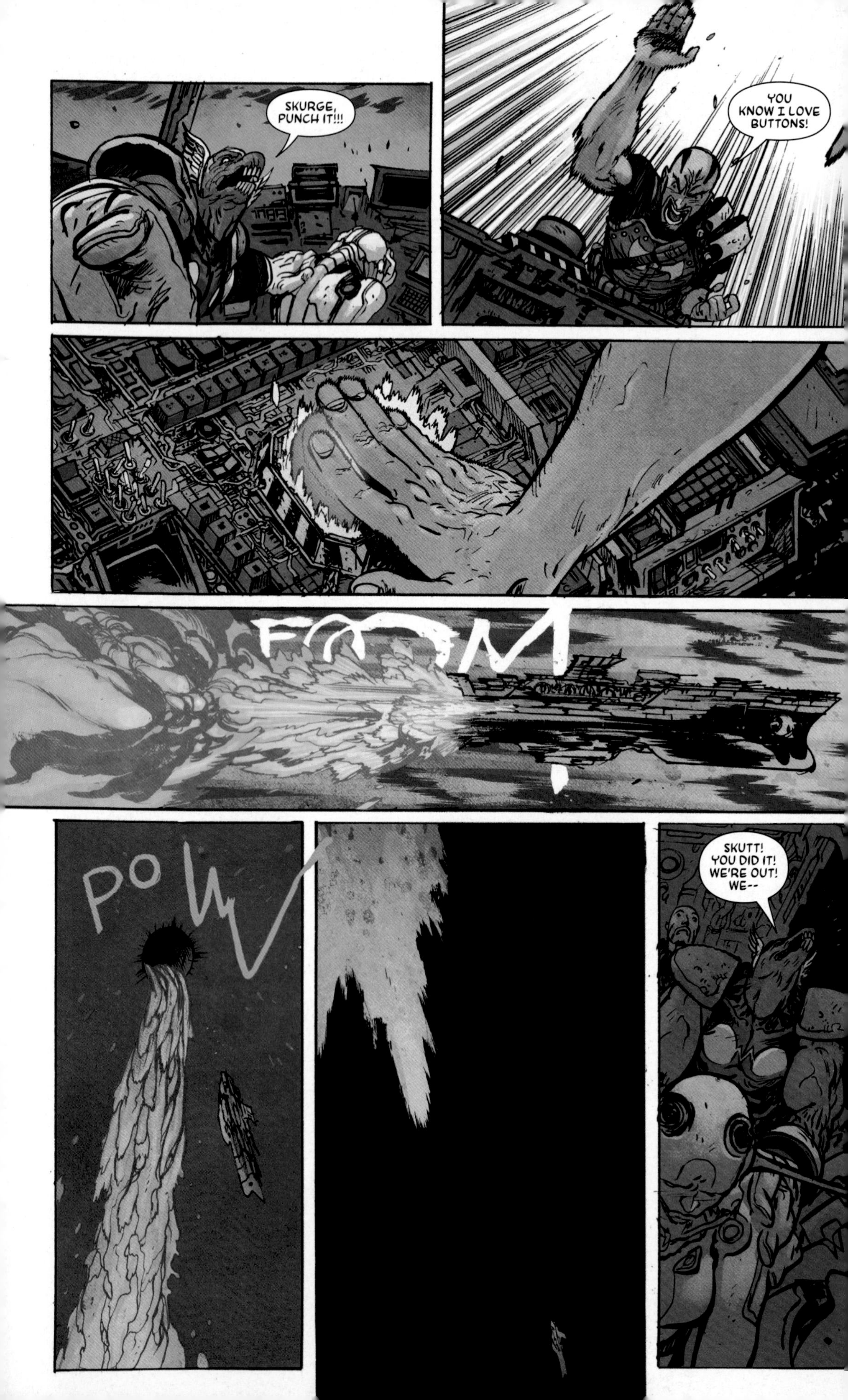
SKURGE, PUNCH IT!!!
YOU KNOW I LOVE BUTTONS!
FOOM
POW
SKUTT! YOU DID IT! WE'RE OUT! WE--

WHAT--
WHAT IS
THAT?

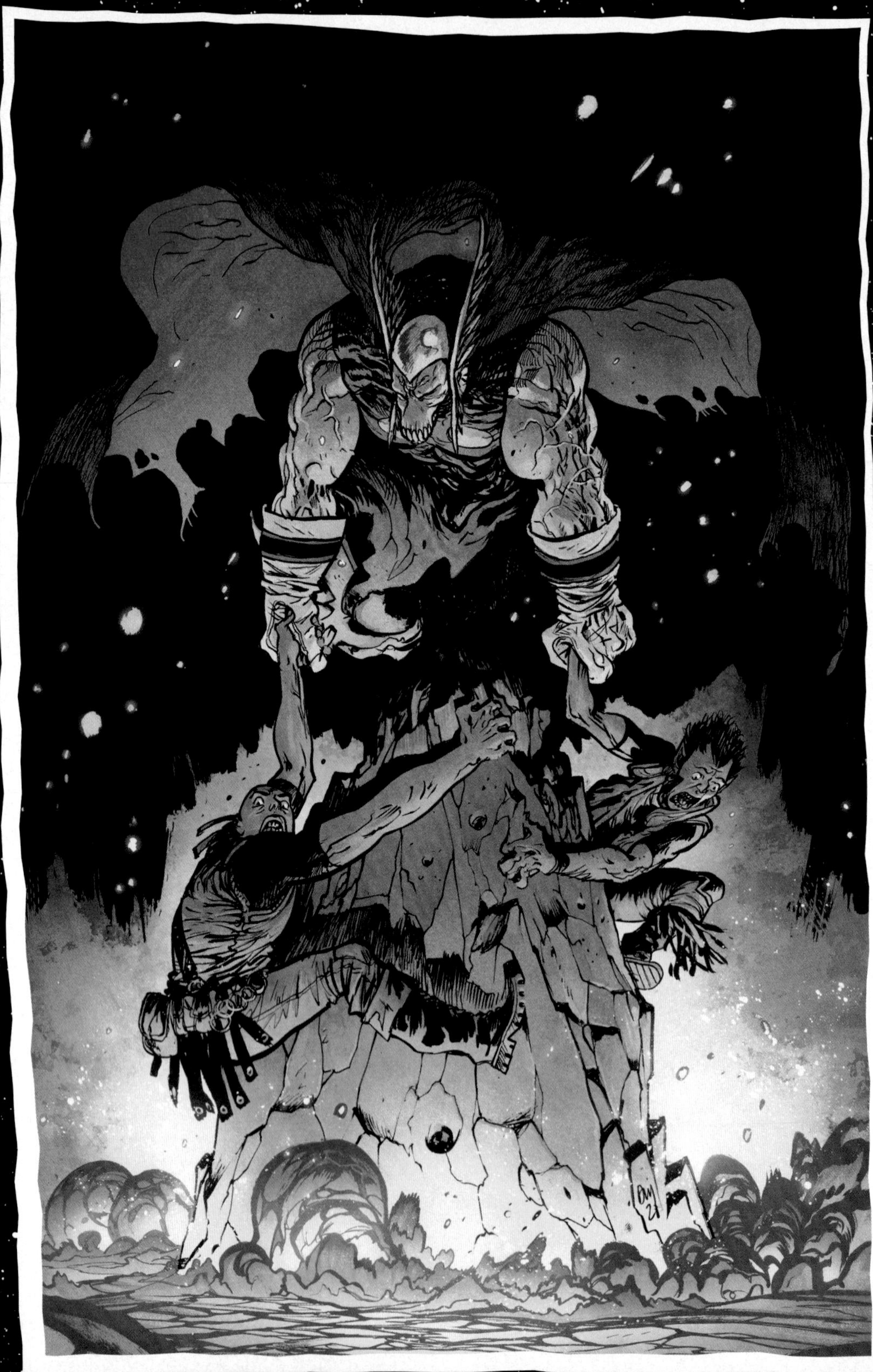

4

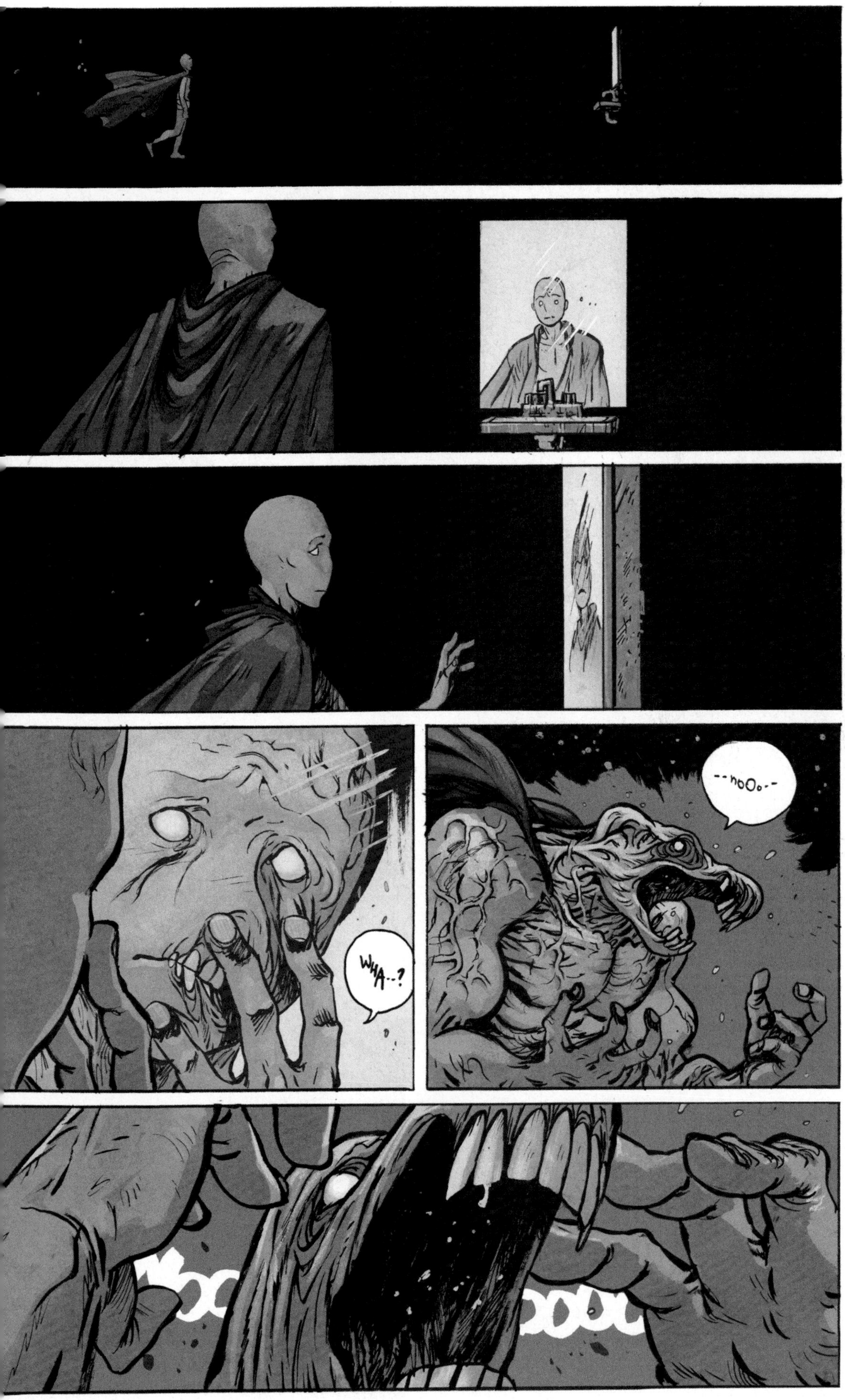
. . .
WHA..?
--noO..-

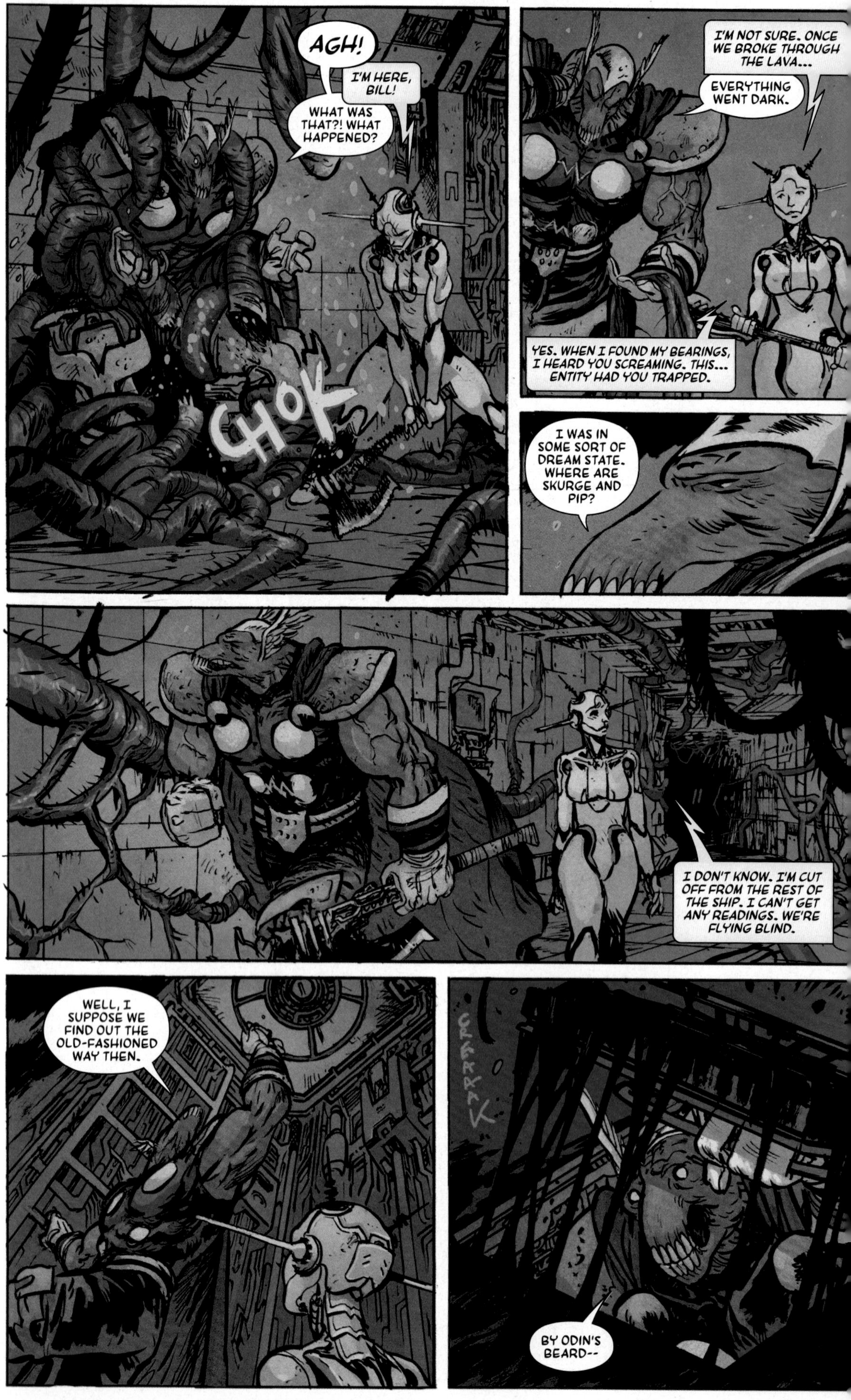
AGH!
WHAT WAS THAT?! WHAT HAPPENED?
I'M HERE, BILL!
CHOK
I'M NOT SURE. ONCE WE BROKE THROUGH THE LAVA...
EVERYTHING WENT DARK.
YES. WHEN I FOUND MY BEARINGS, I HEARD YOU SCREAMING. THIS... ENTITY HAD YOU TRAPPED.
I WAS IN SOME SORT OF DREAM STATE. WHERE ARE SKURGE AND PIP?
I DON'T KNOW. I'M CUT OFF FROM THE REST OF THE SHIP. I CAN'T GET ANY READINGS. WE'RE FLYING BLIND.
WELL, I SUPPOSE WE FIND OUT THE OLD-FASHIONED WAY THEN.
BY ODIN'S BEARD--

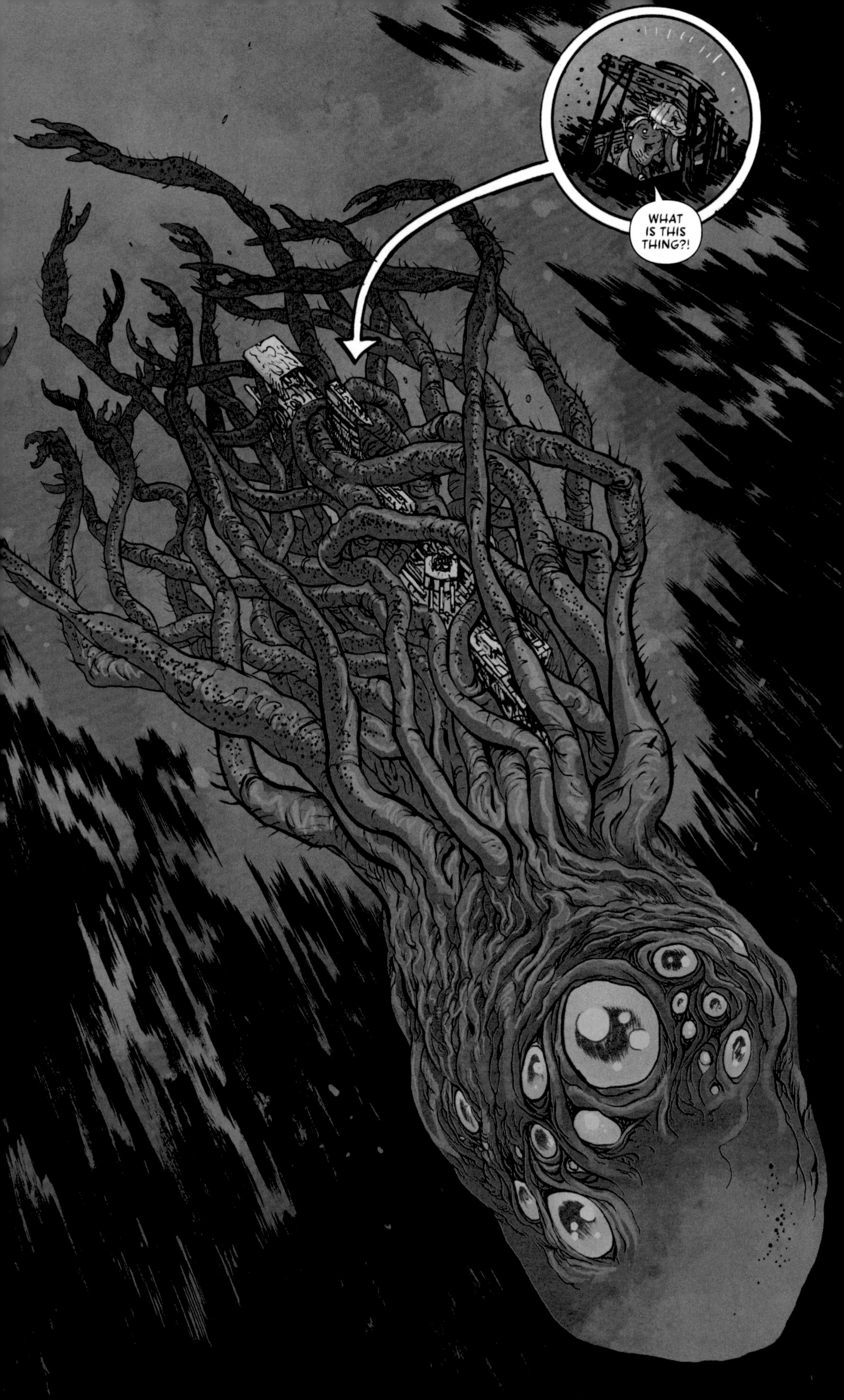
WHAT IS THIS THING?!

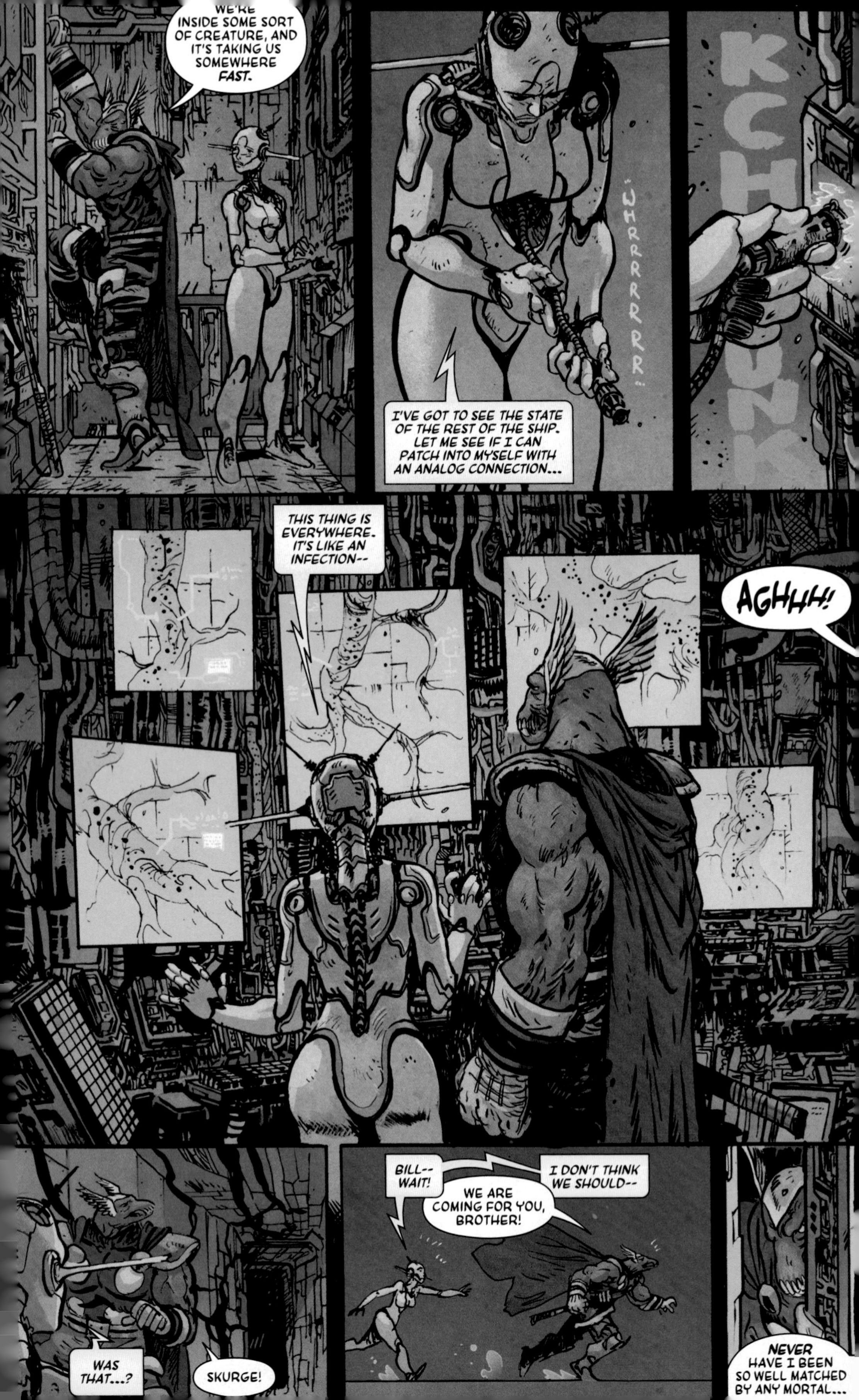
WE'RE INSIDE SOME SORT OF CREATURE, AND IT'S TAKING US SOMEWHERE FAST.
"WHRRRRRRR"
I'VE GOT TO SEE THE STATE OF THE REST OF THE SHIP. LET ME SEE IF I CAN PATCH INTO MYSELF WITH AN ANALOG CONNECTION...
KCHUNK
THIS THING IS EVERYWHERE. IT'S LIKE AN INFECTION--
AGHHH!
WAS THAT...?
SKURGE!
BILL--WAIT!
I DON'T THINK WE SHOULD--
WE ARE COMING FOR YOU, BROTHER!
NEVER HAVE I BEEN SO WELL MATCHED BY ANY MORTAL...

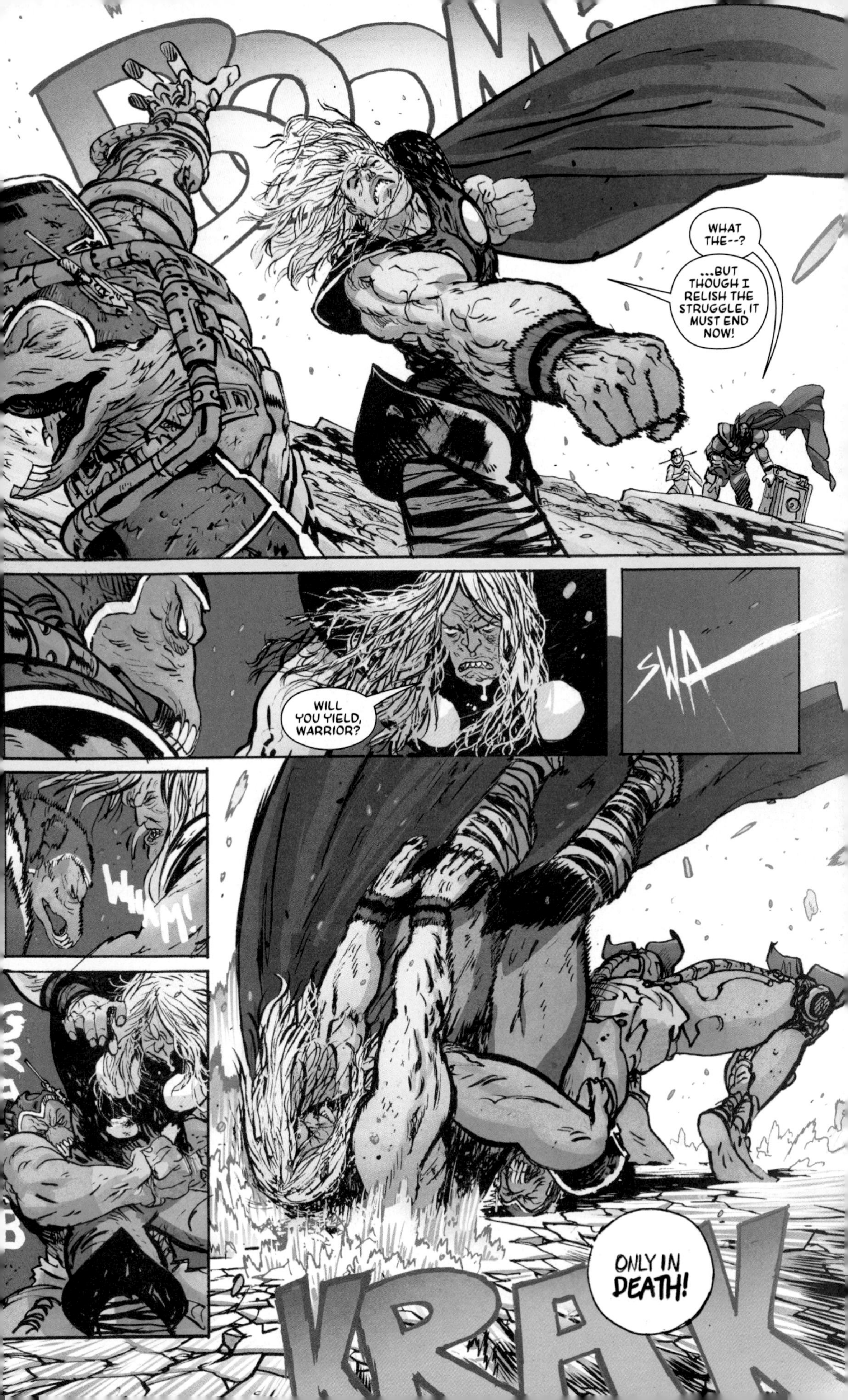
BOOM!
WHAT THE--?
...BUT THOUGH I RELISH THE STRUGGLE, IT MUST END NOW!
WILL YOU YIELD, WARRIOR?
SWA
WHAM!
ONLY IN DEATH!
KRAK

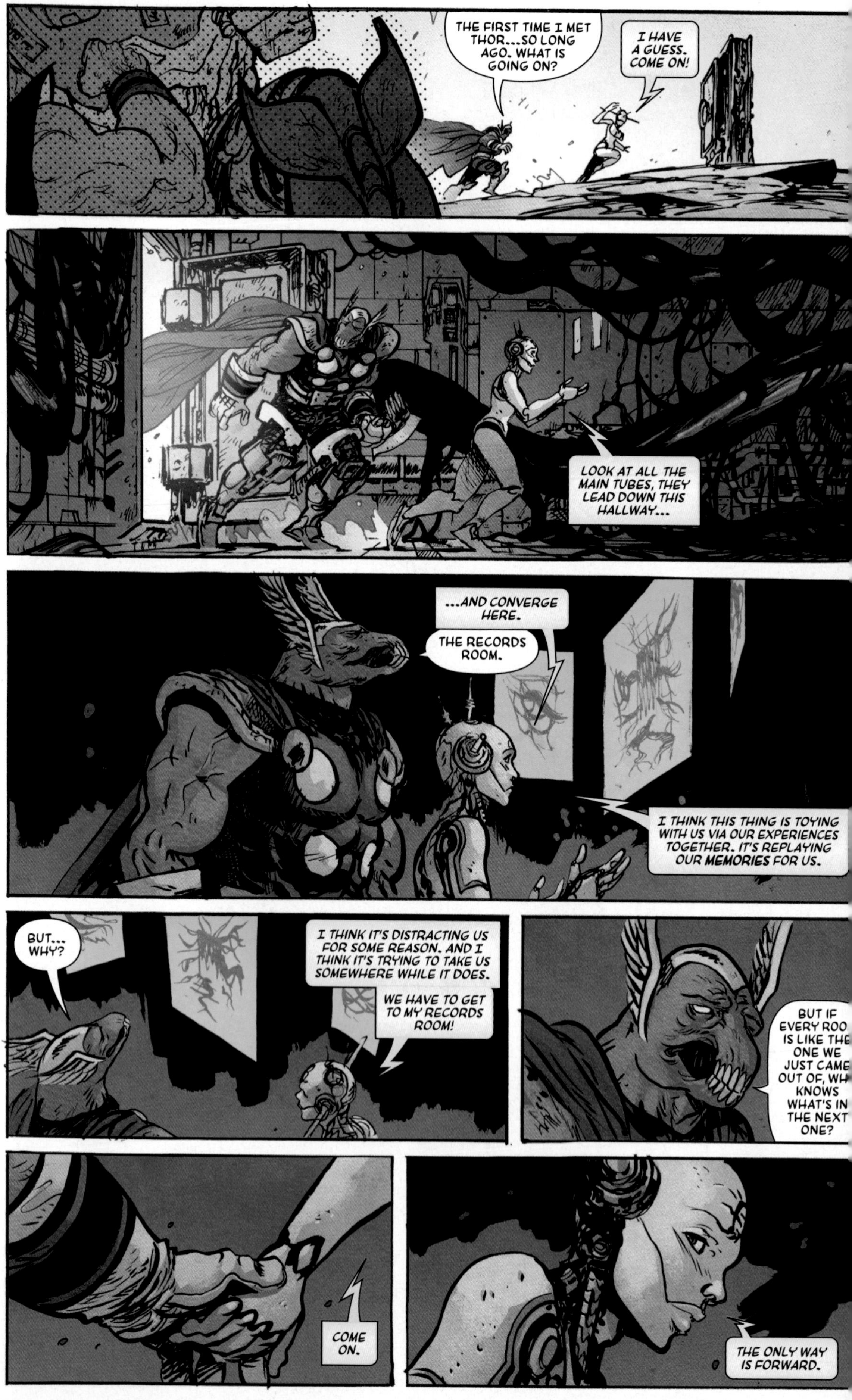
THE FIRST TIME I MET THOR...SO LONG AGO. WHAT IS GOING ON?
I HAVE A GUESS. COME ON!
LOOK AT ALL THE MAIN TUBES, THEY LEAD DOWN THIS HALLWAY...
...AND CONVERGE HERE.
THE RECORDS ROOM.
I THINK THIS THING IS TOYING WITH US VIA OUR EXPERIENCES TOGETHER. IT'S REPLAYING OUR MEMORIES FOR US.
BUT... WHY?
I THINK IT'S DISTRACTING US FOR SOME REASON. AND I THINK IT'S TRYING TO TAKE US SOMEWHERE WHILE IT DOES.
WE HAVE TO GET TO MY RECORDS ROOM!
BUT IF EVERY ROO IS LIKE THE ONE WE JUST CAME OUT OF, WH KNOWS WHAT'S IN THE NEXT ONE?
COME ON.
THE ONLY WAY IS FORWARD.

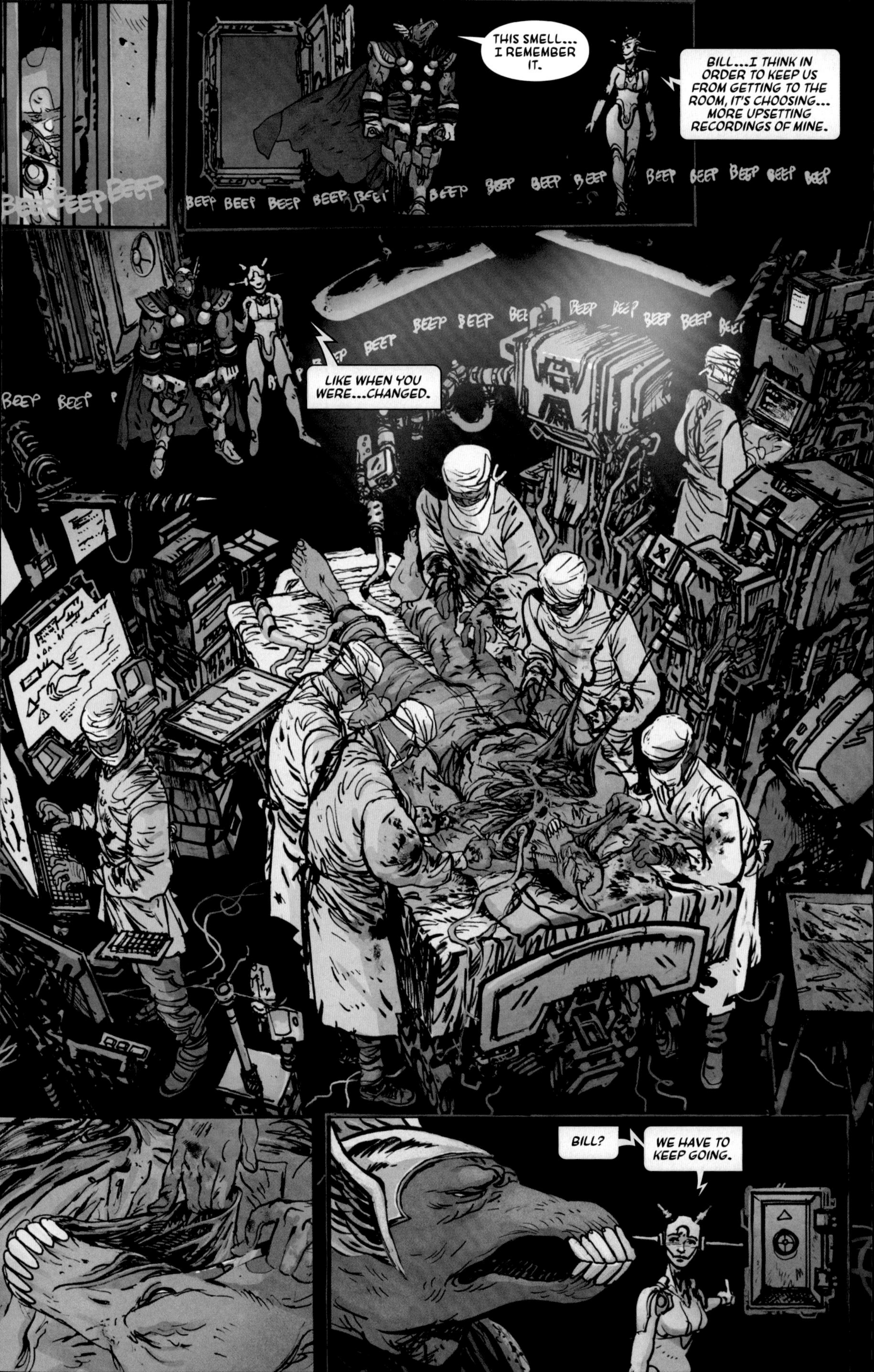
BEEP BEEP BEEP
BEEP BEEP BEEP BEEP BEEP
THIS SMELL... I REMEMBER IT.
BEEP BEEP BEEP BEEP
BILL...I THINK IN ORDER TO KEEP US FROM GETTING TO THE ROOM, IT'S CHOOSING... MORE UPSETTING RECORDINGS OF MINE.
BEEP BEEP BEEP BEEP BEEP
BEEP BEEP
BEEP BEEP
BEEP BEEP BEEP BEEP BEEP BEEP
LIKE WHEN YOU WERE...CHANGED.
BILL?
WE HAVE TO KEEP GOING.

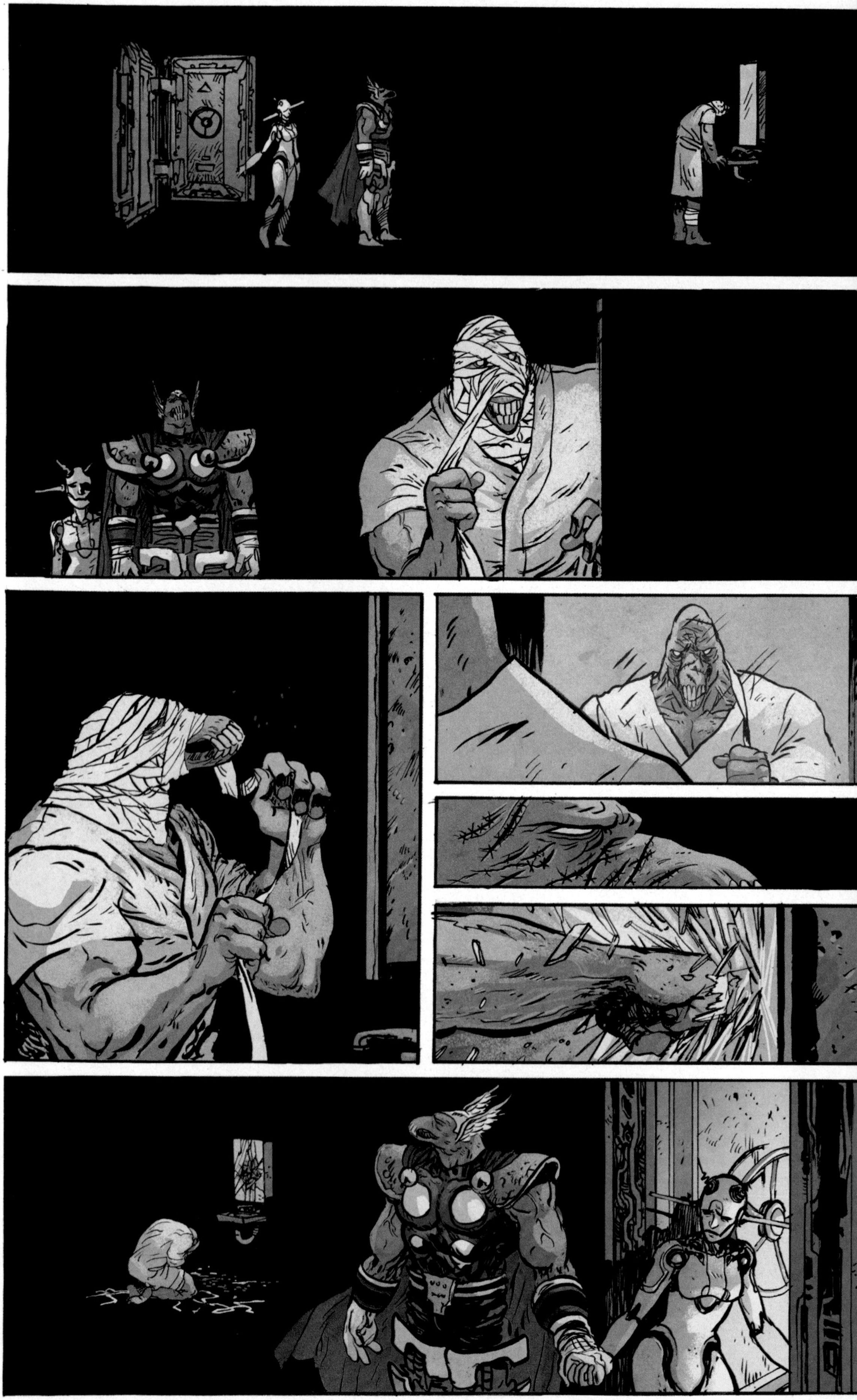

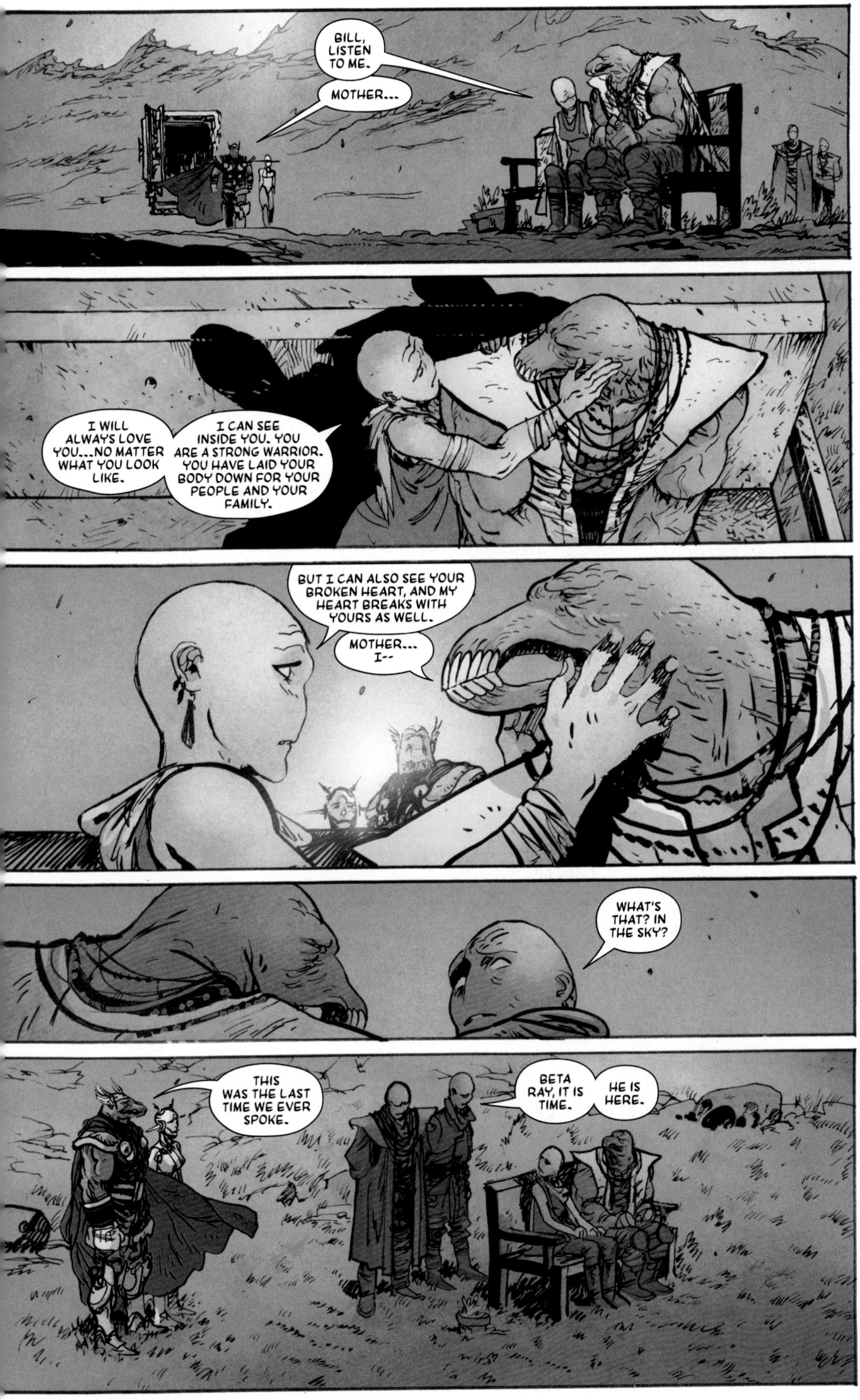
BILL, LISTEN TO ME.
MOTHER...
I CAN SEE INSIDE YOU. YOU ARE A STRONG WARRIOR. YOU HAVE LAID YOUR BODY DOWN FOR YOUR PEOPLE AND YOUR FAMILY.
I WILL ALWAYS LOVE YOU...NO MATTER WHAT YOU LOOK LIKE.
BUT I CAN ALSO SEE YOUR BROKEN HEART, AND MY HEART BREAKS WITH YOURS AS WELL.
MOTHER... I--
WHAT'S THAT? IN THE SKY?
THIS WAS THE LAST TIME WE EVER SPOKE.
BETA RAY, IT IS TIME.
HE IS HERE.

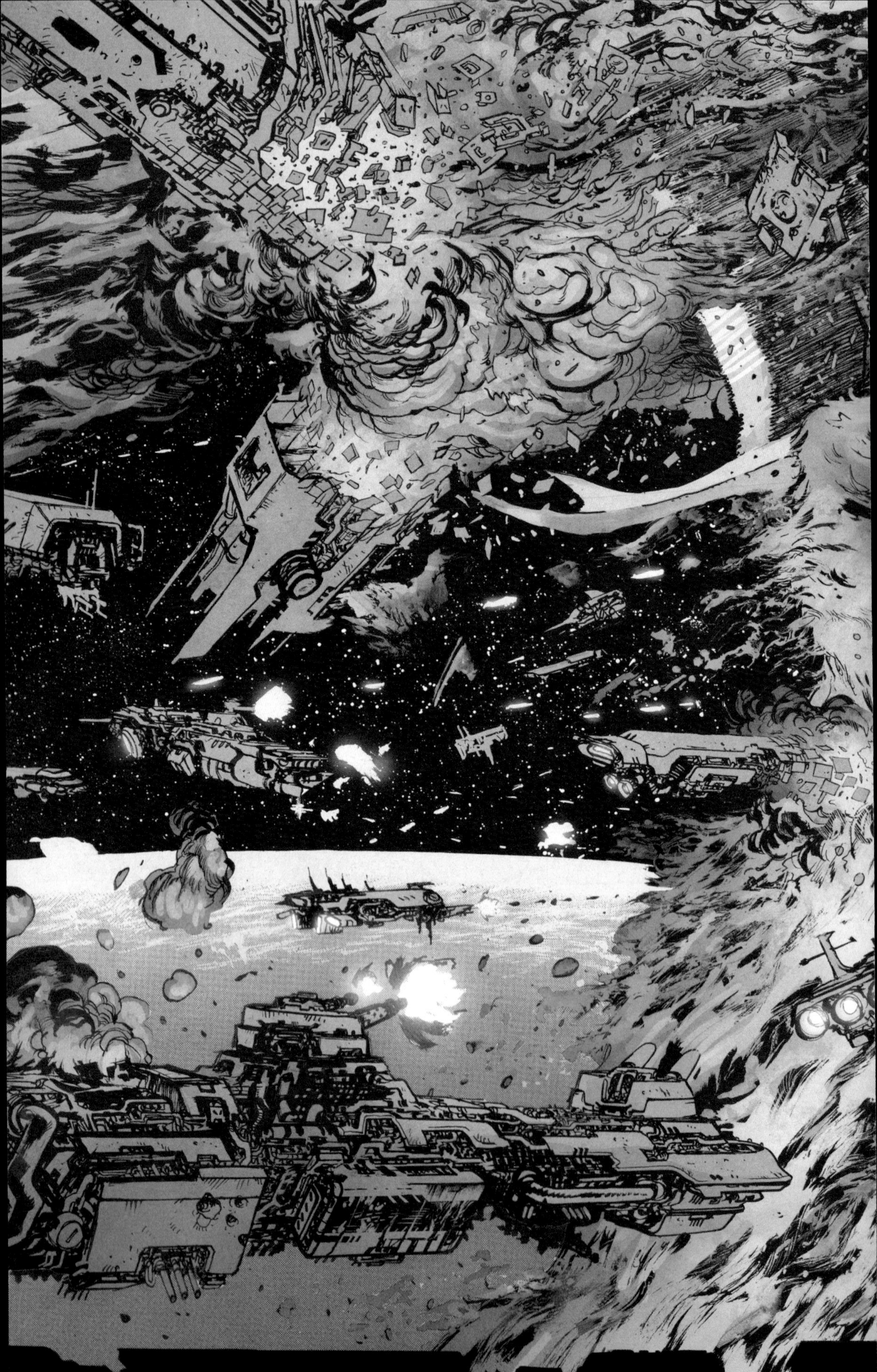

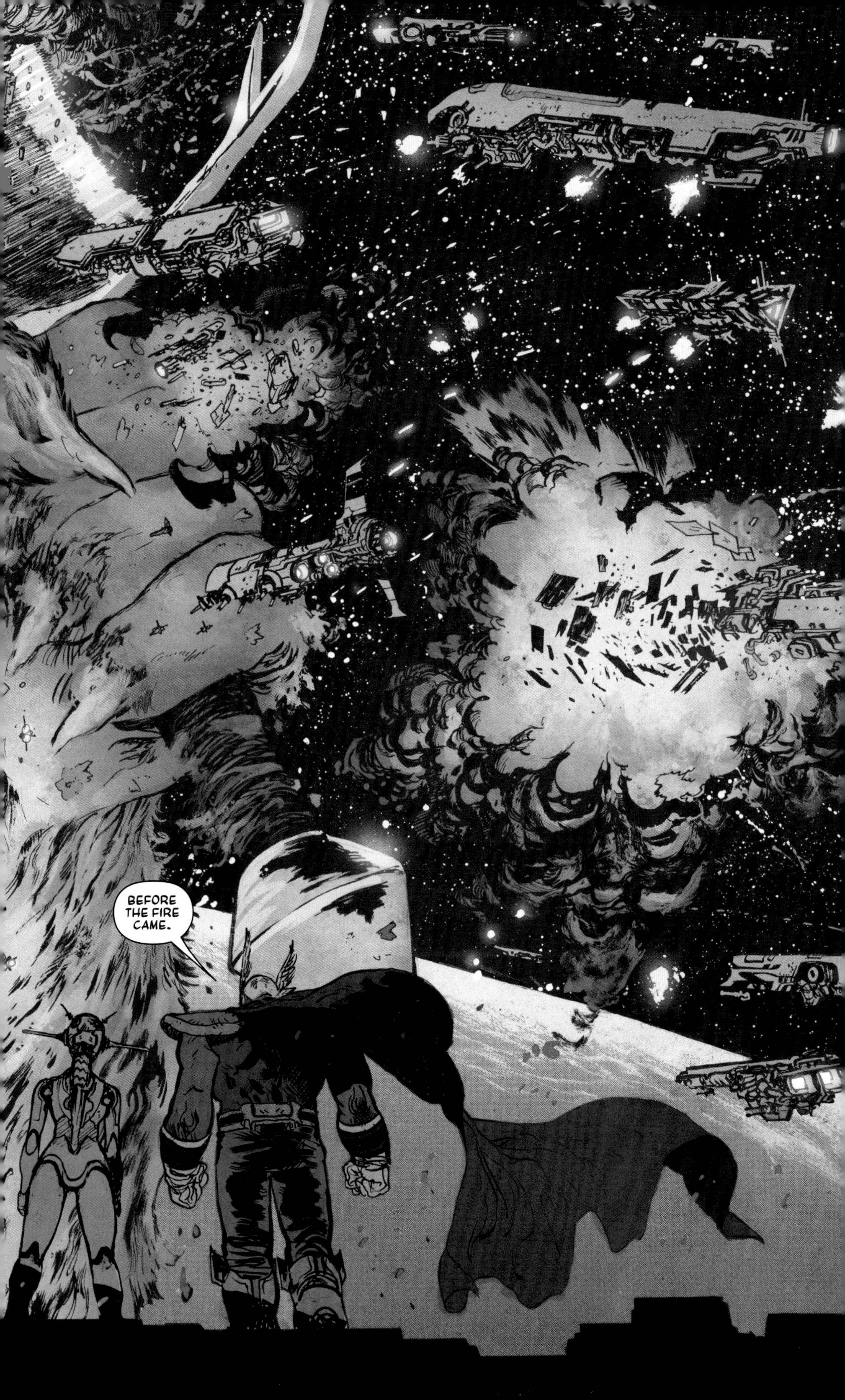
BEFORE THE FIRE CAME.

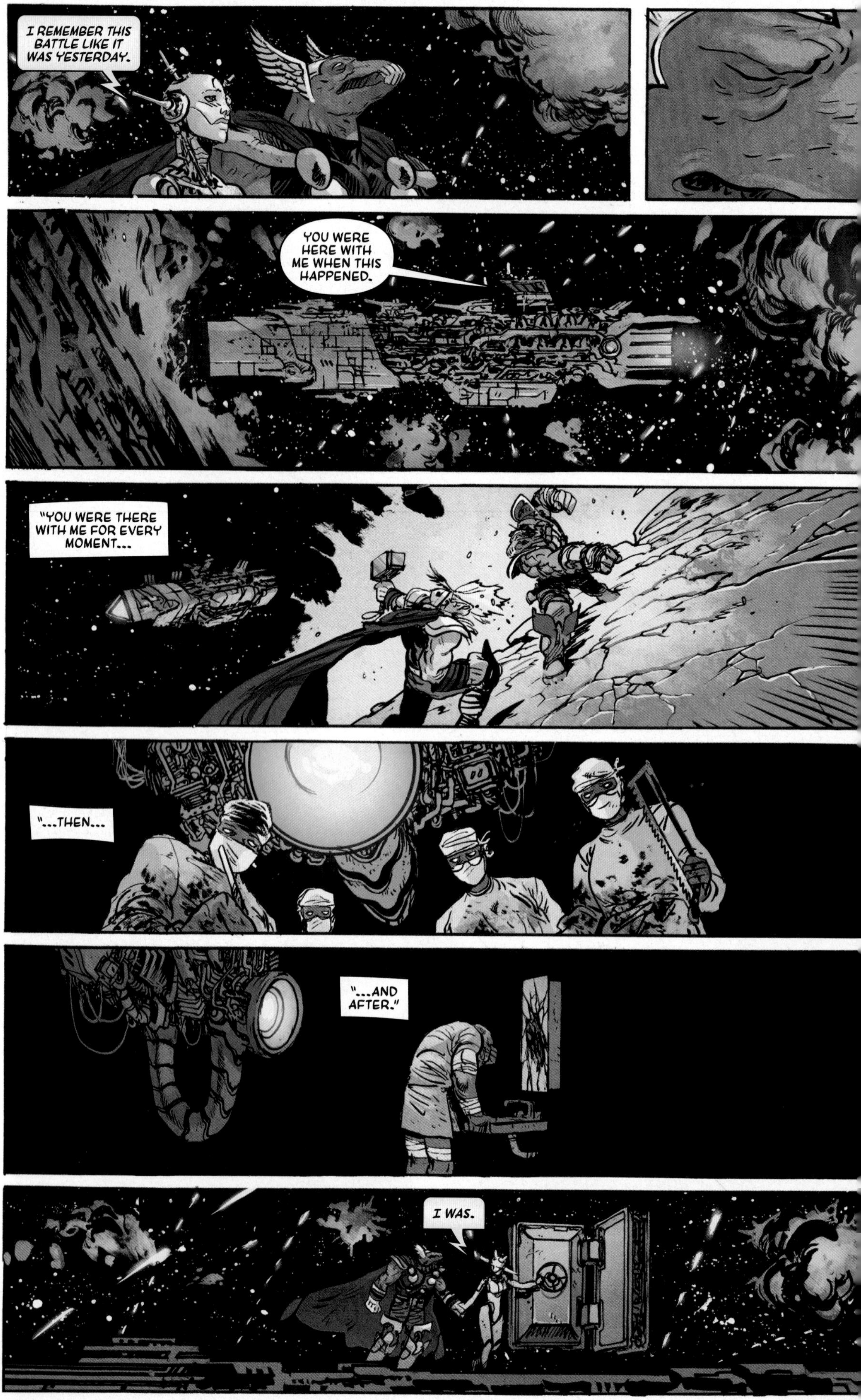
I REMEMBER THIS BATTLE LIKE IT WAS YESTERDAY.
YOU WERE HERE WITH ME WHEN THIS HAPPENED.
"YOU WERE THERE WITH ME FOR EVERY MOMENT...
"...THEN...
"...AND AFTER."
I WAS.

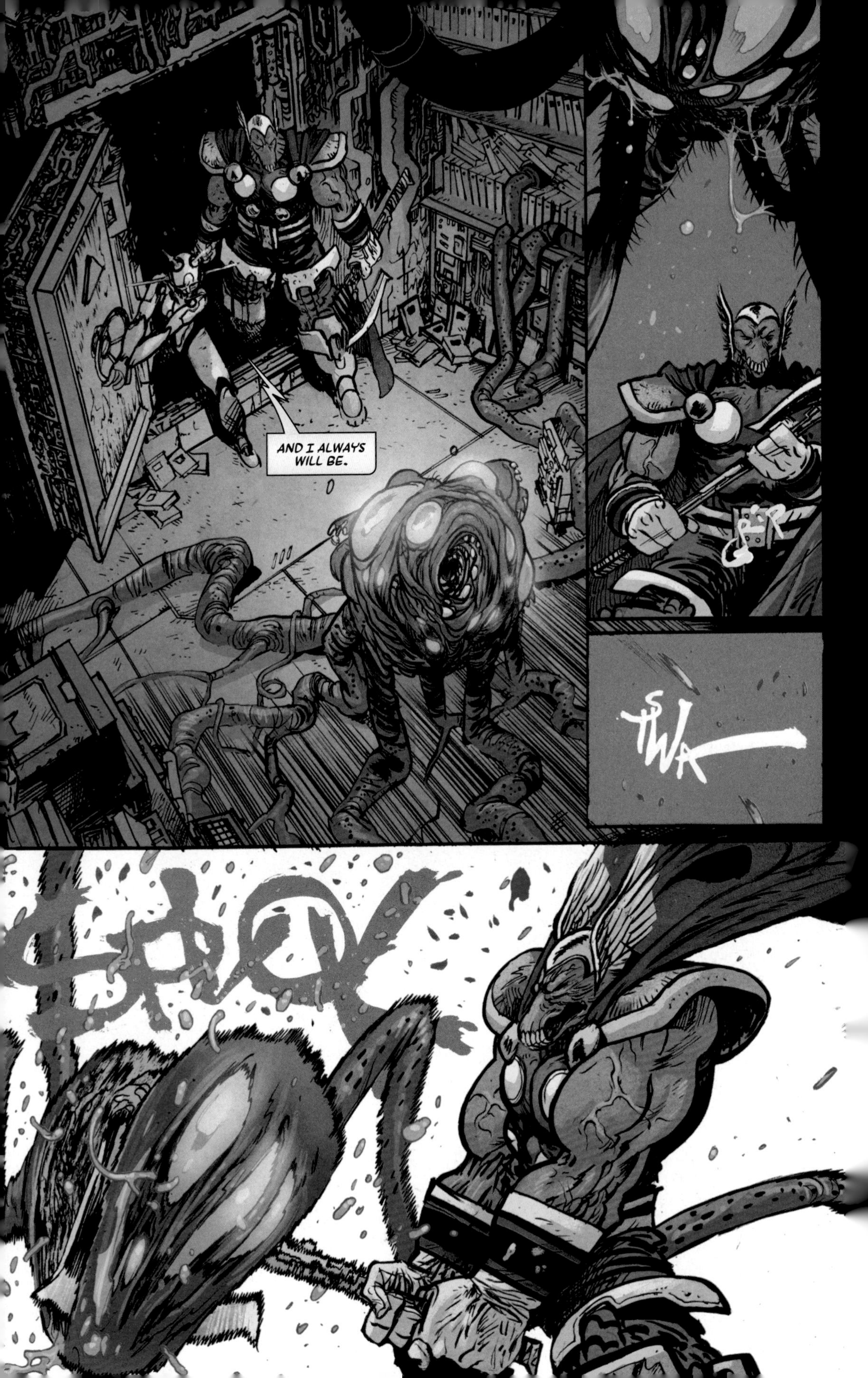
AND I ALWAYS WILL BE.
GRIP
SHWA
SPLOT

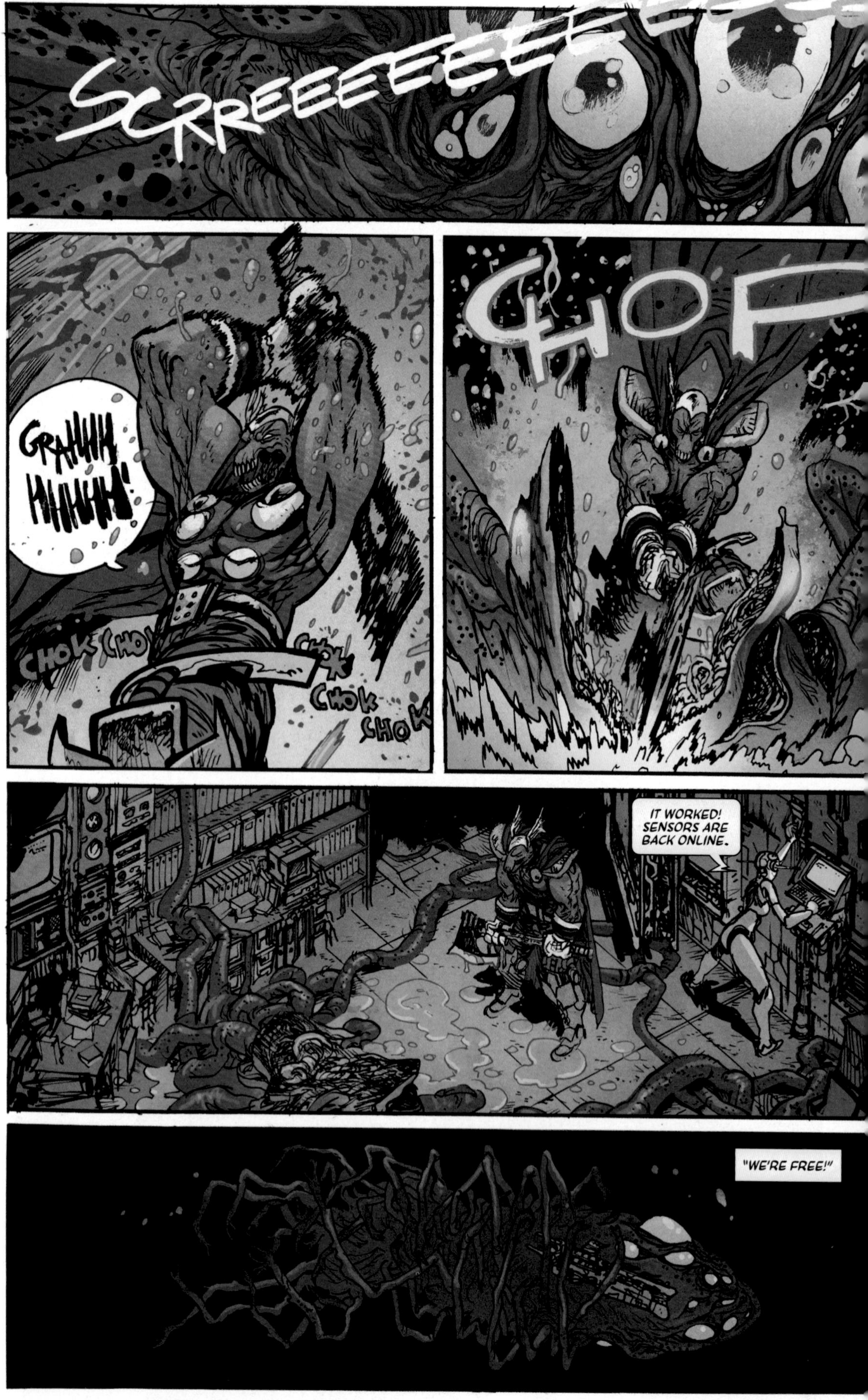
SCRREEEEEEEEEEEEEE
GRAHHHH HHHHHH!
CHOK CHOK
CHOK
CHOK
CHOK
CHOP
IT WORKED! SENSORS ARE BACK ONLINE.
"WE'RE FREE!"

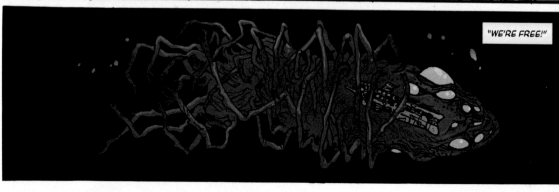

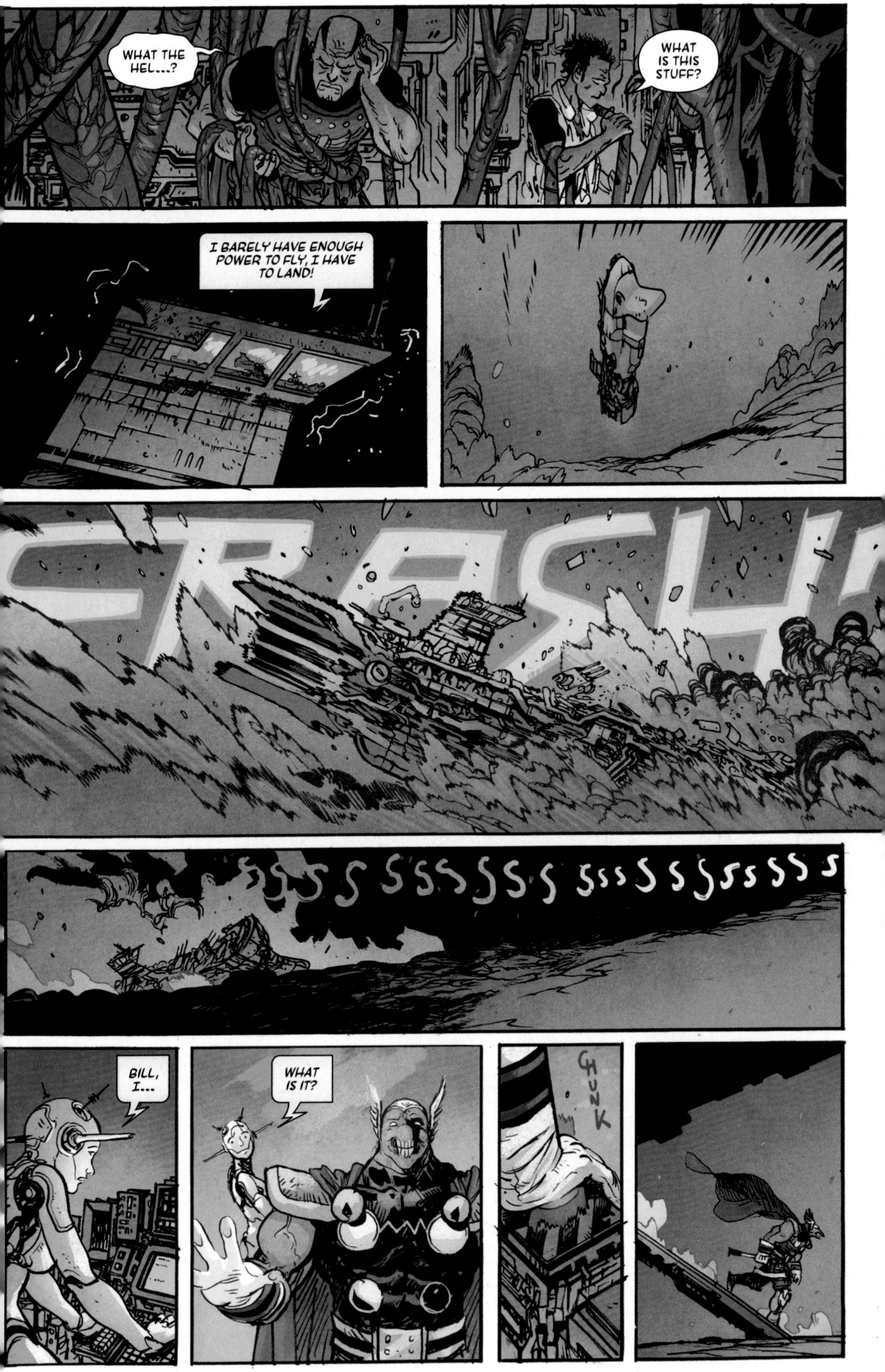

WHAT THE HEL...?
WHAT IS THIS STUFF?
I BARELY HAVE ENOUGH POWER TO FLY, I HAVE TO LAND!
CRASH!
SSSSSSSSSSSSSSSSSSSSSS
BILL, I...
WHAT IS IT?
CHUNK

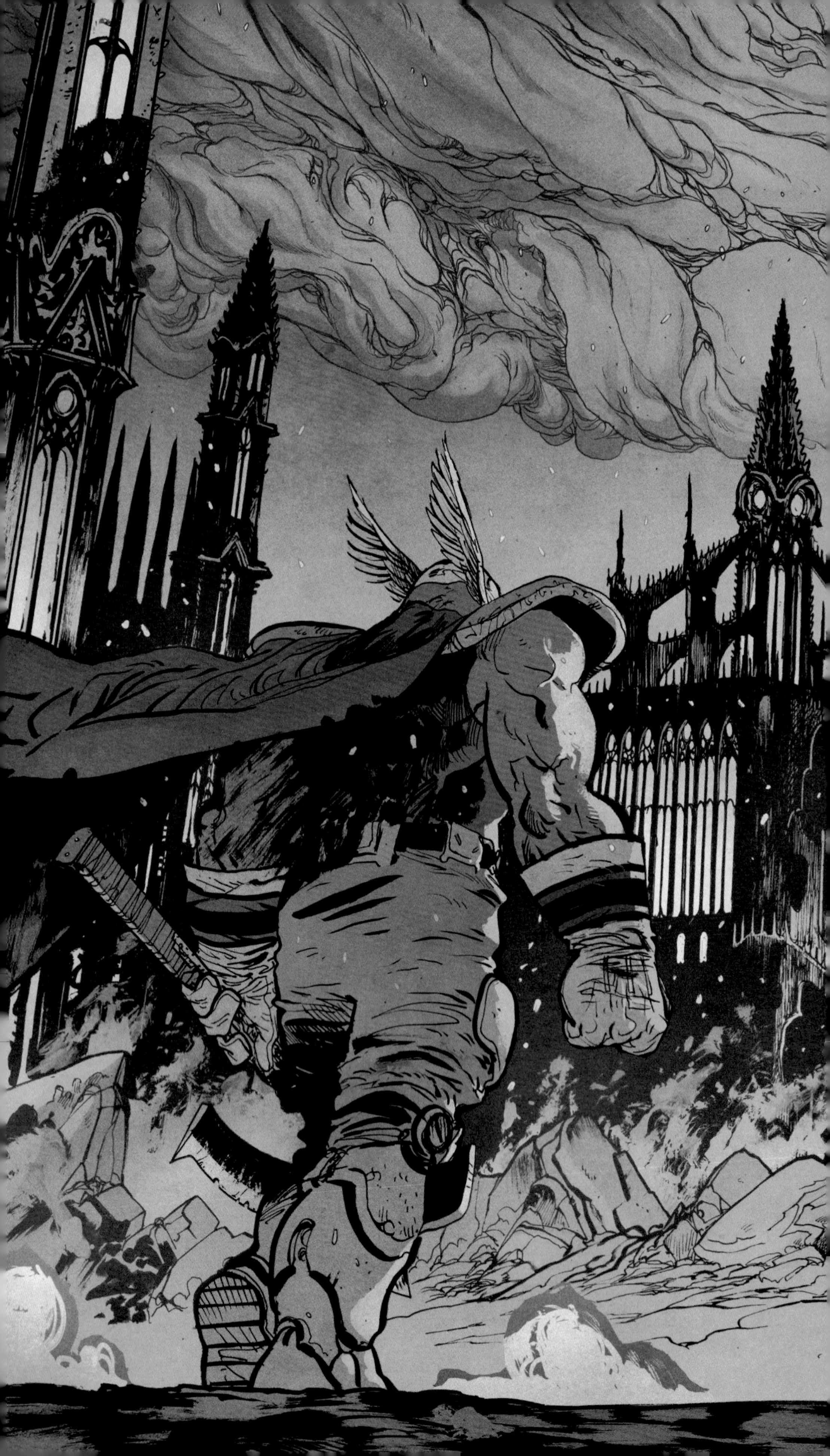

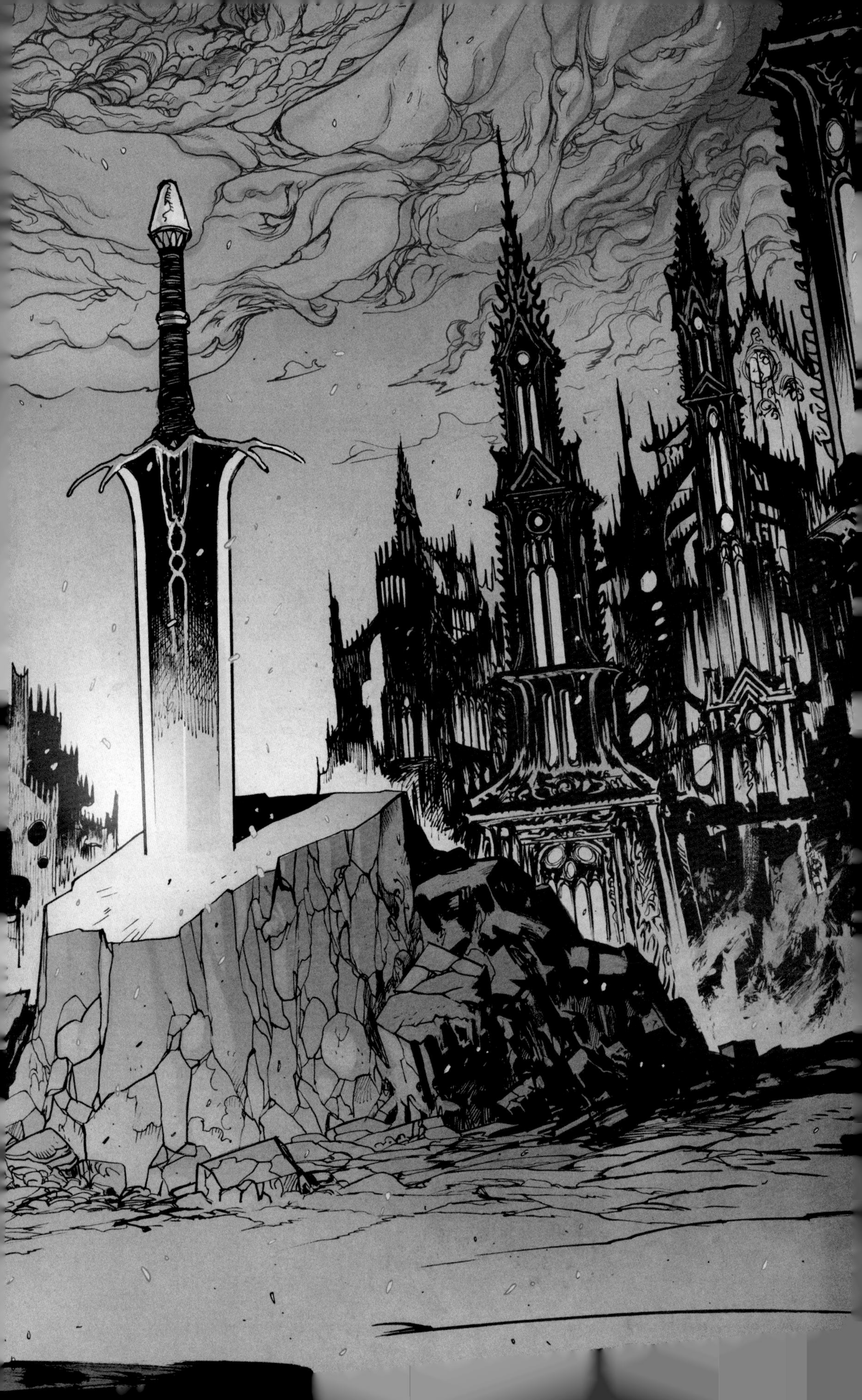

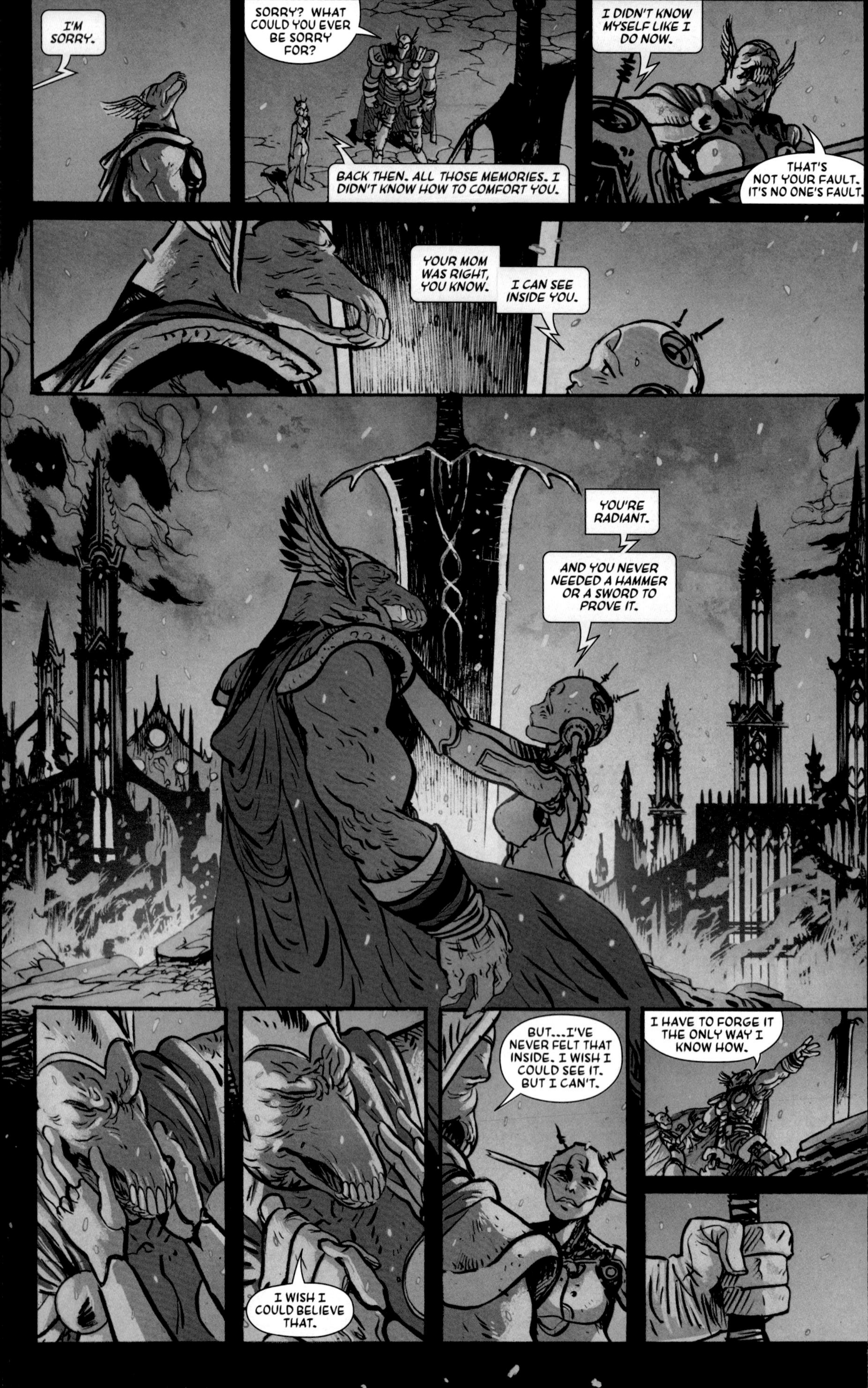
I'M SORRY.
SORRY? WHAT COULD YOU EVER BE SORRY FOR?
BACK THEN. ALL THOSE MEMORIES. I DIDN'T KNOW HOW TO COMFORT YOU.
I DIDN'T KNOW MYSELF LIKE I DO NOW.
THAT'S NOT YOUR FAULT. IT'S NO ONE'S FAULT.
YOUR MOM WAS RIGHT, YOU KNOW.
I CAN SEE INSIDE YOU.
YOU'RE RADIANT.
AND YOU NEVER NEEDED A HAMMER OR A SWORD TO PROVE IT.
I WISH I COULD BELIEVE THAT.
BUT...I'VE NEVER FELT THAT INSIDE. I WISH I COULD SEE IT. BUT I CAN'T.
I HAVE TO FORGE IT THE ONLY WAY I KNOW HOW.

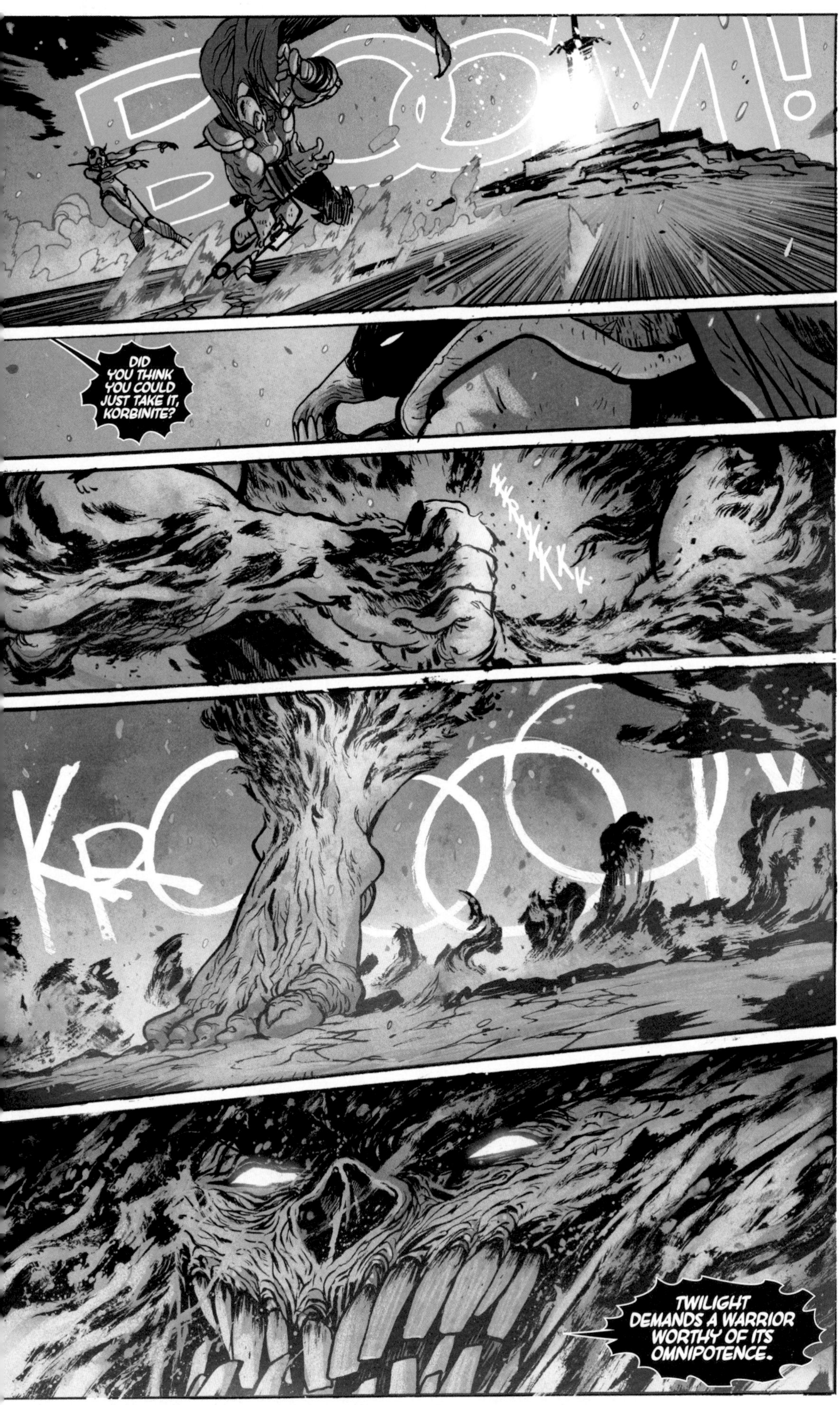
BOOM!
DID YOU THINK YOU COULD JUST TAKE IT, KORBINITE?
KKKRRAKKKKK
KROOOM
TWILIGHT DEMANDS A WARRIOR WORTHY OF ITS OMNIPOTENCE.

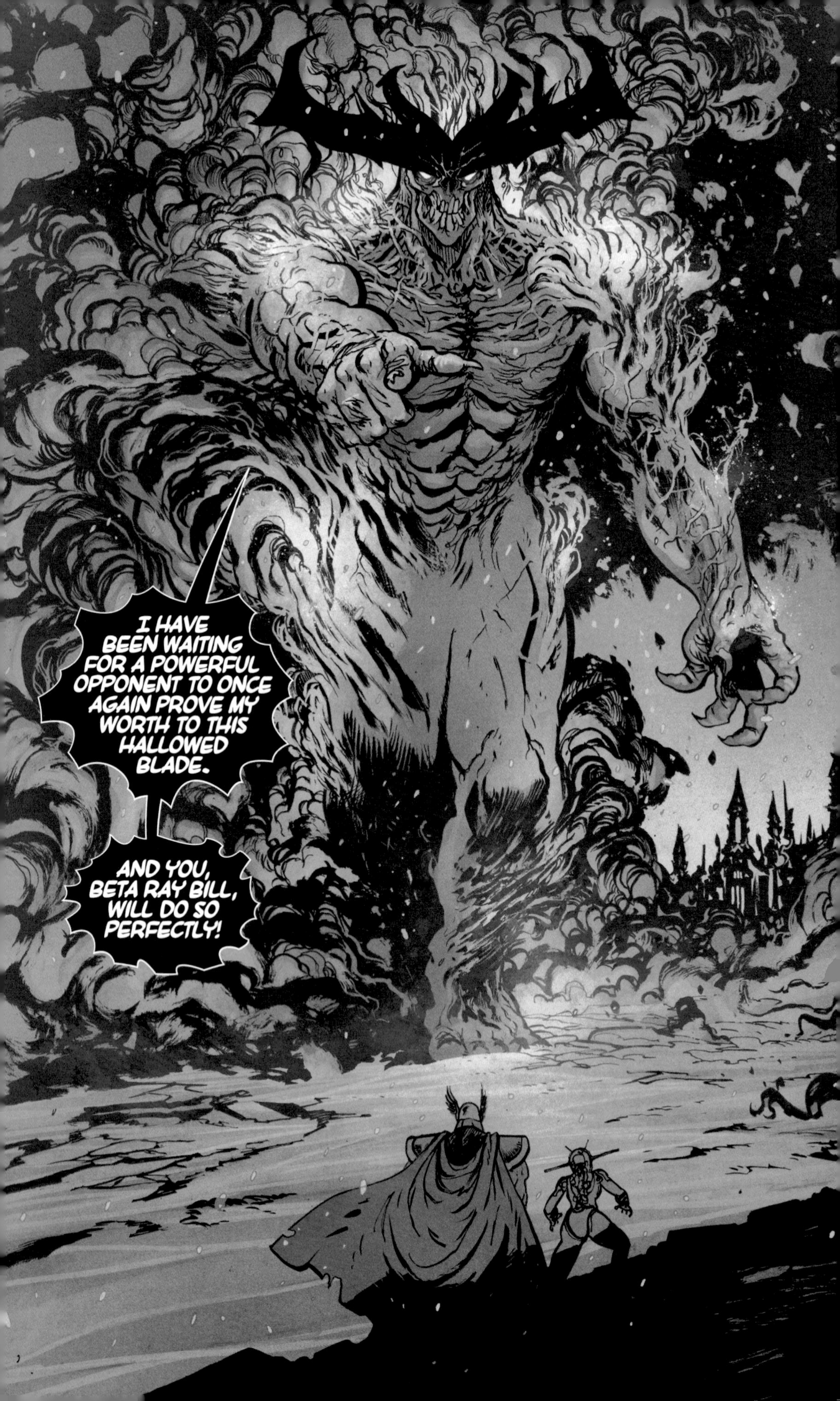
I HAVE BEEN WAITING FOR A POWERFUL OPPONENT TO ONCE AGAIN PROVE MY WORTH TO THIS HALLOWED BLADE.
AND YOU, BETA RAY BILL, WILL DO SO PERFECTLY!

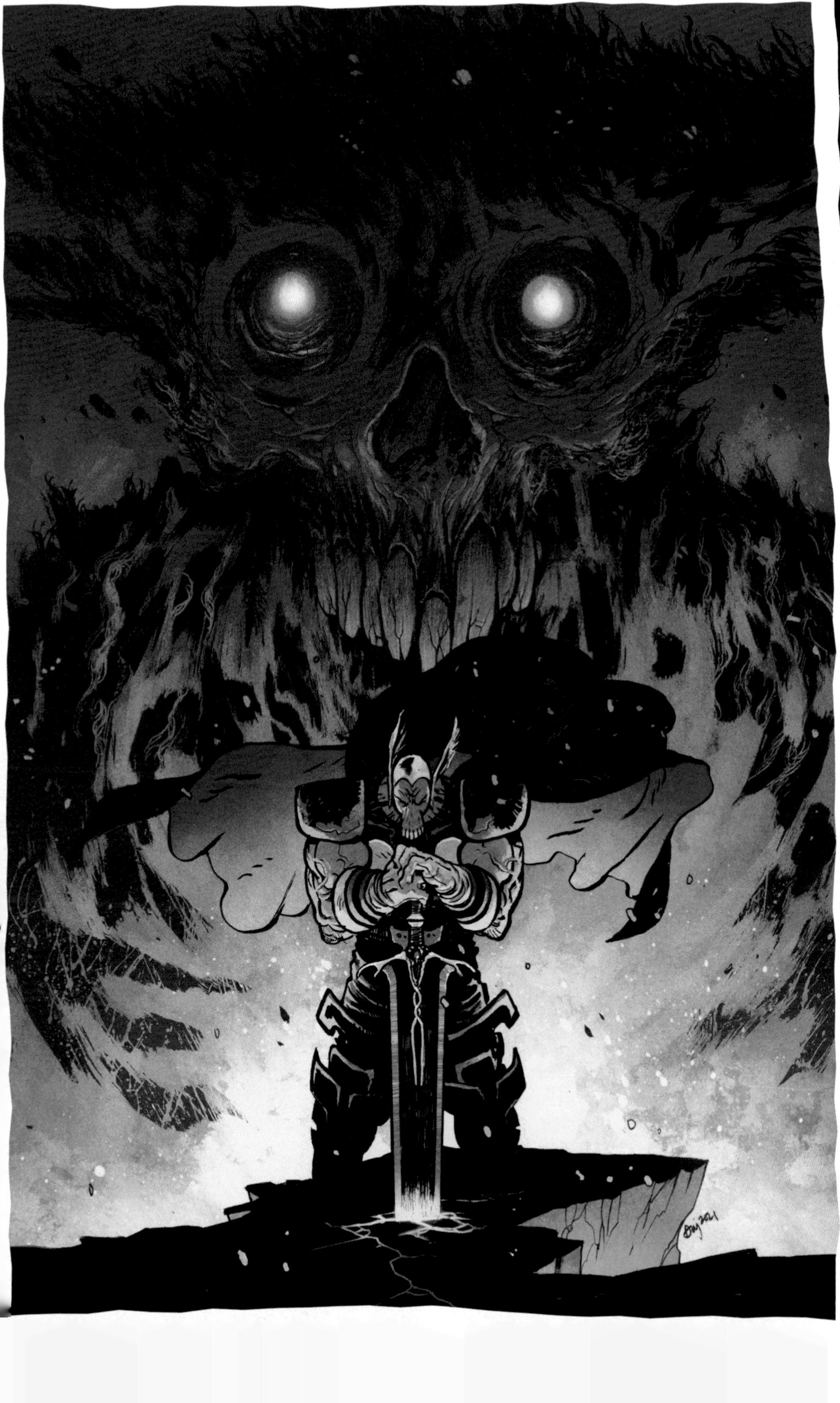

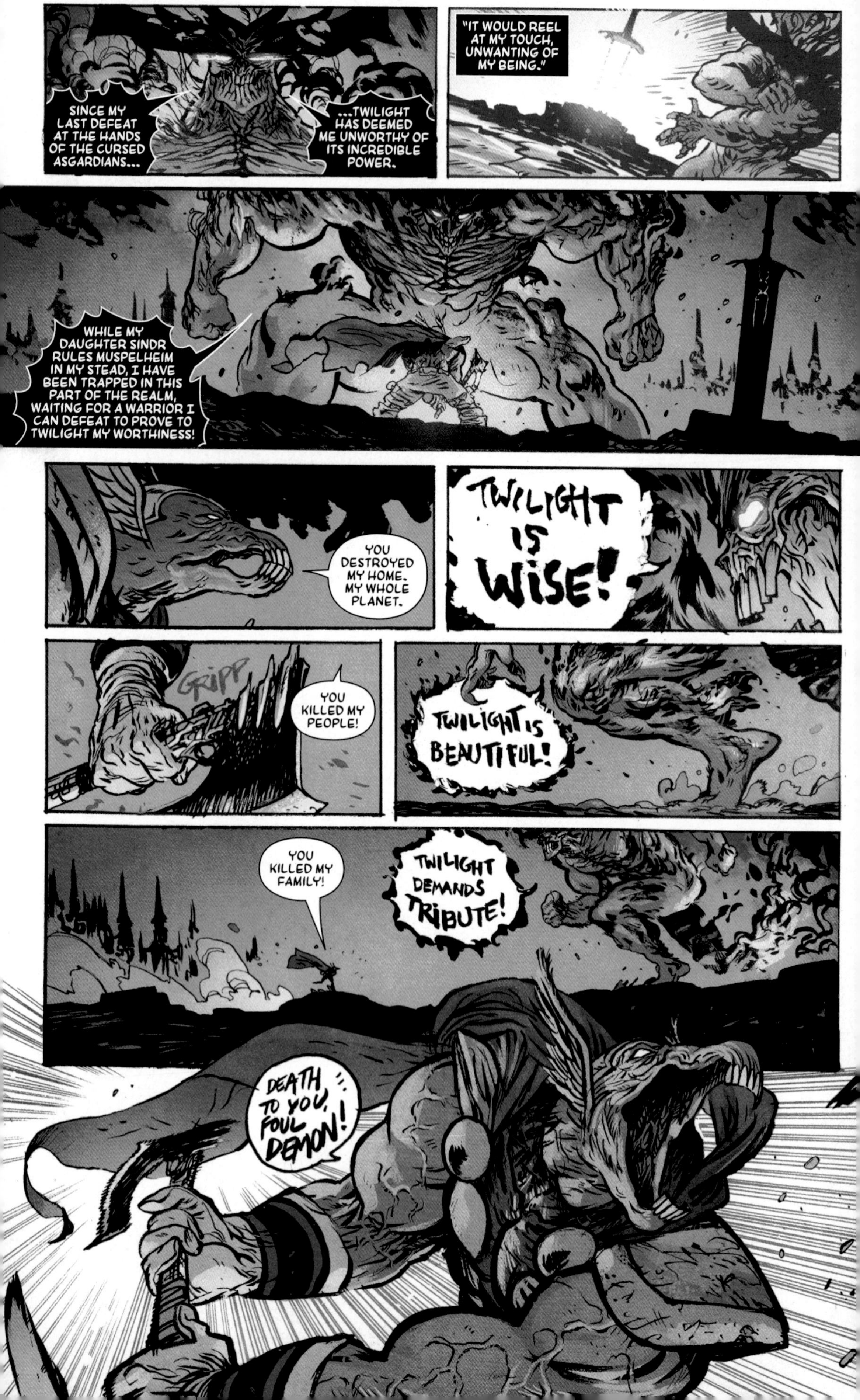

SINCE MY LAST DEFEAT AT THE HANDS OF THE CURSED ASGARDIANS...
...TWILIGHT HAS DEEMED ME UNWORTHY OF ITS INCREDIBLE POWER.
"IT WOULD REEL AT MY TOUCH, UNWANTING OF MY BEING."
WHILE MY DAUGHTER SINDR RULES MUSPELHEIM IN MY STEAD, I HAVE BEEN TRAPPED IN THIS PART OF THE REALM, WAITING FOR A WARRIOR I CAN DEFEAT TO PROVE TO TWILIGHT MY WORTHINESS!
YOU DESTROYED MY HOME. MY WHOLE PLANET.
TWILIGHT IS WISE!
GRIPP
YOU KILLED MY PEOPLE!
TWILIGHT IS BEAUTIFUL!
YOU KILLED MY FAMILY!
TWILIGHT DEMANDS TRIBUTE!
DEATH TO YOU, FOUL DEMON!

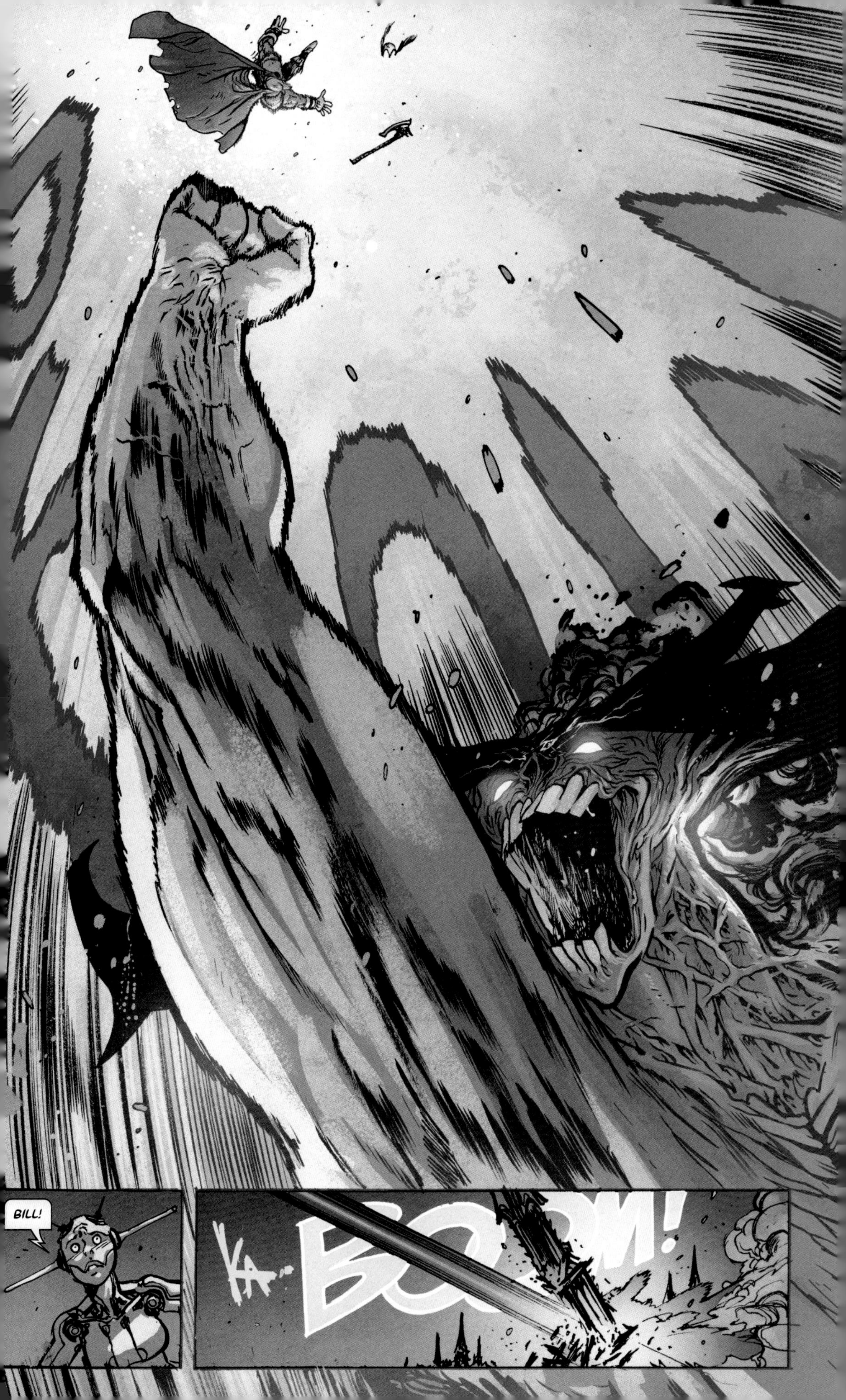
BILL!
KA-BOOM!

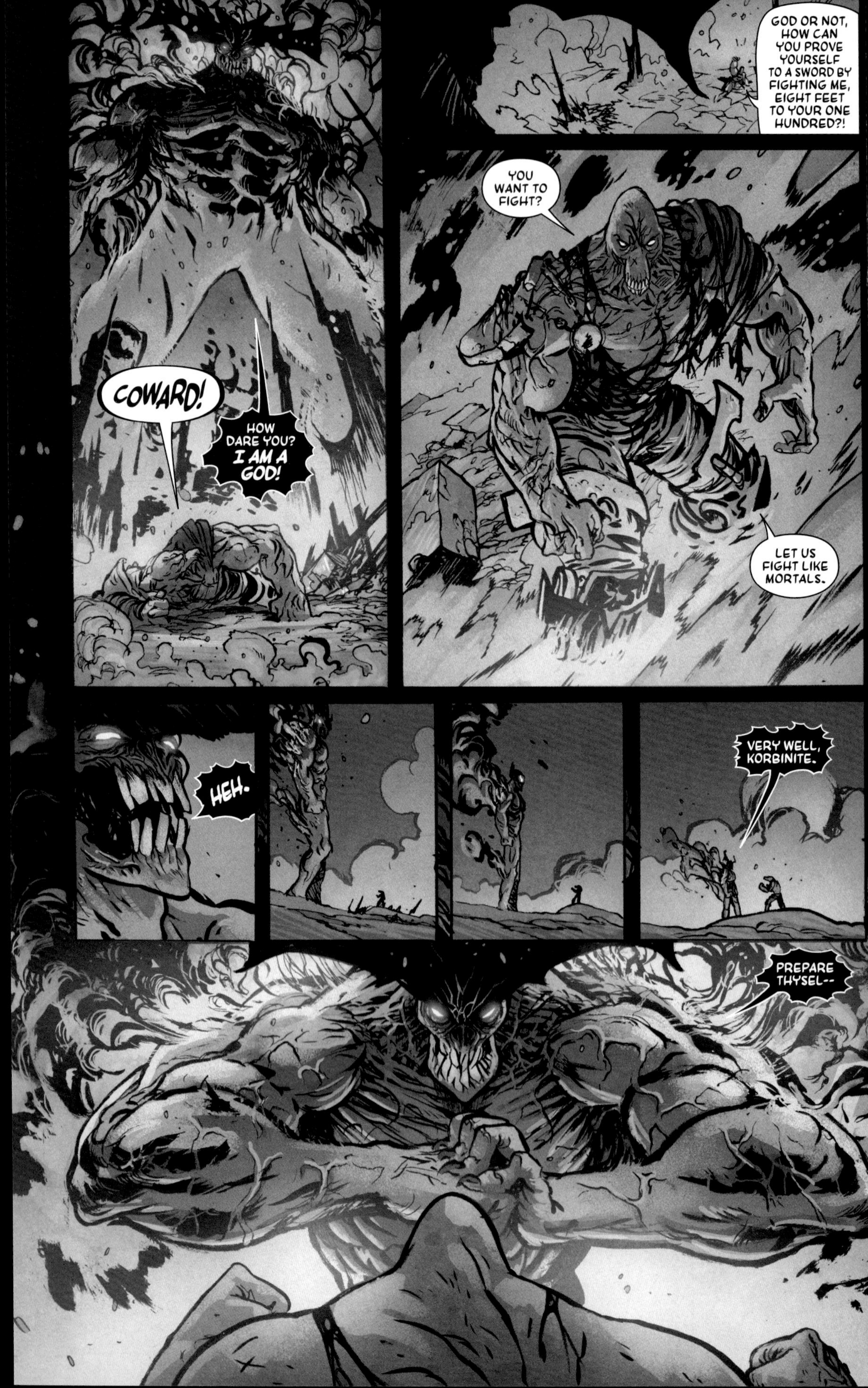
GOD OR NOT, HOW CAN YOU PROVE YOURSELF TO A SWORD BY FIGHTING ME, EIGHT FEET TO YOUR ONE HUNDRED?!
COWARD!
HOW DARE YOU? I AM A GOD!
YOU WANT TO FIGHT?
LET US FIGHT LIKE MORTALS.
HEH.
VERY WELL, KORBINITE.
PREPARE THYSEL--

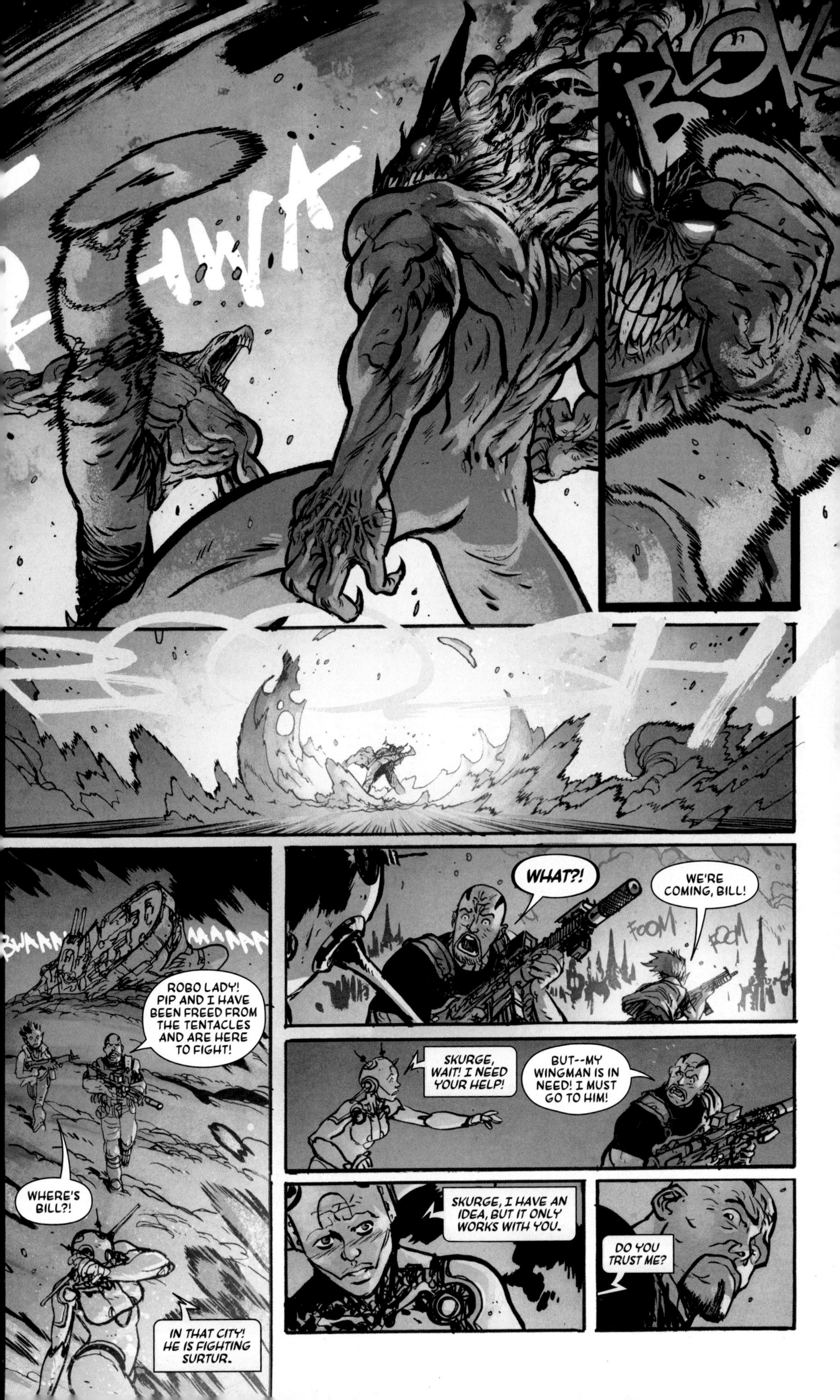

WHAT?!
WE'RE COMING, BILL!
ROBO LADY! PIP AND I HAVE BEEN FREED FROM THE TENTACLES AND ARE HERE TO FIGHT!
WHERE'S BILL?!
IN THAT CITY! HE IS FIGHTING SURTUR.
SKURGE, WAIT! I NEED YOUR HELP!
BUT--MY WINGMAN IS IN NEED! I MUST GO TO HIM!
SKURGE, I HAVE AN IDEA, BUT IT ONLY WORKS WITH YOU.
DO YOU TRUST ME?

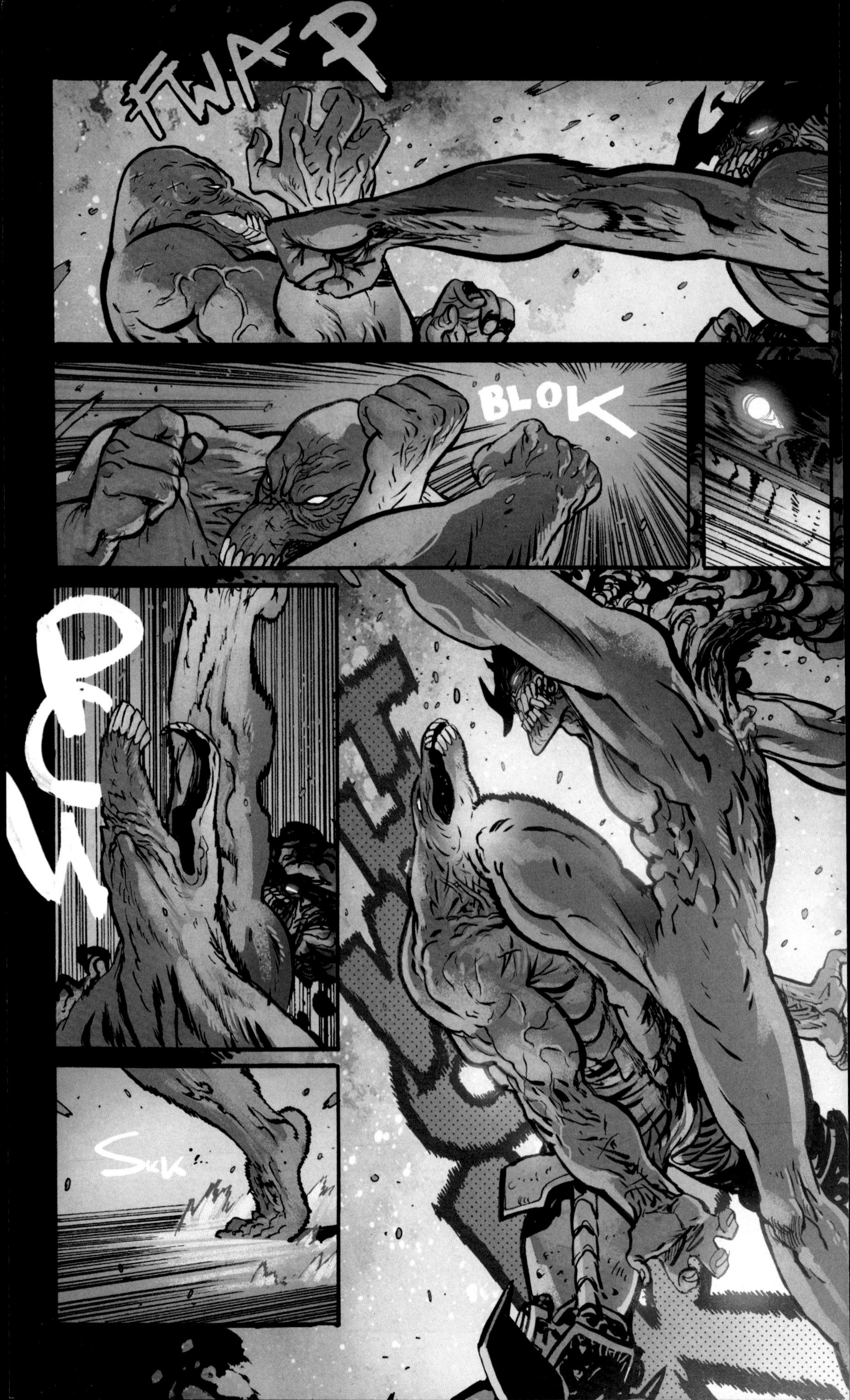
FWAP
BLOK

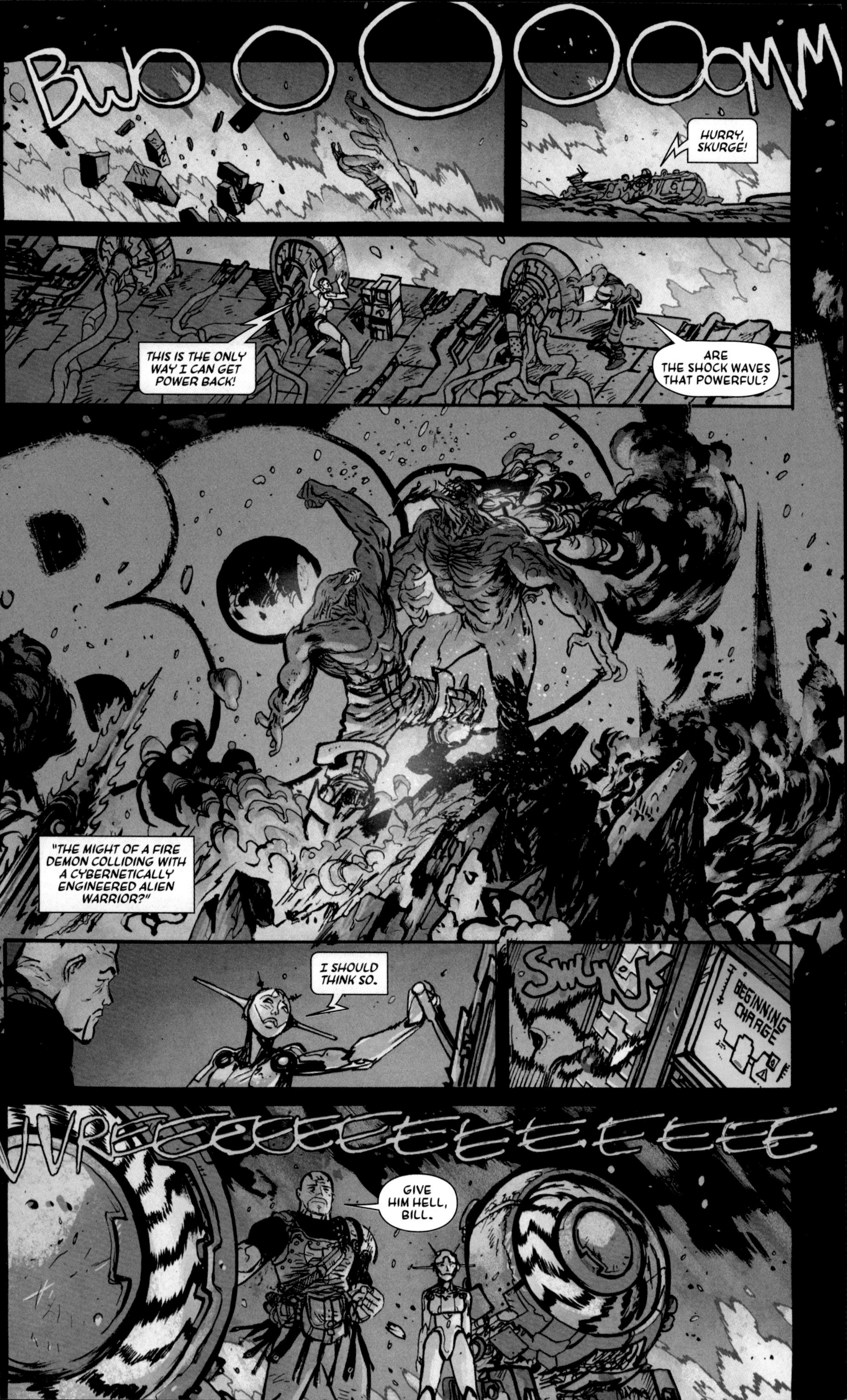
BWOOOOOOOMM
HURRY, SKURGE!
THIS IS THE ONLY WAY I CAN GET POWER BACK!
ARE THE SHOCK WAVES THAT POWERFUL?
"THE MIGHT OF A FIRE DEMON COLLIDING WITH A CYBERNETICALLY ENGINEERED ALIEN WARRIOR?"
I SHOULD THINK SO.
BEGINNING CHARGE
VREEEEEEEEEEEEEEE
GIVE HIM HELL, BILL.

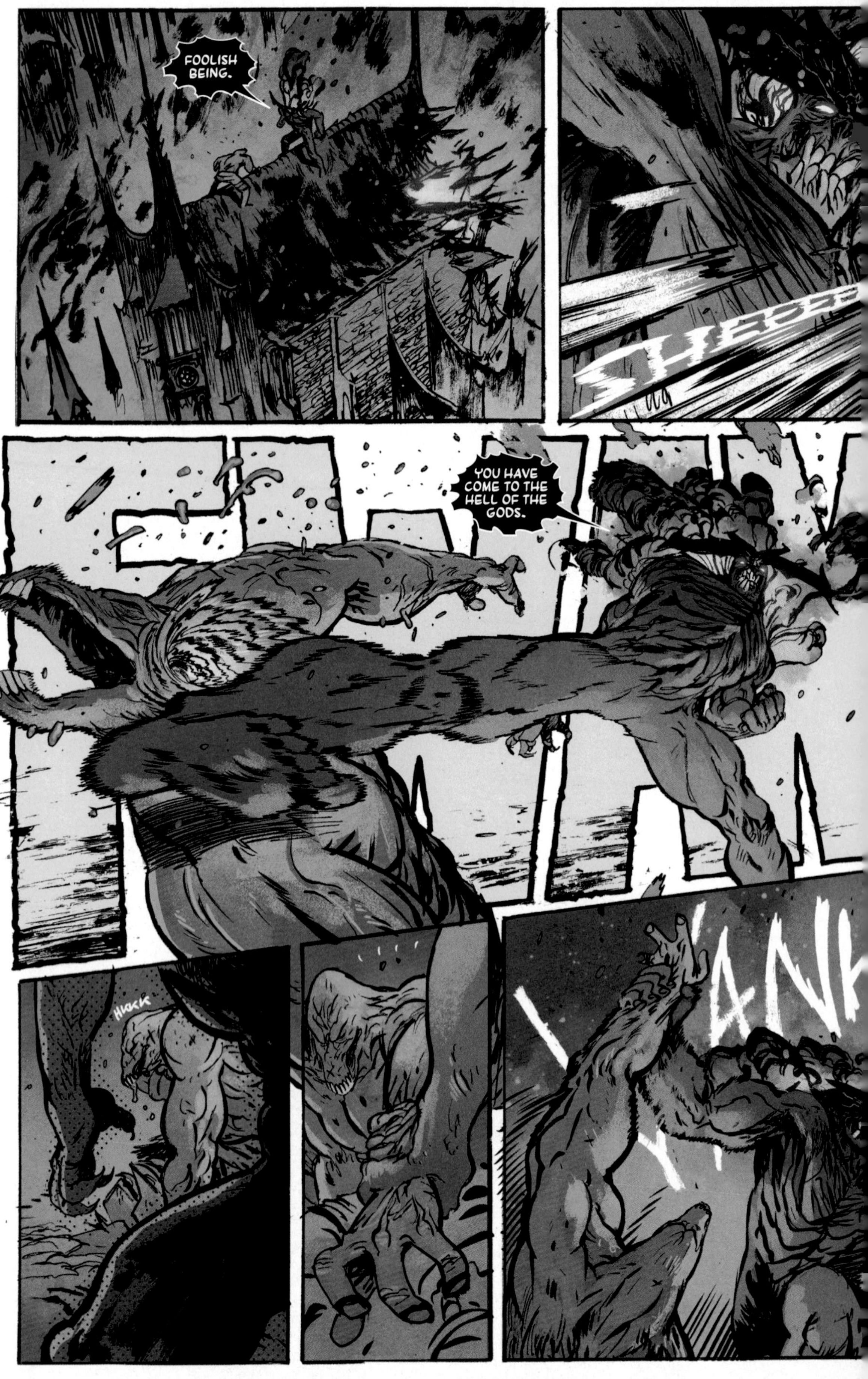
FOOLISH BEING.
SHEEEE
YOU HAVE COME TO THE HELL OF THE GODS.
HUKK

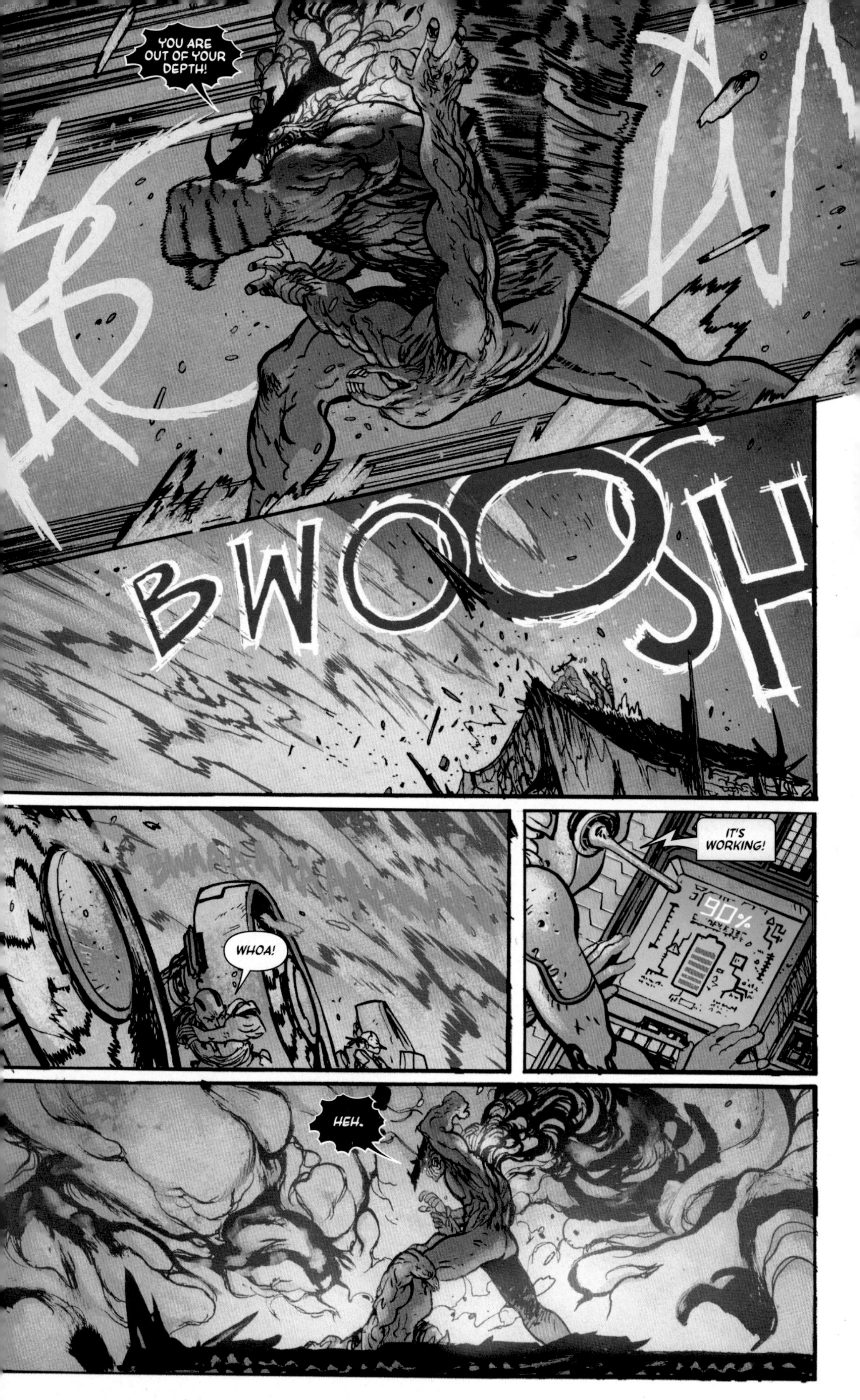
YOU ARE OUT OF YOUR DEPTH!
BWOOSH
WHOA!
IT'S WORKING!
90%
HEH.

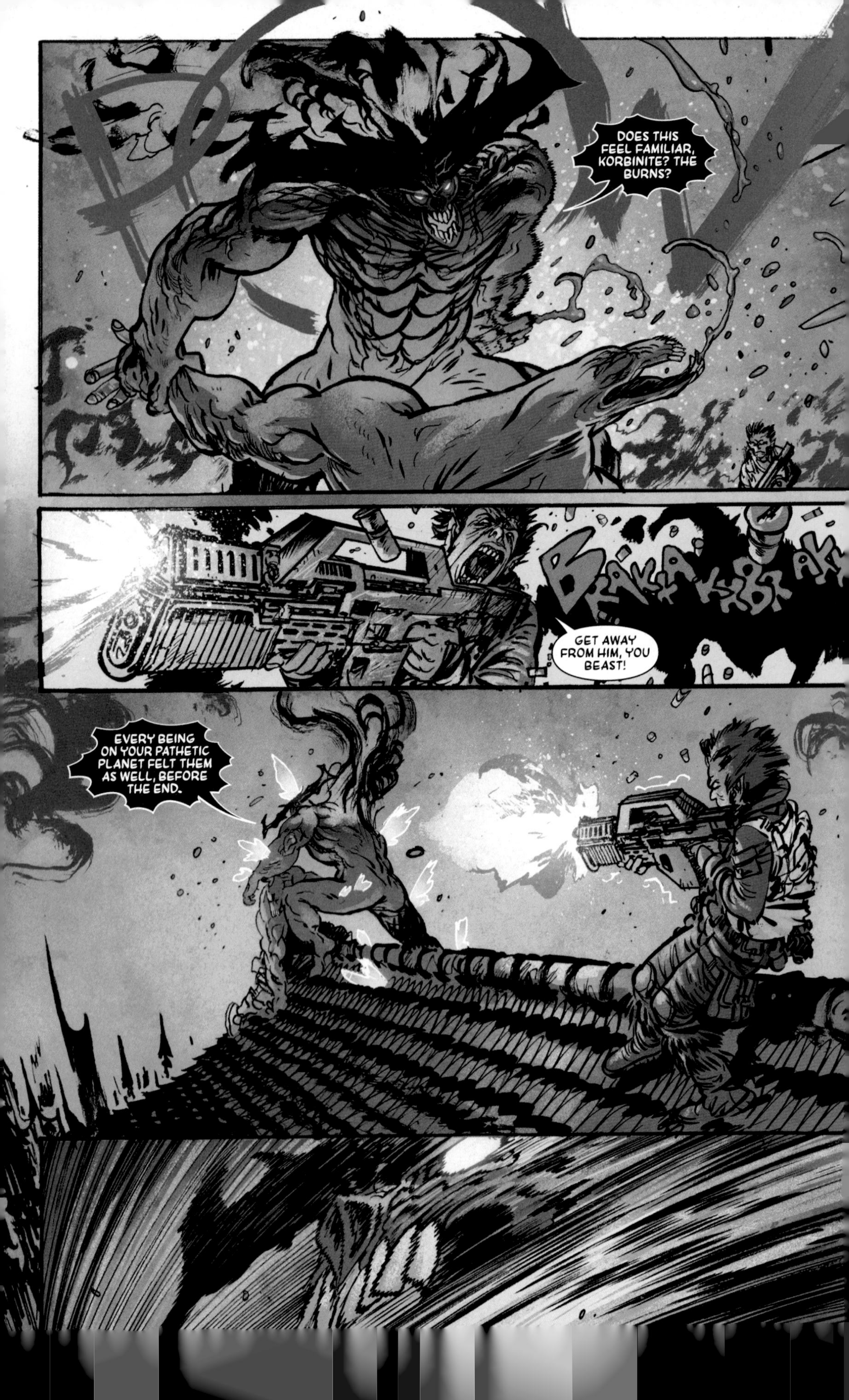
DOES THIS FEEL FAMILIAR, KORBINITE? THE BURNS?
GET AWAY FROM HIM, YOU BEAST!
EVERY BEING ON YOUR PATHETIC PLANET FELT THEM AS WELL, BEFORE THE END.

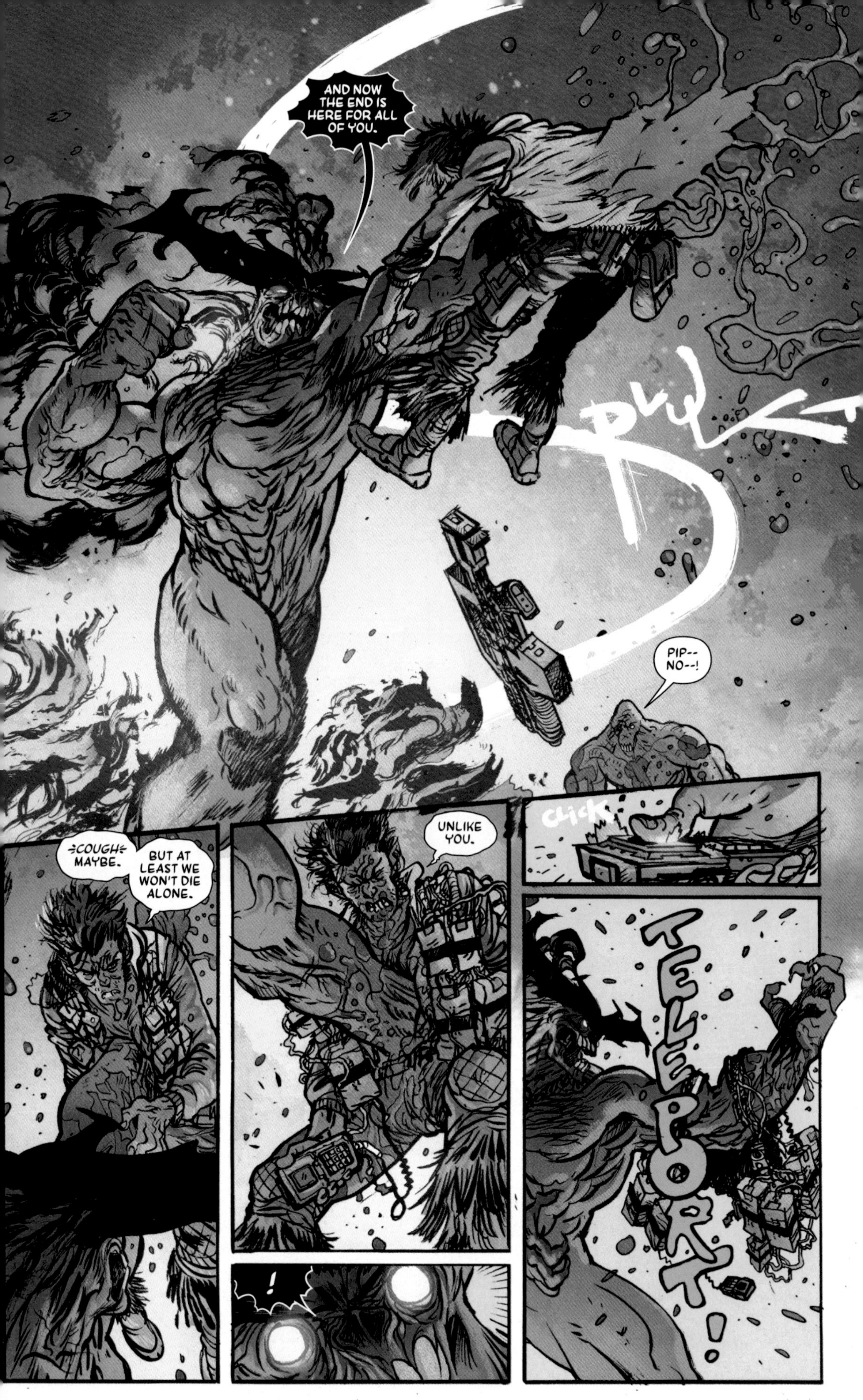
AND NOW THE END IS HERE FOR ALL OF YOU.
PIP-- NO--!
≈COUGH≈ MAYBE.
BUT AT LEAST WE WON'T DIE ALONE.
UNLIKE YOU.
CLICK
TELEPORT!
!

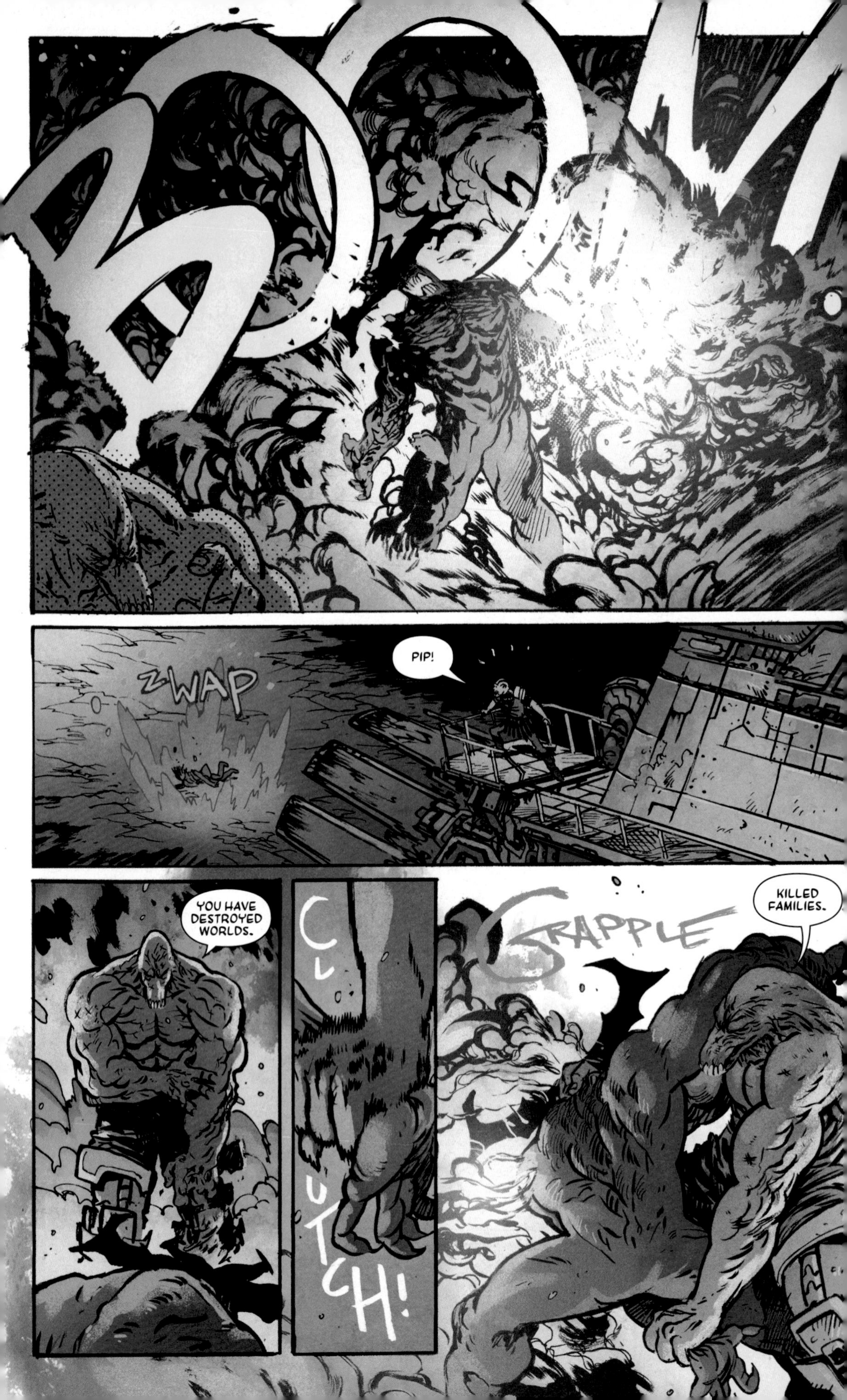
BOOM
ZWAP
PIP!
YOU HAVE DESTROYED WORLDS.
CLUTCH!
GRAPPLE
KILLED FAMILIES.

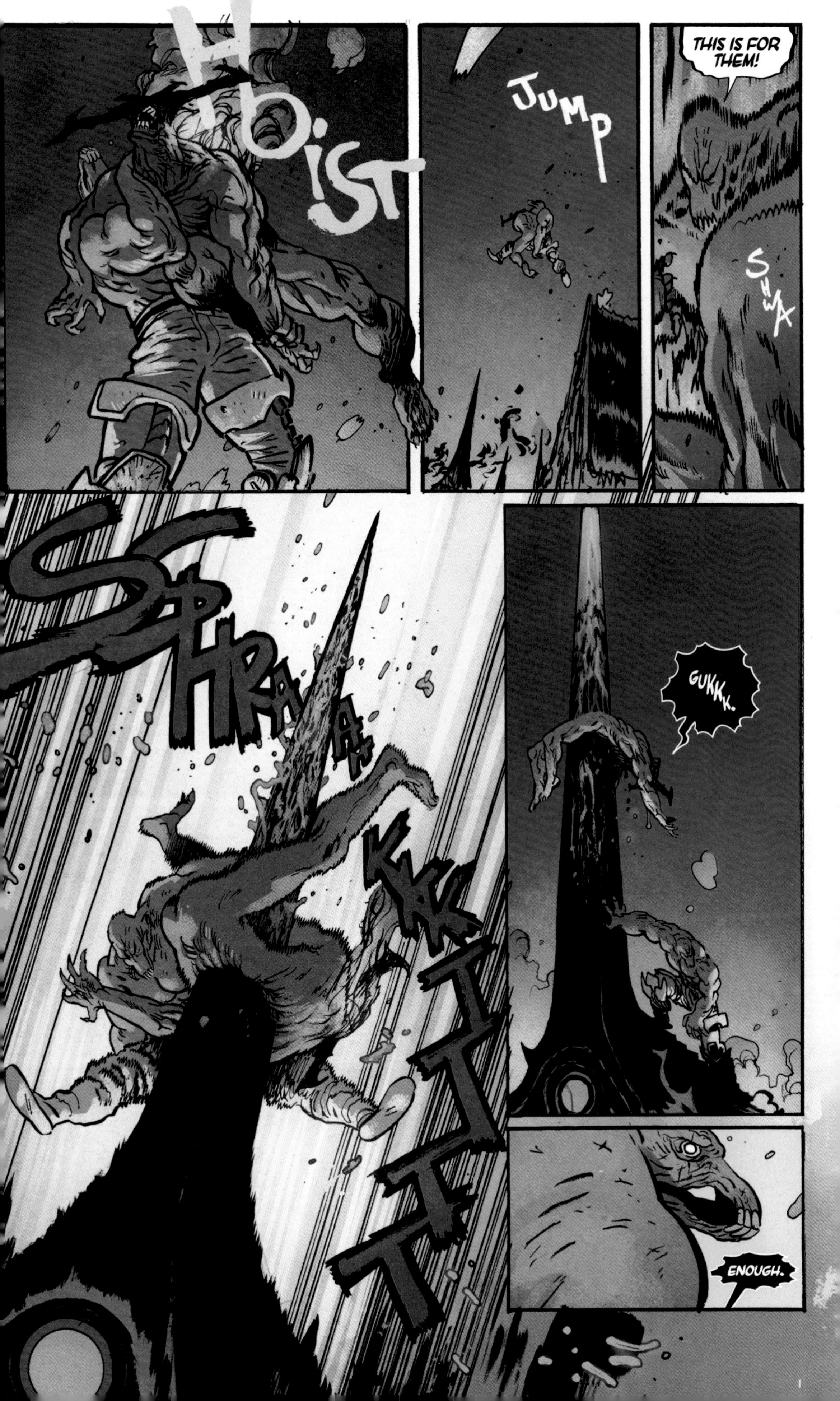
HOIST
JUMP
THIS IS FOR THEM!
SHWA
SPHRAAKKKTTTT
GUKKK.
ENOUGH.

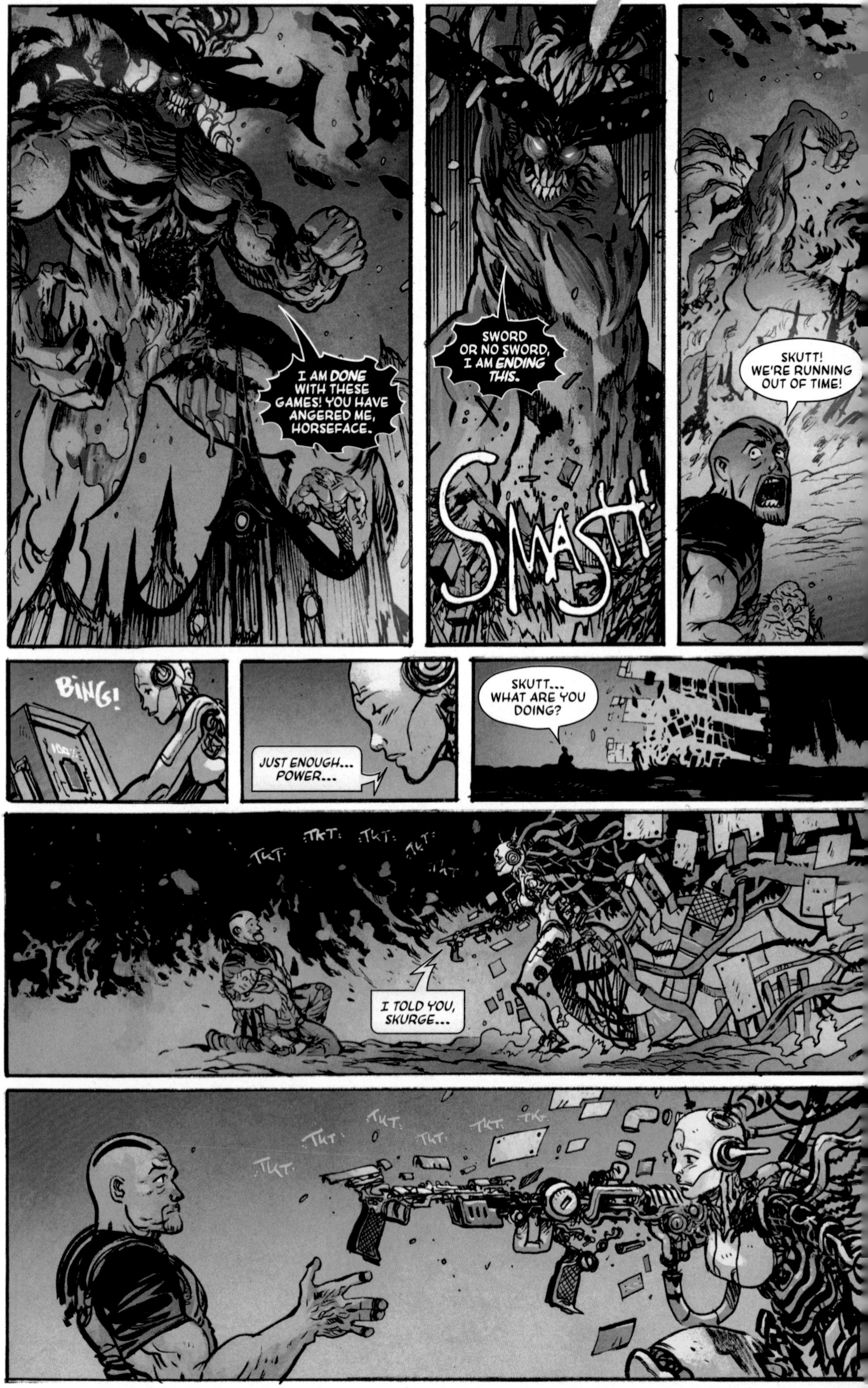
I AM DONE WITH THESE GAMES! YOU HAVE ANGERED ME, HORSEFACE.
SWORD OR NO SWORD, I AM ENDING THIS.
SMASH!
SKUTT! WE'RE RUNNING OUT OF TIME!
BING!
JUST ENOUGH... POWER...
SKUTT... WHAT ARE YOU DOING?
TKT TKT TKT TKT TKT
I TOLD YOU, SKURGE...
TKT TKT TKT TKT TKT TKT

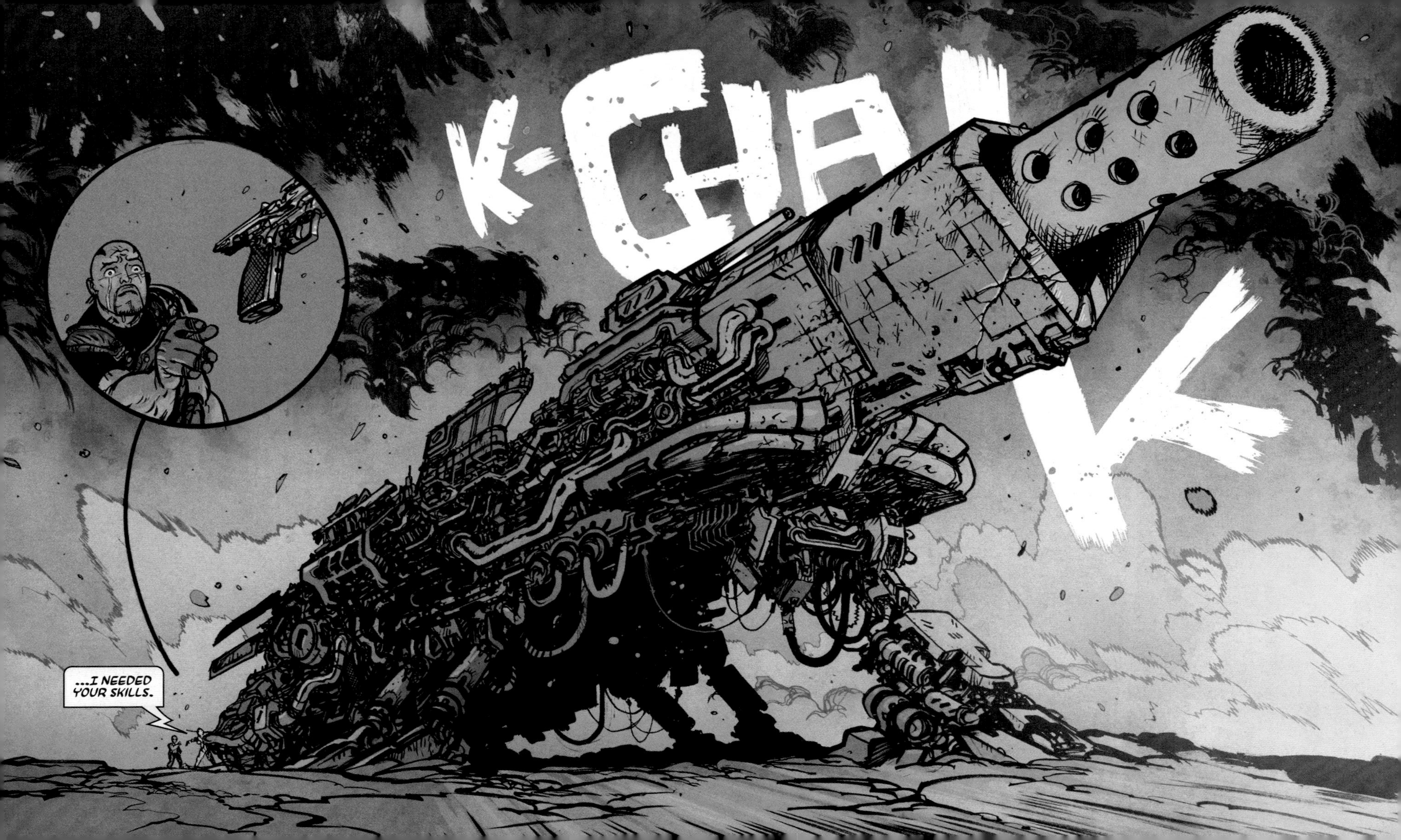
K-CHAK
...I NEEDED YOUR SKILLS.

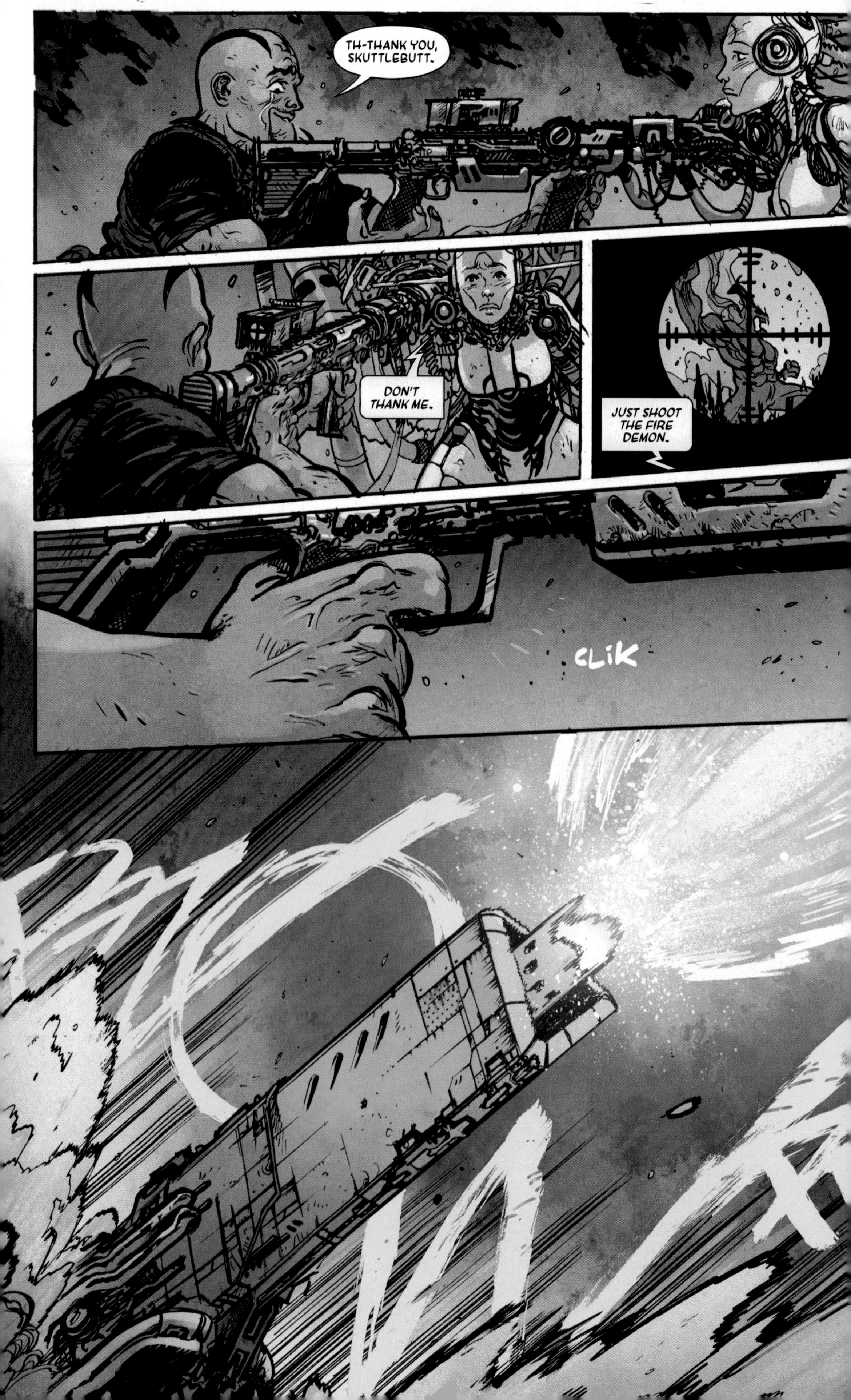
TH-THANK YOU, SKUTTLEBUTT.
DON'T THANK ME.
JUST SHOOT THE FIRE DEMON.
CLIK

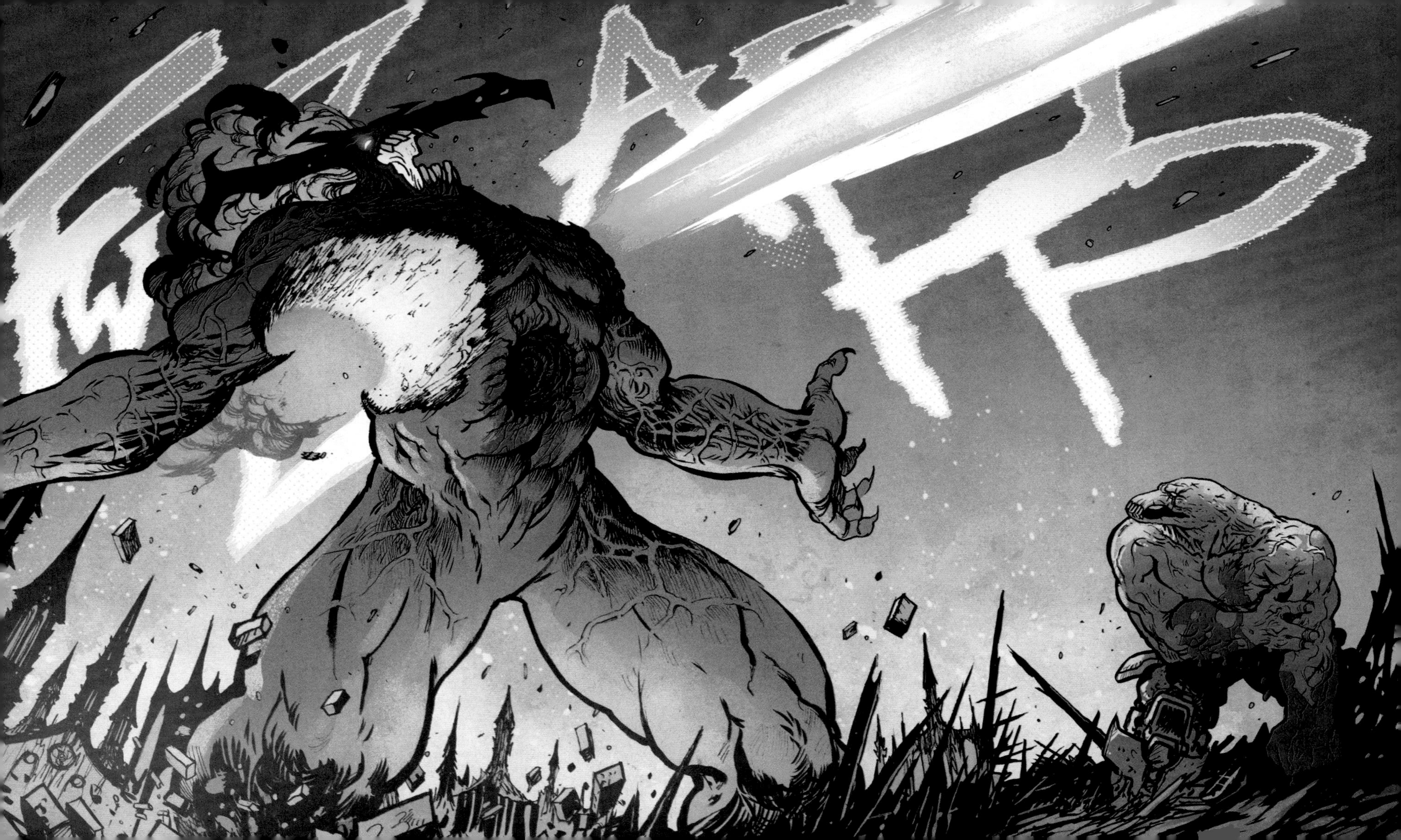

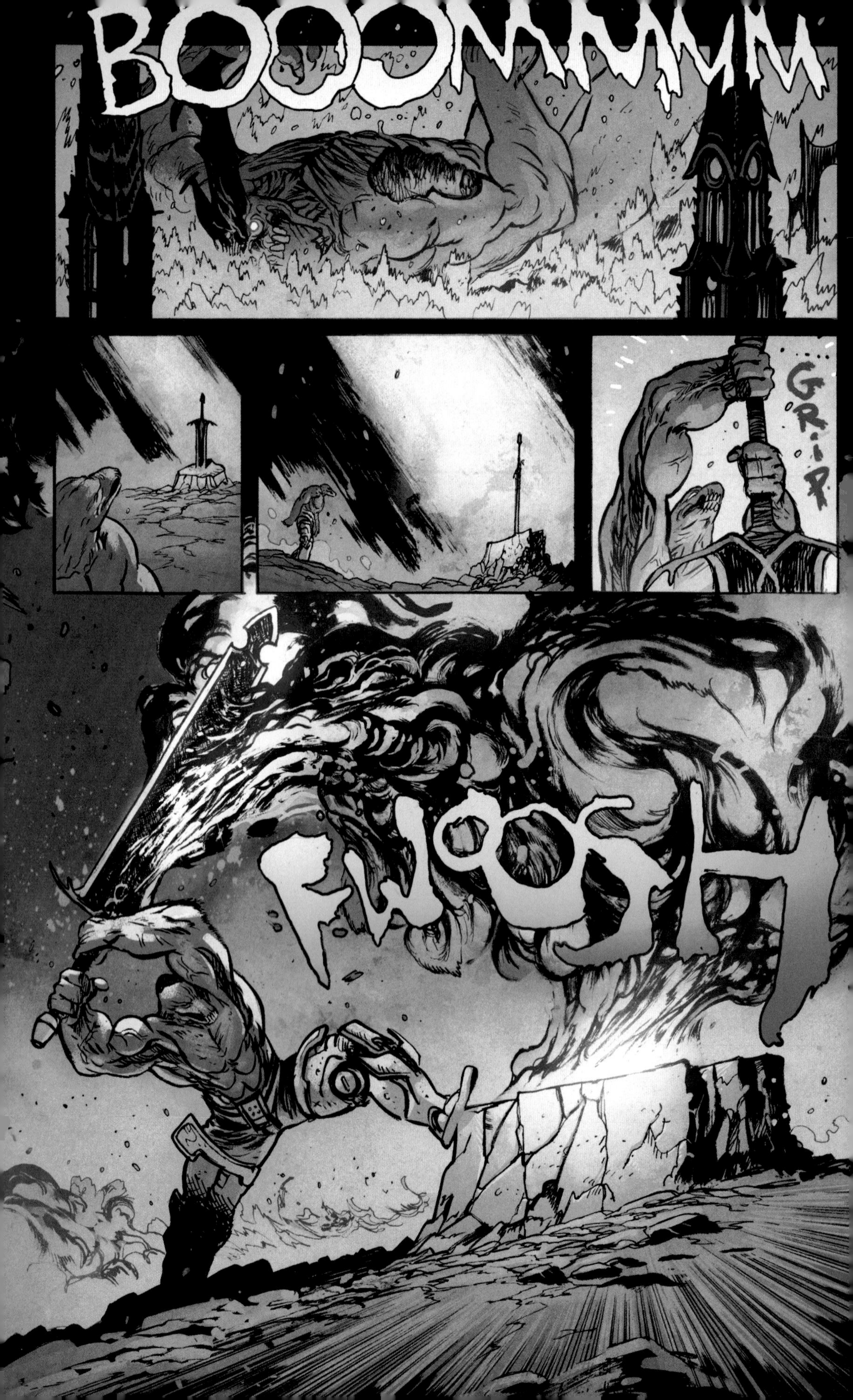
BOOOMMMM
GRIP
FWOOSH

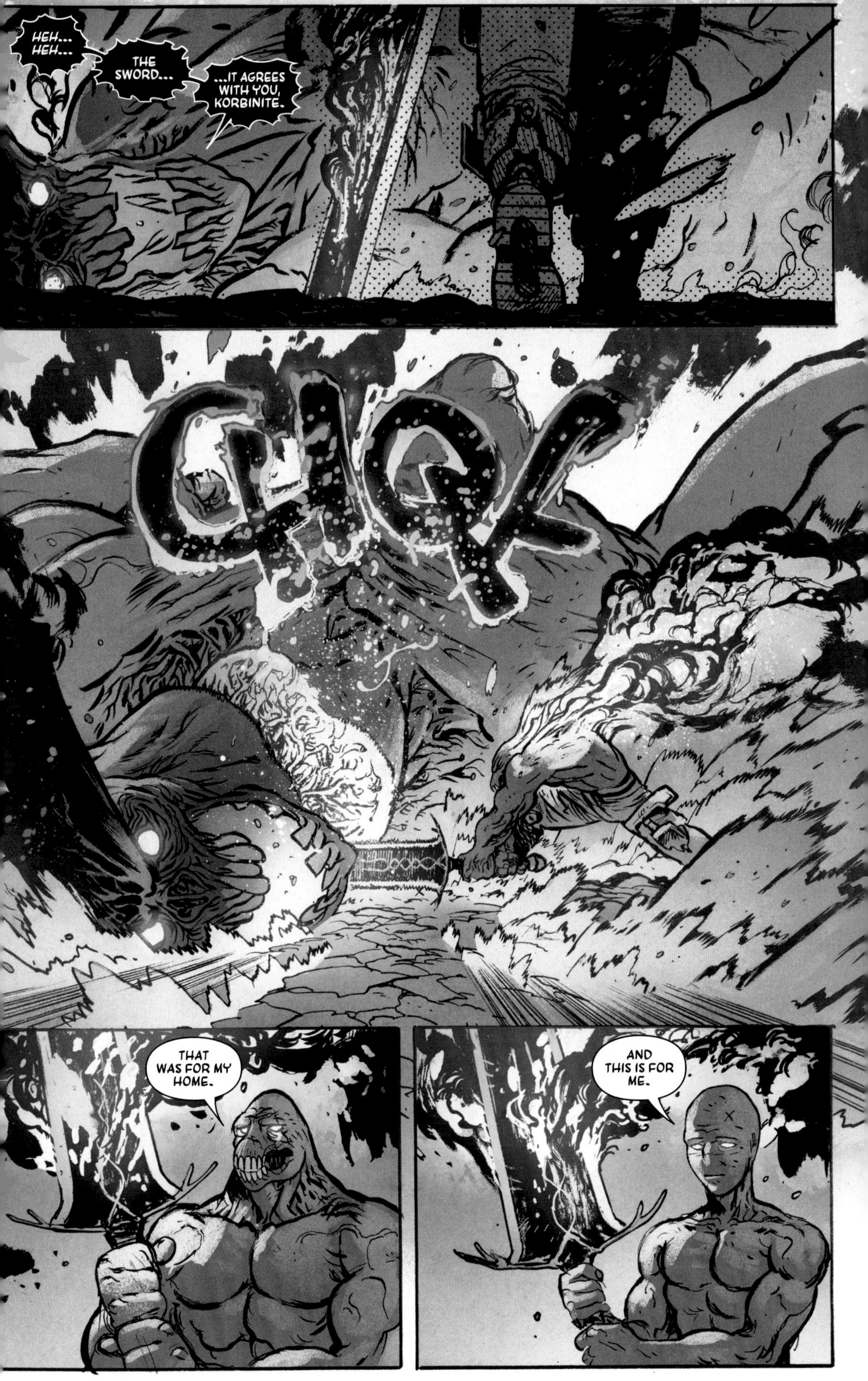
HEH... HEH...
THE SWORD...
...IT AGREES WITH YOU, KORBINITE.
THAT WAS FOR MY HOME.
AND THIS IS FOR ME.

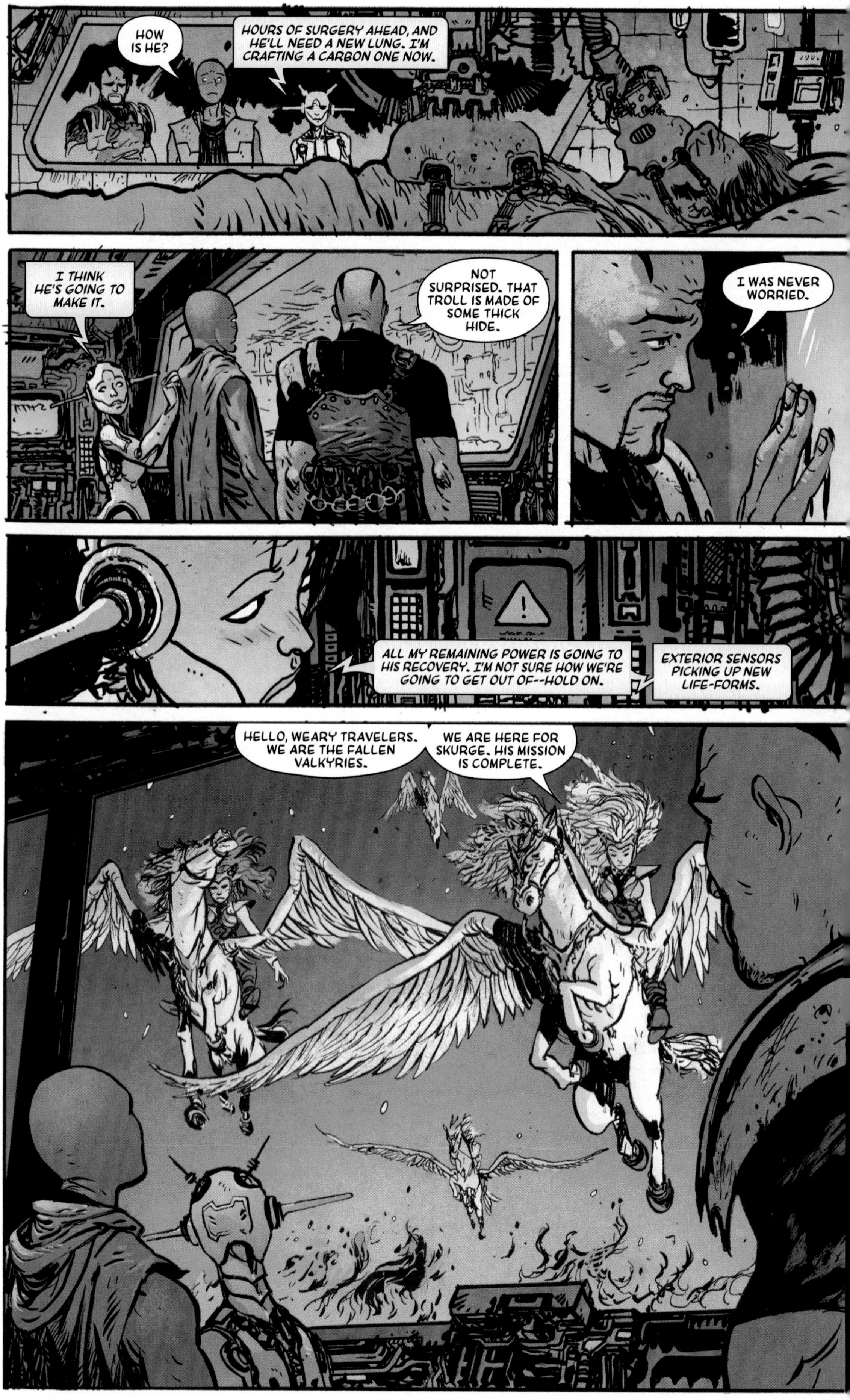
HOW IS HE?
HOURS OF SURGERY AHEAD, AND HE'LL NEED A NEW LUNG. I'M CRAFTING A CARBON ONE NOW.
I THINK HE'S GOING TO MAKE IT.
NOT SURPRISED. THAT TROLL IS MADE OF SOME THICK HIDE.
I WAS NEVER WORRIED.
ALL MY REMAINING POWER IS GOING TO HIS RECOVERY. I'M NOT SURE HOW WE'RE GOING TO GET OUT OF--HOLD ON.
EXTERIOR SENSORS PICKING UP NEW LIFE-FORMS.
HELLO, WEARY TRAVELERS. WE ARE THE FALLEN VALKYRIES.
WE ARE HERE FOR SKURGE. HIS MISSION IS COMPLETE.

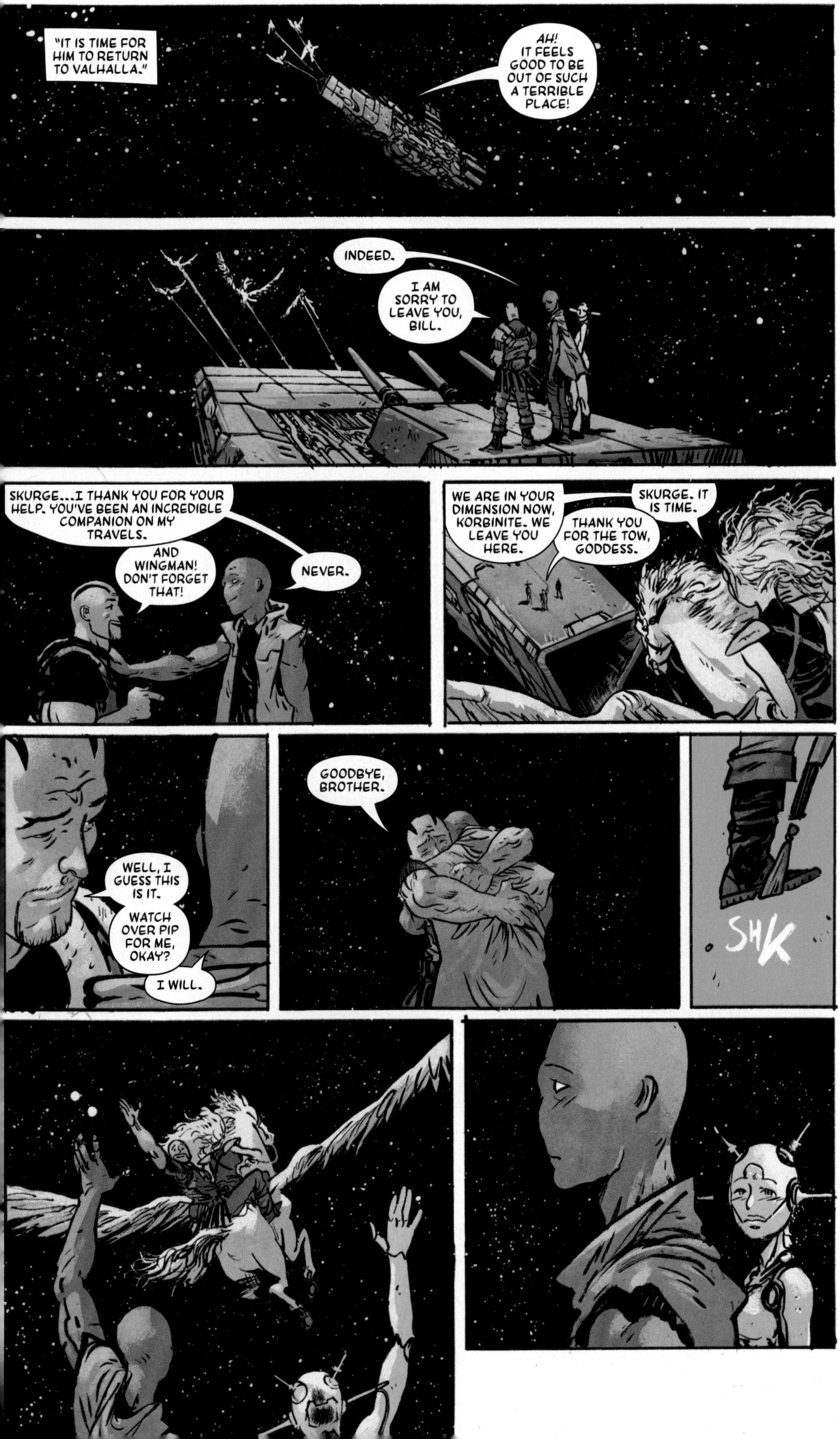
"IT IS TIME FOR HIM TO RETURN TO VALHALLA."
AH! IT FEELS GOOD TO BE OUT OF SUCH A TERRIBLE PLACE!
INDEED.
I AM SORRY TO LEAVE YOU, BILL.
SKURGE...I THANK YOU FOR YOUR HELP. YOU'VE BEEN AN INCREDIBLE COMPANION ON MY TRAVELS.
AND WINGMAN! DON'T FORGET THAT!
NEVER.
WE ARE IN YOUR DIMENSION NOW, KORBINITE. WE LEAVE YOU HERE.
SKURGE. IT IS TIME.
THANK YOU FOR THE TOW, GODDESS.
WELL, I GUESS THIS IS IT.
WATCH OVER PIP FOR ME, OKAY?
I WILL.
GOODBYE, BROTHER.
SHK

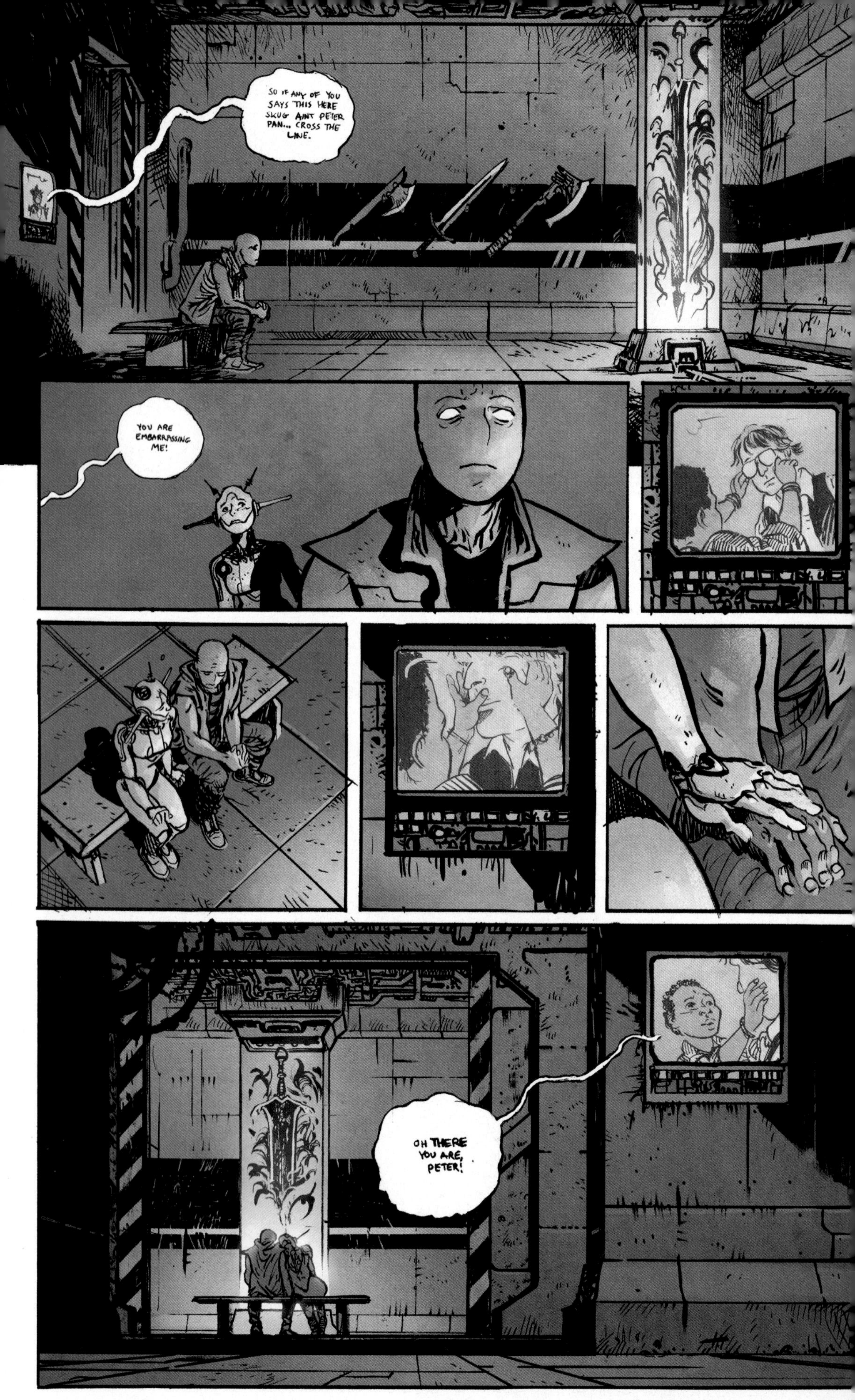

SO IF ANY OF YOU SAYS THIS HERE SKUG AINT PETER PAN... CROSS THE LINE.
YOU ARE EMBARRASSING ME!
OH THERE YOU ARE, PETER!

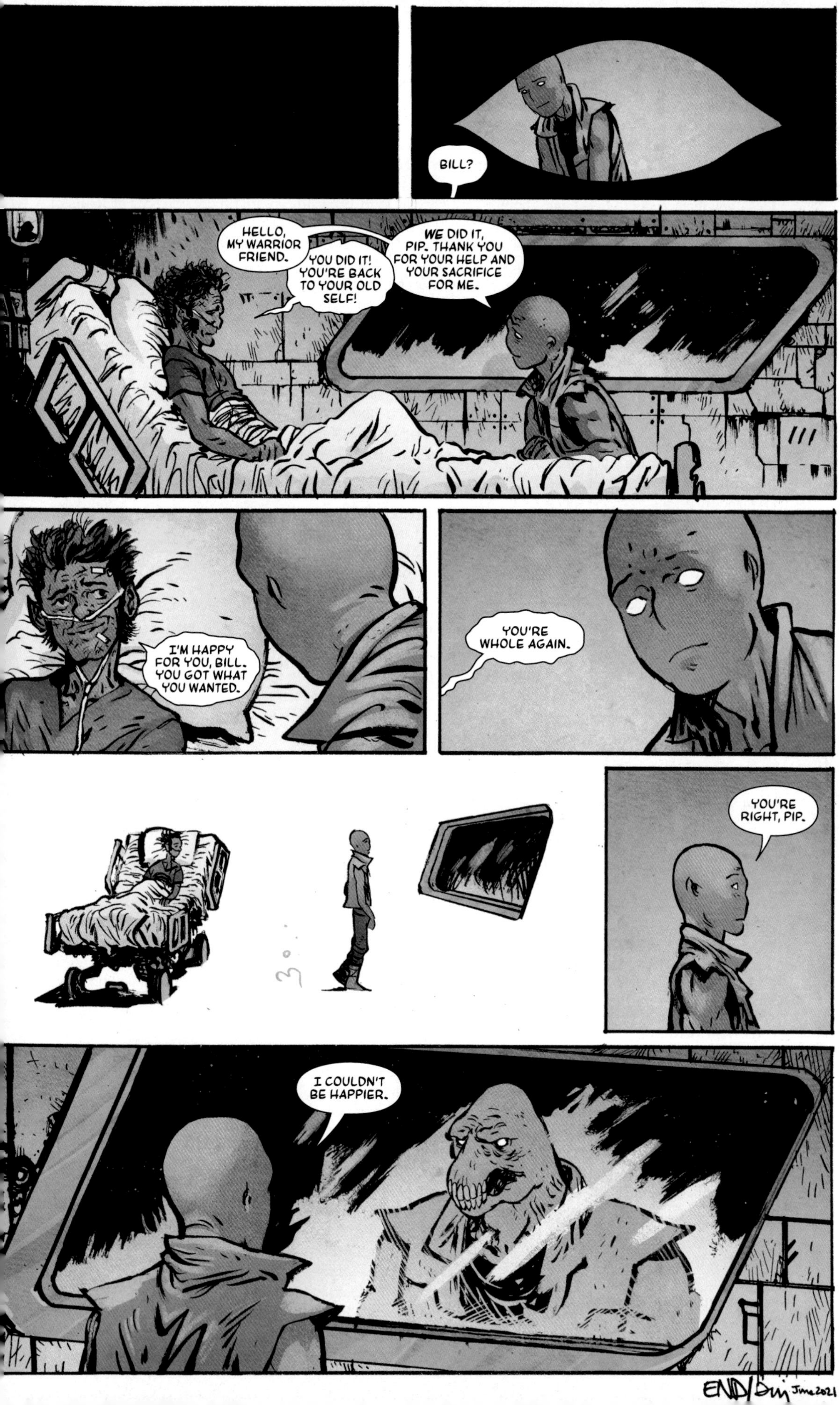
BILL?
HELLO, MY WARRIOR FRIEND.
YOU DID IT! YOU'RE BACK TO YOUR OLD SELF!
WE DID IT, PIP. THANK YOU FOR YOUR HELP AND YOUR SACRIFICE FOR ME.
I'M HAPPY FOR YOU, BILL. YOU GOT WHAT YOU WANTED.
YOU'RE WHOLE AGAIN.
YOU'RE RIGHT, PIP.
I COULDN'T BE HAPPIER.
END

Hey folks! How great was THAT?! Here at Marvel, we're thrilled Daniel Warren Johnson has been able to take some time away from making his incredibly good creator-owned comics like MURDER FALCON and EXTREMITY (and if you haven't read those, you really oughta!) to tell this epic adventure story about your favorite hero and mine, Beta Ray Bill!

We've got a really special "bonus feature"-- an exclusive interview with Bill's creator, the legendary Walter Simonson, conducted by Daniel himself!

A fan-favorite creator pretty much since his start in the '70s all the way up to today, Walter has a long list of beloved projects to his credit (including his kickass current RAGNAROK series from IDW), chief among them a legendary run on THOR in the '80s. Bill debuted in Walter's first issue, #337, and Thor's world has never been the same since.

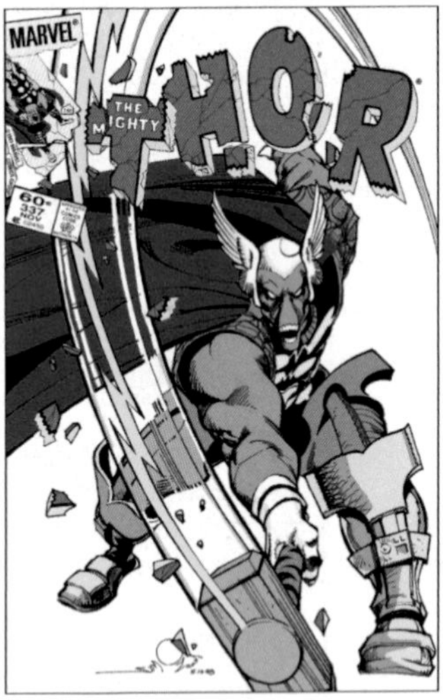
MARVEL
THE MIGHTY
THOR

THE COVER OF *THOR #337*, BETA RAY BILL'S FIRST APPEARANCE. ART BY WALTER SIMONSON.

DANIEL WARREN JOHNSON: I heard that you attended Amherst College (very near to where I grew up, actually!), and that you did a THOR fan comic just for fun. What motivated you to create that, and were there any standout moments during your college life that pushed you into pursuing professional comics?

WALTER SIMONSON: When I was at Amherst in the mid-'60s, I discovered Marvel Comics, which had only been publishing super heroes for about four years at that time. THOR was the first one I discovered. I was already a Norse myth fan from childhood, so I was delighted to find a comic about the gods of the Vikings. I began reading all the Marvel comics (about eleven titles a month at that time). I was inspired to try drawing some comics--a few pages of DR. STRANGE, IRON MAN, ENEMY ACE--over the next couple of years. They were all fragmentary and got longer each time I did a new one.

My first attempt with Dr. Strange was inspired by Steve Ditko's final issue on STRANGE TALES (#146) wherein Eternity and Dormammu faced off. I loved the issue but thought it was too short. (It was half the issue of STRANGE TALES.) So I decided to do the long version of the final battle that I would like to have seen. It turned out that drawing comics was hard work, and I got about four pages done before I ran out of gas. But that was my first serious attempt to draw a comic as an almost-grown-up. I did have an idea for a Thor story based on the Marvel comic and Norse myths and my own thoughts but didn't draw any of it then. During my time at Amherst, I wasn't thinking about going into comics professionally. Originally, I was interested in becoming a vertebrate paleontologist, studying dinosaurs. By the end of college, I had concluded that that was not what I wanted to do. But I had yet to begin to think of pursuing comics as a profession.

JOHNSON: Could you talk a little bit about your time in NYC in the '70s? What kind of creative culture was happening in comics with you and other creators?

SIMONSON: The '70s and the first half of the '80s were a great time to be in comics. There wasn't a lot of money, but all of us who got into the business about the time I did (1972) really wanted to work in the industry. A lot of us thought comics was a dying art, and we wanted to be part of it while it was still around. Didn't turn out that way, but we were full of enthusiasm and a friendly competitive spirit. Back then, there was no overnight delivery, no Internet, no scanners. If you wanted to work in comics professionally, you pretty much had to live in NYC. That meant that I got to know all of the guys in my generation and a lot of the guys in previous generations whose work we all admired. When you were in the office, you saw all kinds of work being turned in by guys like Jack Kirby, John Buscema, Alex Toth, Joe Kubert, Russ Heath, Neal Adams, and all the stuff my generation was producing as well. It was very inspiring.

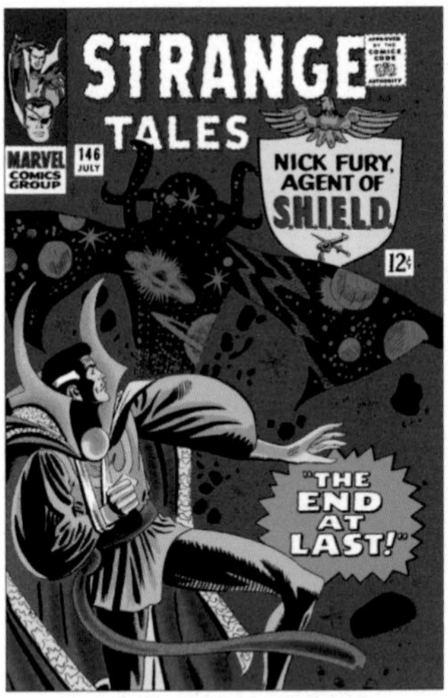
STRANGE TALES
MARVEL COMICS GROUP
146 JULY
NICK FURY, AGENT OF S.H.I.E.L.D.
12¢
"THE END AT LAST!"

***STRANGE TALES #146* COVER. ART BY STEVE DITKO.**

JOHNSON: The first arc of your THOR run that introduced Beta Ray Bill (#337-339) feels incredibly epic. What kinds of things were inspiring you when you created this story?

SIMONSON: Mostly I was just trying to tell a story that didn't feel like it had been told before. Even then, Thor had about 20 years' worth of continuity behind him. I had the idea of somebody else picking up the hammer to utilize the inscription on Mjolnir. It hadn't really been done before, and everything else flowed from that idea. The backstory with Surtur was the tale I had developed in a rudimentary form at Amherst. I'd drawn perhaps 26 pages of it while I was in art school after Amherst, and then 14 years after that, I was able to use some of the original idea as the spine for my first 17 issues or so of THOR.

JOHNSON: Now Beta Ray Bill feels a little bit like a tongue-in-cheek character that is beloved but also maligned as a "horse-faced hero" and so on. Was there any sense of comedy about Bill when first creating him, or was the goal simply to make an intense-looking character?

SIMONSON: Nope. One of the things that I learned from Stan Lee and Jack Kirby is that you can get away with almost anything in a story if you keep a straight face. Bill was never a comedic character to me but more a tragic one who underwent torture and isolation to save his people.

JOHNSON: One thing I noticed when beginning this BETA RAY BILL miniseries is how hard Bill is to draw! After two issues, I'm finally getting the hang of it. Did you struggle with getting his shapes down after initially creating him?

SIMONSON: Bill worked out pretty well for me from pretty early on. I've simplified his face a bit over the years as my own drawing has changed. One thing about his facial structure is that relatively few artists understand his jaw as I drew it. It's not a conventional jaw but a kind of rounded gap behind his teeth, inspired by a horse's skull. But his jaw is not hinged conventionally like a horse's jaw. No idea how that would work in real life, but that's comics. The only real trouble I had was keeping the directions of the zigzag white lines on his torso consistent. I could never remember which ones went up and which ones went down. Now, of course, he has a different costume so that problem is no longer around.

JOHNSON: When looking through your work on that initial Beta Ray Bill story, it seems like your lines have an energy and spontaneity to them that feels organic and lively, and it's one of my favorite things about your drawings. Your lines look like you had fun while making them. Is this a style that you've always had? Did drawing with deadlines ever make you change how you approach mark-making?

SIMONSON: The answer to your first observation about my drawing is that I love marks on paper. I want to make them look like they were slashed onto the drawing--not in a haphazard or sloppy way, but in a spontaneous way that imparts life to the drawing itself just though the marks that comprise it. As a result, I spend a lot of time making the work look spontaneous whereas in real life, as Jon Bogdanove once said, I have a very paper-intensive lifestyle. I go through a lot of stages to get to the point where the drawing looks (I hope) spontaneous.

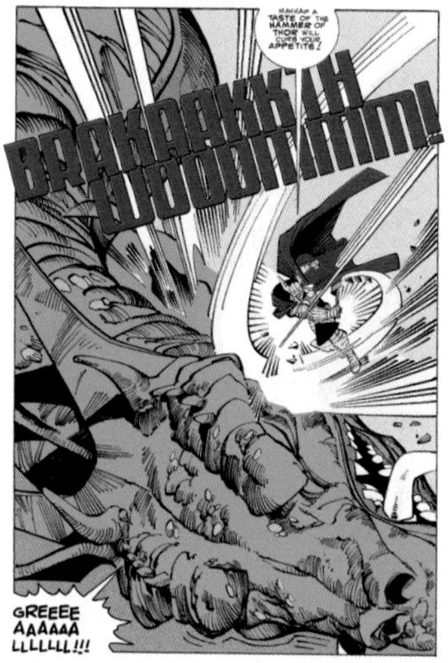
TASTE OF THE HAMMER OF THOR WILL CURB YOUR APPETITE!
GREEEE AAAAAA LLLLLL!!!

A SPLASH PAGE FROM THE ALL-SPLASHES *THOR #380*. WRITING AND LAYOUTS BY WALTER SIMONSON, FINISHES BY SAL BUSCEMA, LETTERING BY JOHN WORKMAN, COLORING BY MAX SCHEELE.

As far as my approach to mark-making, the one serious effect I think drawing for comics has had on my output is that because of my early days in comics, now a long time ago, when comics were printed badly on newsprint, I developed a fairly bold style because I wanted to give the art the best chance to be reproduced on a page in a way that would still contain the energy within the drawings I was trying to achieve. I've gone to finer lines again and more rendering than I used 30 years ago, but some of that boldness in approach still remains, I think. Deadlines also played a role, in that writing, penciling, and drawing a book every month pushed me toward a bold approach without a lot of noodling.

JOHNSON: Nowadays it feels like it's fairly rare for a person to do both writing and art duties on a comic book. What was the culture like back then for someone like yourself who was both the writer and the artist? What did you find to be the biggest challenges of taking on both jobs?

SIMONSON: Back then, pretty much all the doors were open to creative endeavors in mainstream comics by freelancers. Several of us took a crack at writing and drawing mainstream books, and there was the freedom to do so. Even encouragement sometimes. It was a fine time to be doing comics professionally.

And the biggest challenge is always the deadline.

JOHNSON: As a writer, what is the first step when beginning the creative process of making a new story? As an artist, do you think in visuals first, or start somewhere else?

SIMONSON: I don't have a single method of starting a story. Sometimes, as in the case of Beta Ray Bill and THOR where I wanted a story that hadn't been told before, the idea of Mjolnir's inscription came to me as I was thinking about what I might do for my first story arc. In the case of Thor fighting the Midgard Serpent (THOR #380), it came as a flash of inspiration in which the entire story and the approach of using all splash pages literally burst above my head like a light bulb. Other stories I've had to drag out of myself. On books that I work on for a while, new ideas often occur to me. Sometimes it's no more than a thought; sometimes it's a whole plot. I just have to make certain I write everything down, as I've learned the hard way that ideas and plots like that are as evanescent as dreams, disappearing without a trace if I don't capture them immediately.

As a comic book artist, I pay attention to the visual storytelling first when I begin to lay out a tale. It's all about page design, eye direction, panel composition, and how best to tell the story. With my own work, I approach it "Marvel Style," which means that I plot my story first, thumbnail the entire job next--a quick sketch of each page done on copier paper--and then write the script from my thumbnails so that I can see how the words and the pictures work together. Once I have a complete script, I blow up the thumbnails onto artboard, very loosely still, and then place the copy so I can be sure everything lines up. Then I start working out the visuals in detail--figures, costumes, backgrounds, architecture--everything that goes into creating a convincing space in which the story occurs.

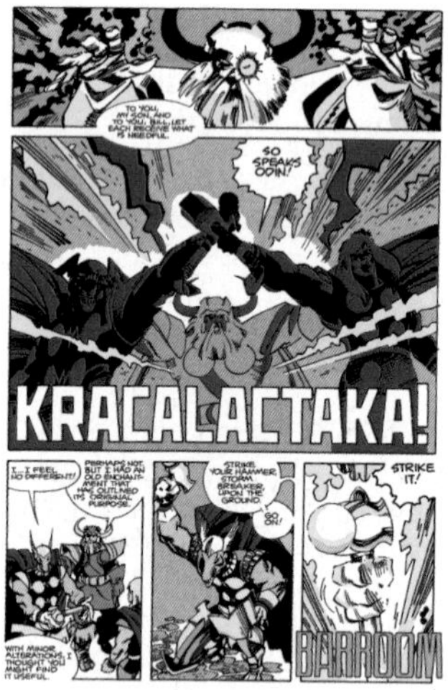
SO SPEAKS ODIN!
KRACALACTAKA!
GO ON!
STRIKE IT!
BARROOM

EXAMPLES OF THE KIND OF SOUND EFFECTS WALTER SIMONSON CREATED WITH JOHN WORKMAN, FROM *THOR #340*. WRITING AND ART BY SIMONSON, LETTERING BY WORKMAN, COLORS BY GEORGE ROUSSOS.

JOHNSON: One of my favorite things about your art is your inclusion of sound effects and the typography used for them. Is this something that you would solely do, or did John Workman (SImonson's frequent letterer, including on his THOR run) also contribute?

SIMONSON: I got interested in letterforms while I was at the Rhode Island School of Design after Amherst. There was a certain emphasis there on lettering in those days. Chancery cursive hand--an italic alphabet based on older letterforms--was popular for a time in the late Middle Ages. A classic pamphlet called La Operina was written in and about chancery cursive by Ludovico Vicentino Arrighi and published in 1522. Students were taught chancery from a translation of the pamphlet as a discipline, and I was interested enough in the subject that I pursued more knowledge of lettering while I was in school there. That knowledge informed my comics, and in my early professional work, I drew my own sound effects and title lettering. When John Workman and I began our collaborations, I found he could do what I wanted to do better than I could, so for the most part I handed the display lettering over to him. I write the titles and sound effects, indicate the size and placement on the art, and then it's up to John to design and letter them.

JOHNSON: As a creator who has worked steadily for so many years, how have you managed to navigate different pop culture trends and different companies? What do you think has kept you relevant all these years?

SIMONSON: Stubbornness and dumb luck.

JOHNSON: Do you find it harder to make things as you get older? Or has the process stayed mostly the same throughout your career?

SIMONSON: It's never really easy. And sometimes I feel now that I don't have the courage of my youth as an artist when a lack of knowledge emboldened me to do all kinds of things that I wouldn't try now. But I hope I make up for it by having learned a lot of tricks over the years. It's also more difficult not to feel that sometimes I am repeating myself in drawing or storytelling solutions. But one does what one can.

JOHNSON: Thanks again so much for your time, Walt. In parting, is there any advice or words of wisdom you could share with the younger generation of creators you've inspired over the decades of your career?

SIMONSON: I taught a comics class for about 11 years over a 20-year period at the School of Visual Arts in NYC. Here's my class in short. No charge, but don't tell my former students I'm giving it away for free.

1. Every time you have a question in your work about the comic you're creating--the writing or the drawing or coloring or lettering or whatever--your direction should always be: Is my answer to this question making my story better? Because that's what you should be doing in your comics--telling stories to the best of your ability. And whatever your answer, if it isn't making your story better, you need to rethink it.

2. Use reference. It'll make your drawing better. There are a million ways to do this, of course. You don't need to copy or trace a photo, but you need to learn to see the world. What you see, really see, goes through your eyes into your brain, gets scrambled, and comes back out through your hand. So you need to train both your eye and your hand and their interaction with your brain, because that is what makes both training and improvement possible.

3. Comics is hard work.
Get used to it.

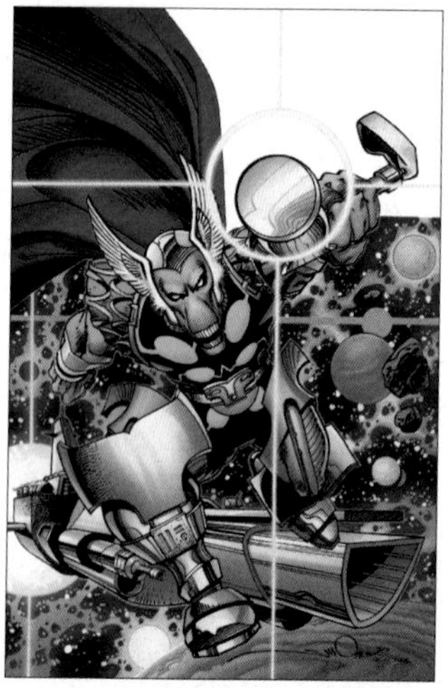

***BETA RAY BILL #1* VARIANT COVER ART BY WALTER SIMONSON, COLORS BY LAURA MARTIN.**

Okay, that's all we have room for here! For the full interview, including what work of Walter's long, celebrated career he is most proud of, go to Marvel.com! And if you haven't read Walter's classic THOR run, it's available in trade paperback and on Marvel Unlimited -- trust me, it's every bit as insanely awesome as you've heard. - Wil